D0363619

THE HOLLOW DRUM

_12_

Arnold Kemp

THE HOLLOW DRUM

SCOTLAND SINCE THE WAR

MAINSTREAM
PUBLISHING

EDINBURGH AND LONDON

To Jackie and Sue

Copyright © Arnold Kemp, 1993

The moral right of the author has been asserted

First published in Great Britain in 1993 by
MAINSTREAM PUBLISHING COMPANY (EDINBURGH) LTD
7 Albany Street
Edinburgh EH1 3UG

ISBN 1 85158 588 5

A catalogue record for this book is available from the British Library

Typeset in 10/11 Linotron Sabon by Servis Filmsetting Ltd, Manchester

Printed in Great Britain by Bookcraft, Avon

Contents

Acknowledgments

This book is called a personal history. Some may say this title is simply a device to excuse the fact that it is not systematic or comprehensive. It is, however, a necessary qualification, for newspaper editors do not have time to be punctilious historians. What I have tried to do is to cast light on important events which have affected Scotland during my lifetime and which in some way impinged on me as a journalist. I did find that my first, insouciant approach had to be altered. Soon I was immersed in the literature of the period and the history of the preceding years. Newspaper cuttings accumulated as if in a blizzard. I also quickly realised that I must amplify both my memory and contemporary accounts by interviewing some of those involved. During this latter process I discovered that a kind of Parkinson's Law operated. Each person interviewed would suggest a dozen more people that I really had to see. And so it went on until the publisher's deadline called a halt.

This is a work of journalism, not of scholarship, and I have avoided foot-notes. I have indicated in the text where statements are attributable, to a source or person, and a list of the full titles of books cited or consulted is given at the end. Some of those interviewed preferred not to be quoted directly, because many of the events with which I deal remain sensitive. And of course, in the tradition of journalism, I occasionally take the plunge and offer my own interpretation: I hope that these passages will also be self-evident. A particular word of gratitude goes to Michael Foot who, after our lunch in the Gay Hussar, sent me an invaluable note about the fall of the Callaghan Government in 1979.

A great host of other people helped me and I thank them all. First, the librarians. To David Ball, Marie Campbell and all the library staff at *The Herald* I give admiring thanks. The speed with which they verified dates or retrieved cuttings was invariably stunning. The same applies to the picture librarians of *The Herald* and *Evening Times*. To the journalists on whose work and advice I relied I am indebted too – particularly Geoffrey Parkhouse, our Political Editor, William Russell, our London Editor, Murray Ritchie, our European Editor, Alf Young, our Economics Editor, Ronald Dundas, our Business Editor, Derek Douglas, our Chief Reporter, Stuart Trotter, our Political Correspondent, Stephen McGregor, our Parliamentary Correspondent, William Clark, our Scottish Political Correspondent, and Alan MacDermid, our Medical Correspondent. I was also extremely grateful to John Warden, our former Political Editor and now, in retirement, a columnist for us on the politics of health; he sent me an insider's account of the Government's reaction to the Hamilton by-election of 1967. It is very reassuring for an editor to be reminded of the authority, amplitude and excellence of the archive which our journalists have created. I am in debt to Roy Petrie for the cover.

I am also much indebted to Endell Laird, Editor-in-Chief of the *Daily Record* and *Sunday Mail,* for giving me permission to consult his chief librarian, Mrs Patricia Baird, to whom I also express my gratitude. The *Record* has a splendid set of cuttings from the Thirties when the independence movement was burgeoning and the paper was engaged in a circulation war with the *Scottish Daily Express,* then newly opened by Beaverbrook in Glasgow. They outbid each other in their Scottishness. Generally, the newspaper houses of Scotland in combination hold an archive of enormous value, and it would be good if they could be brought together and made more widely available.

To the new school of historians active in Scotland I also acknowledge a debt. Their work is casting light on our past and our understanding of the present. But one of the most useful books was written by a journalist. Andrew Marr's *The Battle for Scotland* is an excellent account of modern Scottish politics and its history. I have tried to avoid going over too much of the same ground.

My sincere thanks go to all who spared the time for an interview. Some prefer not to be named; the identities of the others emerge from the text. I very much enjoyed the many conversations, and found them professionally valuable as well as essential for an understanding of the period. My thanks to them all.

My directorial colleagues had to put up with a great deal as my manner grew increasingly distracted and my eyes glazed over more than usual. I am indebted in particular to Liam Kane, our managing director; Iain M. Forbes, our deputy managing director; Big Ron MacDonald, our long-suffering financial director; Alex Hastie, our production director; and my fellow director and editor, George McKechnie of the *Evening Times.* I owe special thanks to all my duty editors – Ron Anderson, *The Herald*'s executive editor; Anne Simpson, Bob Sutter and John Duncan – and to my secretary Isabel Barnes.

My neighbours Annie Good and Ian Murray, two people who light up the West End of Glasgow with their friendship and conviviality, undertook to read the manuscript. I thank them for this signal act of kindness. They spotted many slips, and the errors that remain are mine. My trusty old legal companion, Alistair Bonnington, cast his sharp eye over the text, and I was most grateful. Bill Campbell and Peter MacKenzie of Mainstream must be thanked for wanting to publish the book in the first place, although my gratitude sometimes felt strained as I laboured on in what seemed infinity. Without the help of Eva Collins chaos would have submerged the effort.

Harry Reid, my deputy, must take some of the blame for the book since he prodded me into writing it. I benefited greatly as work progressed from his incisive and knowledgeable commentary and I value greatly the friendship and support he has given me so unstintingly down the years. My brother David, too, helped enormously, filling many gaps in my own memory and stimulating many ideas, quite apart from the erudite and entertaining discourse with which he habitually beguiles us at our Sunday suppers. I give thanks most of all to Anne Simpson, who has seen the book travel from optimism, through fatigued pessimism, to completion; to her go my gratitude and love.

PART I
INTRODUCTION

CHAPTER ONE

A Tanfield nationalist

Across from the house there was a corporation park and, in a corner of it enclosed by a tall hedge, a bowling green. At the bottom of the back garden the Water of Leith ran through the district known as Puddocky, named after the frogs; it was usually a gentle and inoffensive river, if never completely clean because of the effluent of paper mills upstream. In the basement next door lived an old man called Mr Easton who had worked as a navvy in a gang that had cleared the silt from the river, at the time an open sewer. 'You know, Mr Kemp,' he told my father, 'I dug oot a' that silt and I never saw a single germ.'

At the end of the street, on the main road and in the district known as Tanfield, there was a pub which drew many of its customers from the printing works opposite, where the Scottish edition of the *Daily Mail* was published for some years. This was an enclave of bourgeois Scotland. Warriston Crescent in North Edinburgh was a curving terrace, just at the northern fringe of the Georgian New Town, although one resident richer than others; the leading local businessman and sometime Lord Provost, Sir Andrew Murray, lived in a house with an extra storey which broke the graceful line of the roofs and prevented the street from achieving true distinction. This was regarded as a sign of extreme pretentiousness by my parents.

My father was the writer Robert Kemp. My mother, Meta Strachan, was a schoolteacher. Most of our neighbours were clearly middle-class. Some were even English, with the eccentricities to be expected of them. The gardens of the crescent ran down to the river and were separated from it by a wall. We fished for minnows and sticklebacks and dodged the leeches that lurked in its mud. It was mostly an insignificant stream but in spate it grew brown, swift and menacing.

A likeable and artistic English family who lived a few doors along the street acquired a duck to keep in the garden. Hens were more the thing in 1947, when eggs were hard to come by; but in their eccentric way our friends preferred a duck. They thought that it would prosper more if it could have access to the river and decided to make an opening for it in the wall, in the way that a hatch may be let into a door for the nocturnal passage of cats. A few of the local urchins, myself among them, were asked to help, and a merry little party we were. Armed with primitive tools like old bits of railing and iron bars, we spent a most agreeable summer's evening knocking a hole in the wall. We were proud of that hole and felt the glow of achievement.

Some weeks later we went on holiday to the depths of Angus. Newspapers then did not penetrate to the head of Glen Clova until the day after publication,

11

and the first we knew that anything was amiss was a telegram from my grand-mother saying cheerfully: 'Don't worry, firemen pumping water out.' My father's face went as black as the Angus skies and he departed rapidly to Edinburgh. At home he found an appalling mess. The summer rains had produced an enormous spate. The swollen Water of Leith had poured through the duck's hole; its force knocked down the dividing wall, wrecking Sir Andrew's garden which he had primped in preparation for the first Edinburgh Festival. Then it flooded the houses of the crescent and neighbouring streets. Mr Easton was discovered calmly eating bacon and eggs at his table, his legs in a foot of floodwater, his trousers rolled up.

When the waters fell and the silt was cleared from countless basements, our English friends encountered a certain *froideur* and had to move to the wilds of Trinity. Their chief persecutor was another Englishwoman of a particularly officious nature. My father's reflections were rueful, since my mother and he had shortly before our holiday been at the dinner party where the duck had been on the menu, but they were tempered by *schadenfreude* over the damage to Sir Andrew's garden, comeuppance for a show-off. Eventually my father came to see the funny side of the story. I was able to confess my part of the crime, and he dined out on that duck for the rest of his life.

My elder brother David, in an article in *The Herald* in 1992, vividly evoked our happy childhood where he and I grew up with Robbie and Christina. He wrote that he spent the 'happiest years of my life in Warriston Crescent, a shallow arc of graceful, two-storeyed Georgian houses on the edge of the New Town.' He continued:

> We lived there in ungentrified period splendour, an astragal above the door and great stone flags throughout the basement. There was even a wrought-iron butler's tray fixed to the banister at the top of the steeply curving stairway that led to the top floor. It was indeed the perfect place to be a child ... As we got older, we crossed the park, first to Eildon Street, where my grandmother lived, and then to Warriston Woods behind, occasionally glimpsing (and always care-fully avoiding) the bulldog from Warriston House.
>
> What I remember, above all, is the quality of silence then. It had the effect of sharpening distant sounds like the clop of hooves from the milkman's or coalman's horse (there was still a stone horse trough at the end of the street), the lazy hum of the sawmill on the heights across the river, the distant clank of a goods engine shunting on the railway downriver towards Leith, or the late-night roar of the two Buick V8s leaving Tanfield, on the other side of the main road, with the Glasgow edition of the Scottish *Daily Mail*. Very occasionally, there were mysterious revelries, with singing and raised voices, in the Northern Bowl-ing Club, normally a model of genteel decorum, just across the way.

I had forgotten the bulldog at Warriston House but not so long ago I strolled by the wall from which David dreeped and broke his arm. In my mind it was precipitous; in reality, of course, about five feet high. David was the leader of the bourgeois boys who stravaiged the district. In the Scotland that emerged from the Second World War, society was not so segregated as it has since become because of post-war housing. The monstrous schemes had not yet been thrown up according to rigid criteria invented by central government to produce the lowest possible unit cost. And so all sorts lived not cheek by jowl but within shouting distance of each other, even if the quality of housing available to the poorer people showed a sudden deterioration.

The tenements at the end of the street, across the main road, were of the best kind. The word itself in Scotland does not really have the pejorative flavour that it has earned in England or Ireland. These tenements of the superior sort survive to this day and where they have escaped the slum clearance programmes have been extensively restored and refurbished; as a form of housing they have much to recommend them. The common stair is often dark, the stone steps perpetually dank from the weekly washing, but the flats themselves are usually light and airy, with generous rooms. In modern times the entry phone has transformed the entrances. The famed good neighbourliness of the tenement is perhaps an invention of nostalgia. Neighbours are good and bad wherever you are. But the tenement certainly lacks the impersonality of much of the housing that was built with understandable urgency after the war. When you heard a step on the stair, you were liable to know whose it was, and the scents would announce with some clarity the eating habits of the families next door.

My father evoked the atmosphere of the common stair in his comic novel *The Malacca Cane* (1954). His tenements were in 'Bleachfield', a light disguise for Tanfield at the end of our street:

> Mrs Thin was a trifle late, and as she mounted the eighty-three steps an assortment of odours assaulted her olfactory nerve, as beauty queens might compete to pet a stray kitten. What an aromatic orchestra, blending in the ripest of chords! Bat-eared musicians, they claim, can put a name to all the notes that are blared and sawed forth at one simultaneous second. So could Mrs Thin disentangle the thorough bass of cod cooking in deep fat from the brassy fanfares of sausages on the grill or fresh herring as they leaped in the pan. To this symphony finnan-haddocks, as they baked in milk, supplied their gentle flutings, and somewhere pickled beetroot cut through with the acerbity of a triangle. When she rested on the top landing, all these vapours swirled round her head with intoxicating bravura. She entered and prepared to vary the tone with the full, oily tone of her pair of kippers.

The respectable working class lived in those tenements, law-abiding, churchgoing, Conservative-voting, devoted readers of the Edinburgh *Evening News* (it was slightly raffish to support the Hibs rather than the Hearts and to read the *Dispatch*). Their children played football and cricket with us in the park, gravitating naturally into bourgeois alliances.

Round the corner, in darker, dingier tenements, lived the poorer, more anarchic working class. Led by David, we fought running battles with Tommy Cairns's gang, trading abuse, punches and kicks, none of which left any permanent damage. The worst of Scotland's social deprivation has been banished from the inner cities but then it was there just a minute away, often tucked away behind some broad Georgian terrace. And stepping down the economic and social scale you found the tenement could be a grim place indeed. The official statistics of the day tell the story coldly but after the war large numbers of houses in Scotland had no lavatory of their own and many had no running water. Nowadays it is fashionable to identify the failures of housing in Scotland with the public sector. What we had then was the failure of private landlordism, for complicated reasons flowing from the Lloyd George Act of 1915.

Like the other Scottish cities Edinburgh was compact, crowded and smoky. The privations of the war persisted with rationing. There were, for some years, few sweets. At the end of the road Mr Coia, who had migrated to Scotland before the war from northern Italy, presided over his cafe with enforced exiguousness. He spoke the broken Italian Scots so beloved of generations of Scots comics. He once went to London in a bus and on his return pronounced a condemnatory verdict. 'The trouble with England,' he said, 'is that there are nae hills. It's a' flat.' He eventually married a cousin, also called Coia, because, as he told us, it was cheaper than paying her to be his housekeeper. Thereafter they quarrelled volubly and incessantly in the back shop, and I felt there had been a certain loss of happiness and innocence. But as children, in Mr Coia's magical café with its fizzy ice-cream drinks and jars of sweeties, we had our first inkling of the enormous contribution Scottish Italians would make to the pleasures and achievements of our national life. At first, of course, the ice-cream Mr Coia sold was a sorry imitation of the real thing, made from substitute ingredients which produced a grey and unappetising travesty, but the product rapidly improved.

In the shops like the 'fruiterers and florists', a portmanteau phrase I always associate with the fluting Edinburgh speech, bananas or exotic fruits did not reappear for some years. Adults spoke longingly of bananas. When they eventually returned to the shops, the news caused great excitement. People came running down the street to tell everybody of their arrival. The fruit was a distinct anti-climax, bringing the first taste of disillusion I can remember. When a friend prancing round in his clumsy boots accidently killed my brother's pet rabbit it was my first recognition of death, and I wept inconsolably all night. One day I ate a berry in the garden which, I had been warned, was poisonous. I spent a miserable if short season as a condemned man contemplating his own extinction, staring moodily from the bus at the beloved scene I should leave so soon. After two sleepless nights I confessed my fears to my father and they instantly evaporated.

Shortages were made worse for a long time by the peculiar Scottish prejudice against vegetables. To her dying day my mother disliked them, with a particular detestation of salad which she contemptuously described as rabbit food. She came from a large family which grew up in Rosehearty, a fishing village on the coast of Aberdeenshire, and sang the praises of the traditional Scottish diet of herring and oatmeal, supplemented when you could get it with fish and meat. She believed that such a diet was hard to beat, and she herself was a fine cook. No doubt the old diet was nutritious, but in modern times it became hopelessly corrupt. Porridge disappeared from the breakfast table; when rationing ended, sweets became universal. The frying pan was the reality in modern Scotland, not the old barrel of salted herrings. Honest poverty maybe made a healthy race, but that was never the case in industrial Scotland. To our addiction to sugar, booze and fat we owe some of the health statistics which put us at the bottom of almost every league, whether of heart disease or cancer. A historian wrote once that Scots owed the lilies in the kailyard to the English; and it is to our English settlers, I think, that we owe at least in part the rapid improvement in the quality and variety of fruit and vegetables on sale nowadays in Scotland.

My parents had an idealised view of what Scotland should be, perhaps. They revered the grammatically confident Scots Tongue of the old countryside; and they reviled the slipshod speech of the towns. There could be no greater sin at table than to utter some solecism picked up on the streets or, horror of horror, drop your ts with the glottal stop (a marked characteristic of Scottish urban language).

Yet old Scotland was already disappearing beyond recall.

Reithian rectitude and conservatism still ruled the air waves. Scotland had, since the nineteenth century, indulged in an intermittent flirtation with the modern forms of nationalism, and indeed had elected an SNP member to the Westminster Parliament at a by-election in 1945, where he sat for a few months before being swept away in the general election of that year. Even so, the Conservative vote was remarkably resilient. In the 1955 General Election the Tories achieved more than 50 per cent of the vote, a feat never emulated by Labour in Scotland for all its subsequent dominance. For a couple of decades after the war, the old Tory alliances held good – Unionism still reinforced by echoes of the Reformed tradition and rooted in Protestantism; it was subscribed to by the industrial barons and their upwardly mobile offspring, the urban kirk-going bourgeoisie, the respectable working class, the Orange Order, and the deferential workers in the countryside like gamekeepers and shepherds. Even in the Seventies I came upon a shepherd's wife who believed that those in the 'Big Hoose' knew how she voted and thought this was the purpose of the counterfoil on the ballot paper. To be a member of the Church of Scotland meant it was more than likely that you voted Conservative (in the West of Scotland, particularly, voting behaviour was much more heavily influenced by religious affiliation than class interest). This was the Toryism of the toffs and the genteel; but it was also the Toryism of the petit bourgeois, the master plumber and the lock-keeper on the canal. The industrial proletariat was for the moment confined in the old cities. Clearing the slums and creating the sprawling estates changed the political as well as the physical complexion of Scotland: it meant that the electoral system was more bounteous to Labour than the Conservatives.

But the old songs were already giving way. Popular culture was transatlantic in its inspiration. The simple airs of the old Scots tradition, which my father valued so much, were not the ones they sang in the pub on a Saturday night or on the nights the bowling club took to drink. The keening, mawkish cadences of the sentimental ballad would float through the night air. That was the urban reality, and the values of urban life and of a political system which constantly bid up material expectations were all the time chewing away at the Arcadian vision of a thrifty but resourceful Scotland. Distaste at the industrial process is a recurring theme in twentieth century literature, for example in the work of D.H. Lawrence, and it was a strong element in my father's attitudes. He had been brought up first in Orkney, then in the hard farming lands of Buchan. When he was a teenager his parents moved to Deeside (his father was a minister). He was amazed by the woods: he had never seen so many trees. But he came to dislike the snobberies of Deeside and perhaps found there early evidence of the anglicisation of Scotland which gathered so rapid a pace in later years, particularly in Edinburgh and parts of the countryside. (David, when we discussed this point, recalled that our paternal granny was exceedingly deferential to the petty lairds of Deeside.)

Like that of so many Scots my father's attitude to the English was complex, a mixture of irritation and admiration. After a spell in journalism and broadcasting in Manchester and London (he was, he said, the last reporter to have been appointed to *The Manchester Guardian* by the great C.P. Scott), he returned to Scotland to pursue a career in his own country and with the specific aim of adding to its literature and tradition. Yet he never lost the desire that his work should find a wider stage. He took pleasure in the fact that his publisher was an Englishman, Lord Horder. Indeed, when he eventually was able to buy a car, a Ford Consul, he became enormously proud of it, and took Lord Horder for a drive round the King's Park. 'Bit of a biscuit box,' said Horder. My father always remembered and thereafter his cars were always second-hand Wolseleys, Rovers or Rileys, and occasionally he would look longingly at the second-hand Bentleys in the Rossleigh showroom. Similarly, he never stopped hoping that his plays would find acceptance in the West End. Although his work enjoyed great popular success in Scotland, and was often shown on television or heard on radio, although his comedies were written with well-constructed grace and with a sure ear for Scottish speech, this was an ambition that eluded him; and the paradox of his life, spent in Scotland and in Scotland's service, was that this was a disappointment for him.

His dislike of the industrial culture extended to the sciences, for which he had a contempt also. Of this split in our culture, much has been written. He believed that literature and the imaginative arts were superior to the desire to measure everything. His dislike of science went to the extent of tacitly encouraging me to slack at it in school and diverting David from an early preference for science into Greek, Latin and English. The Edinburgh Academy was at that time dedicated to producing recruits for the law, the civil service and the ruling classes. Science teachers were in my day a bit of a joke. Our hero was the classics master who, it was said, consumed a bottle of whisky for breakfast and had verses published from time to time in *Punch*. I gather that life at the Academy is much changed.

My father's attitude I never quite understood but guess that it partly arose from his own family background, from which science had been missing; his father had mild literary ambitions and his mother wrote a host of unpublished romantic novels. They encouraged his own literary hopes and at Aberdeen University he took the gold medal in English. As a son of the manse, he would also still have been influenced by the Darwinian controversies of the nineteenth century. In 1859 Darwin's work, *The Origin of Species*, was furiously denounced by the clergy. This controversy, which began half a century before my father's birth, would certainly have washed into the manse in Orkney where he grew up.

Hostility toward science has seen something of a revival in the 1990s. After the war, confidence in science reached a high point. System building would free people from insanitary slums. Nuclear power offered a cheap and trouble-free route to universal electricity and prosperity. New technology's white heat propelled Harold Wilson to electoral victory in 1964: it would transform our industrial future and give us an exit from industrial decline. The green revolution offered the poor world freedom from hunger.

These hopes have proved false. The public housing boom produced its own disasters. The nuclear industry has faltered on a combination of unforeseen cost, contamination and human incompetence culminating in Chernobyl and concern about the impact on health of long-term low-level radiation. The new technologies have allowed competitors rapidly to undermine the industrial dominance of the old powers. They are extruding labour and creating a political and economic crisis as the industrialised world struggles to generate new employment or come to terms with more or less permanent unemployment at a level which would not so long ago have been regarded as politically unacceptable. The green revolution has been negated by political corruption: in the Third World the few rich have grown richer and the poor have grown much poorer. Desertification, hunger and Aids have spread across Africa. The contemporary dislike of science reflects a misdirected political and popular disillusion. The quick fixes that science seemed to offer are found not to work. A new strain of mysticism is also attacking science, and with it are carried echoes of the old Darwinian controversies.

My father's hostility to science was partly bound up in his regret over the price paid for progress and the degenerative effect on the Scottish people of their industrial life and the erosion of their native traditions. A Marxist might have called this alienation but my father was no Marxist. From a bourgeois standpoint that did not consciously filter everything through ideas of class struggle he nevertheless perceived that somehow the industrial experience had been coarsening and imprisoning. Adam Ferguson, in his *Essay on the History of Civil Society*, in 1767, wrote of the way the labourer may have no possibility of understanding the system which he serves:

> Any mechanical arts require no capacity; they succeed best under a total suppression of sentiment and reason; and ignorance is the mother of industry.

From such bondage socialism struggled to free people through education and by state transfers of resources like health care. If my father was no Marxist, he was no socialist either. Raised in the Church of Scotland, he was in part at least a Tory of the Sir Walter Scott school, torn between his love of order and his sense that the dear old ways were being cheapened and eroded. His political attitudes I remember as being often to the Right. My mother's father had been a Unitarian but she had been brought up in the United Free Church and therefore in the old Liberal tradition. I suspect that she voted Labour on at least some occasions. What one commentator has called romantic antiquarianism, certainly a large element in my father's nationalism, was mixed with an anger over the way that his countrymen had been exploited. One of his comedies lovingly celebrated the skill of a baker who, as a craftsman on his own account, avoided the fate of the uneducated manual worker selling his labour. I also remember his distress one Sunday, when I accompanied him on one of his favourite walks, to Leith Docks. He loved the sniff of maritime commerce. It reminded him of his Orkney boyhood. A gang of dockers, seated on the back of a truck, gave off a ripe balloon of bad language as it passed us. The Sabbath still meant something to my father but the language would have distressed him on any day. He turned to me and apologetically explained that I should forgive them: their swearing betrayed the poverty of their vocabulary. Social theorists would advance more complex explanations, that such language was a means of group and class bonding, but my father would have had little enough time for such ideas.

As the reader may have gathered, my parents had nationalist leanings. By that I mean they were concerned about the future of their own country, which was Scotland, and celebrated its traditions. But Scotland is an unusual country. It is a nation but not a state, and Scots combine their national feelings with their sentiments of loyalty to Britain, in whose affairs they have taken so active a part. The result for all of us is a certain emotional disorientation resulting from trying to deal with conflicting impulses. My mother cherished the old Scots speech. When she fell into it she would rebuke us if we did not understand her. I would reply that she should not have sent us to a school heavily influenced by English attitudes and models. My father toyed with the idea of standing for Parliament on behalf of the SNP, but wisely decided not to. His essentially gentle personality, though his gentleness was occasionally punctured by irritability, would not have suited him to the political life; it would have made him choleric. Indeed, the anger he felt at the council's plan to drive a ringroad through Edinburgh – it would have lopped the end off the crescent – hastened his death. He died before we learned that the campaign against it, in which he played a leading part, had been successful.

This book is not biography, or indeed autobiography. It is a series of reflections about my own country, and the things that have happened to it in my lifetime. My starting point has been my parents and how they looked at things. All the confusion that marks modern Scottish attitudes was present in them, as they are present in me. Scotland vested its personality in a Union from which it has received, as far as these can be measured, economic advantages. It has no capital city. Edinburgh, which formally holds that title, is little more than a centre of law and administration. None of the transactions of power take place there. The real capital, London, lies outside its borders, not just because London is the centre of the UK political system but because Scotland is composed of four or five city states none of which has achieved dominance. That has made it very hard for Scotland to develop political coherence within its own boundaries, and helps to explain why it has adhered to the Union for so long, if with flawed enthusiasm. It also explains why it has permitted itself to be ruled in a way that smacks of the proconsular. The academic attempts that have been made to understand Scotland's acquiescence in the Union offer various explanations. Some say that an alliance of the capitalist and mercantile interests at a British level delivered political stability and obedience; and this alliance has been strengthened by the tacit support given to it by formally anti-capitalist forces which have nevertheless been committed to the Union. Labour's periodic flirtation with home rule habitually comes to nothing. There remains something of a conspiracy, or at least an agreement to share power, between Conservative and Labour in Scotland. Through the Eighties, the Tories had the Scottish Office. Labour dominated large chunks of the local government system created in 1974 and enjoyed substantial political patronage at this level of government (Strathclyde, with a population of more than two million, is greater in size than some countries with affiliation to the United Nations). To that basic partnership sustaining the Union, Labour holds true: its plan for a Scottish parliament envisages it as part of a new political arrangement for the UK. The decisive political debate in Scotland is between Labour and the SNP, who aspire to the full restoration of Scottish sovereignty. In their opposition to the SNP, the business class and the Labour Party remain united. Until or unless Labour abandons the Union, Scotland will remain within it. Ian Hamilton QC, of whom more later, wrote memorably in an article in *The Herald* in 1993 that the bread of Unionism stuck in his craw; most Scots swallow it effortlessly.

Yet it is also wrong to represent Scotland as being in some colonial thraldom. For a start colonial status implies domination by outsiders while the Scots themselves have delivered their country to the Union and operated pervasively and successfully within it. In modern times Scotland has experienced nothing like the Irish subservience to the Church which marked the first half century of the Irish State. Indeed, since the war, it has thrown off the Church with startling rapidity and has adopted secular values to a point where something of its old familial culture has been damaged. And, as I have noted, explanations of colonialism do not carry conviction when the ruling group is so heavily composed of Scots. It was Lord Reith who, by creating the centralised and bureaucratic BBC, solved the problem of diverse cultural and national aspirations by inventing the 'regions', of which Scotland was one. Later, after the postwar rise of Scottish nationalism, these were modified. Scotland and Wales were called 'national regions' in BBC terminology.

The theory of class and sectoral alliances, of religious and regional tensions externally moderated, is much more convincing than any scenario of quasi-colonial subordination. Anyone who moves around the Scottish business community will testify to its enduring fear of separatism, even if that prospect, now that we are all in the European Community, must be theoretically remote. Indeed, the idea of national independence in any real or meaningful sense is hard to sustain. It is not just in Scotland that external ownership of the major industrial and commercial enterprises has become commonplace. The international economy defies regulation by the governments of major countries. National treasuries, even in cartels and combinations, find foreign exchange dealers to be powerful and influential adversaries. The best a national government can hope for is to take its cut in taxation and hope that economic activity and employment can be stimulated by its policies. For Scotland an open economy remains a necessity and an open culture an inevitability. This leaves a gap in the hearts of Scots. There is a hollowness there which too often is perceived as arising from economic causes or having economic explanations. That, I believe, is to misunderstand it; and in this book I shall try to arrive at an explanation for it. Like my fellow countrymen, I am a confused traveller, but I travel hopefully.

CHAPTER TWO

Agonised deference

In few cities of Europe can the question 'Which school did you go to?' have as much importance as it carries in Edinburgh. In Glasgow, it was often asked of applicants for jobs to determine their religious affiliation so that they could be excluded if they were Catholic. With the decline of the older industries, the dilution of the old Protestant mercantile class and, with them, the nepotistical and exclusive craft unions, such attitudes have begun to dissolve, to be replaced by prejudices of more recent vintage. In Edinburgh, the question is designed not to elicit religious adherence but to determine social standing. Broadly there were in Edinburgh in the Forties and Fifties about five kinds of school for boys (education for girls in Edinburgh has been definitively chronicled by Muriel Spark in *The Prime of Miss Jean Brodie*), with the Academy occupying a cagetory on its own. The public sector had grant-aided schools of academic excellence among which the Royal High was pre-eminent, with a long and ancient lineage as the tounis college, the school of Sir Walter Scott and Lord Cockburn. In the last decades before comprehensivation – and its removal from Regent Street to Barnton – it had a period of fecundity. In *Memoirs of a Modern Scotland* the critic Karl Miller wrote movingly of his great English teacher at the Royal High, Hector McIver. Apart from literary talent the post-war generation at the High School produced a school of British jazz musicians whose leading member, the late Sandy Brown, achieved excellence by all international levels even if he remains somewhat under-rated by jazz students today.

For those who failed the eleven-plus and did not make the High School or Boroughmuir, there was the secondary modern. It is still, in some Edinburgh circles, social death to admit that you went to one. In the private sector the Merchant Company schools, Watson's, Heriot's, Stewart's and Melville's, attracted much support from the mercantile and professional middle class. In my mind Watson's was associated with swots (Mary Erskine's had the same reputation for girls), a breeding ground of civil servants; it also produced Malcolm Rifkind who as Secretary of State for Scotland broke the Tory mould of aristos or public-school products. No doubt it is unfair to characterise Watsonians as polite, punctual and parsimonious, but that is how they dwell in my mind. Heriot's I associate with a gifted generation of rugby players, among whom Kenny Scotland was pre-eminent. Watson's was in the genteel suburb of Morningside, the Edinburgh of kippers, pianos, fur coats and no drawers, the Edinburgh of 'you'll have had your tea?', the classic expression of the city's legendary inhospitable *froideur* (a reputation, I may say, never justified in reality – in my experience Edinburgh is convivial to a fault). Heriot's seemed to have arisen from a more robust and demotic tradition, perhaps because the Edinburgh jeweller George Heriot (1563–1623), known as Jinglin' Geordie, left his estate to found a hospital for poor children. The difference was summed up in the popular joke about two boys interrogating each other about the badges on their blazers:

Knock knock, who's there?

(In a Prime of Miss Jean Brodie *voice):*
Emma Watsonian. Who're you?

(In gruffer demotic tones):
Humphrey Heriots.

Stewart's and Melville's were regarded, no doubt without any justification, as more effete than either; they later combined. Then there were the public schools more or less completely modelled on the English system – Fettes, Merchiston Castle and Loretto. These were most patronised by expatriates, the English or by wealthy parents from the rest of Scotland and, to the best of my knowledge, a day school was the preference of most Edinburgh families. Fettes, Bryce's exuberant riot of Victorian neo-Gothic, was as a piece of architecture reviled by my father, who every time he passed it denounced it as a revolting and pretentious pile and compared it unfavourably with Heriot's Hospital, built more simply in the era of Inigo Jones but, according to Professor A. J. Youngson's *The Making of Classical Edinburgh*, not designed by him as has been suggested.

The Edinburgh Academy fell somewhere between the Merchant Company schools and the public schools. In no setting could you find more clearly apparent the various contradictions with which Scots have to grapple. It was proud of being Scottish yet deferred to the English system. It was a member of the Headmasters' Conference and regarded itself as a public school. In its organisation it followed the English model, with houses which competed against each other in sport and cadet-force exercises, and the delegation of punishment to prefects. My brothers and I were members of the house named after the famous judge Henry (Lord) Cockburn (1779–1854), a zealous Whig and a founding father of the school. But because it was mostly composed of day boys, it was never fully imbued with the cloistered atmosphere of the public school: the flavours of the town washed through it and it was always possible to find relief from it, either at home or in the promenades along Princes Street ogling the girls from St George's (the female equivalent of the Academy in that it was the preferred school for the daughters of judges). When the Academy in the 1990s had to seek an interdict to prevent the publication of an article about pot-smoking among schoolboys, its lawyers ran through almost a dozen names before they could find a judge who hadn't been to the school.

The Academy prepared most of its pupils for the Scottish exams, with their wide range of subjects. Yet it also pushed its brightest pupils towards the more specialised English A-levels and Oxbridge. If boys won exhibitions or scholarships to Oxford or Cambridge then a holiday was declared in celebration. My brother David recalled that when he decided to enter the Edinburgh University bursary competition, the Academy displayed total indifference. He had to go up to the Old Quad and find the syllabus for himself. At the time I resented this and scoffed at what I regarded as the school's excessive and deferential respect for English criteria. Now I have come to regard such confusion as an inevitable part of the Scottish condition. Locally, Academy boys felt themselves most keenly in rivalry with Fettes, a kind of compliment since Fettes was a real public school but also because Fettes was entirely imbued with the English ethos whereas, at the Academy, the Scottish dimension remained dominant if ambiguously regarded.

The Academy was founded in 1824. It arose, in the first instance, because of dissatisfaction with the state of classical education in general and in the High School in particular, and in the context of growing agitation for political reform. Edinburgh was a disputatious, contumacious place as the Whigs increasingly challenged the political supremacy of the Tories. Warring newspapers and periodicals traded insults, and duels were sometimes fought to expunge libels. *The Scotsman* had been founded by the Whig side in 1817. In *Memorials Of His Time* Lord Cockburn wrote that Edinburgh was peculiarly ripe for the use of libel because there was no place where the contrast between the new and the old internal systems was so strong.

> The whole official power of Government was on one side (the Tory side), nearly the whole talent and popularity was on the other; and the principles espoused by each admitted of no reconciliation.

Lord Cockburn recounts that he and his fellow Whig Leonard Horner (1785–1864), the educationalist and geologist, had often discussed the causes of the decline in classical education and its possible remedies. 'We were at last satisfied that no adequate improvement could be effected so long as there were only one great classical school in Edinburgh, and this one placed under the town council, and lowered, perhaps necessarily, so as to suit the wants of a class of boys to more than two-thirds of whom classical accomplishment is foreseen to be useless.' The non-classical thrust emerging in the burgh academies may have given nineteenth-century Scots a pre-eminence in science and technology. But as a means of preparing the sons of the Scottish proconsular class for the home and imperial civil service or for a life in the law, or of giving them access to English centres of influence and patronage, the emerging deficiencies of the system had become all too obvious to Cockburn and his contemporaries.

> So one day on the top of one of the Pentlands – emblematic of our foundation of the extent of our prospects – we two resolved to set about the establishment of a new school. On taking others into council we found that the conviction of the inadequacy of the High School was far more general than we supposed. [Sir Walter] Scott took it up eagerly. The sum of £10,000 was subscribed immediately; and soon after about £2,000 more. We were fiercely opposed, as we expected, by the town council; and, but not fiercely, by a few of the friends of the institution we were going to encroach upon. But, after due discussion and plotting, our contributors finally resolved to proceed, and in 1823 the building was begun.

The opening a year later, Cockburn concluded, was an important day for education in Scotland, 'in reference to the middle and upper classes'. The popular explanation for the building of St Stephen's Church in St Vincent Street, which our family attended, was that it represented revenge for the betrayal of the High School. It seals the vista from Princes Street, blocking out any glimpse of the Academy. Magnus Magnusson, in his readable account of the Academy's history, says that although it's a good story it isn't true: the town council had bought the land in 1822 and Playfair had been commissioned to design it a month before Cockburn and Playfair took their walk in the Pentlands.

William Burns's classical building for the Academy, with its Doric portico, eloquently advertised the school prospectus. In its classicism the Academy swam against the tide of Scottish education. Nor were the English models beyond criticism. The historian and journalist Peter Hennessy has written that Oxford and Cambridge practised sloth and anglican bigotry for much of the nineteenth century. The public school system was hardly in better shape. My grandfather was named after Dr Thomas Arnold of Rugby (1795–1842), a man revered by the Victorians, and so I too owe him my name. History has not been kind to his reputation. Lytton Strachey definitively debunked him in *Eminent Victorians* and George Macdonald Fraser has given us that memorable extension of *Tom Brown's Schooldays,* the legendary bully Flashman.

Yet this was the example that the Academy was largely to follow, even if the High School was its first influence. Sir Walter Scott was a director and in his Journal is to be found agonising over the question of corporal punishment. He opposed it but regretted that it was a necessary evil without which there could not be discipline. 'I was indifferently well beaten at school; but I am now quite certain that twice as much discipline would have been well bestowed.' Later he worried over whether the pronunciation of Latin taught at the Academy should conform to that adopted in England. It was a dilemma typical of an age which struggled to reconcile tradition with inevitable change.

Although the Academy adopted the classics as its foundation, it contrived to produce one of the great scientists of the period, James Clerk-Maxwell (1831–1897), the first professor of experimental physics at Cambridge whose best-known researches dealt with electricity and magnetism. But in my time the masters at the school, nearly all of whom were English, seemed more proud of another old boy, Archibald Campbell Tait (1811–1882), and his picture was displayed with greater prominence in the hall. Like Maxwell he penetrated the highest levels of English influence. Born in Edinburgh of an Aberdeenshire farming family, he was raised as a presbyterian but became Dr Arnold's successor as headmaster at Rugby and ultimately Archbishop of Canterbury. He was an early example of the Scot on the make, than which Barrie was later to say there were few more impressive sights in the world.

Like English public schools, the Academy was very proud of its 'traditions', which if analysed were no more than grafts or inventions designed to secure bonding and instil esprit. An old Scots ball game called hailes, vaguely akin to shinty, was played in the yard with the clacken, a bat shaped like a very large and flat wooden spoon. This was a tradition, certainly: but it came from the High School. Magnusson claims it was also used as a weapon for battles in the play-ground or with local 'keelies' as the little bourgeois boys called their proletarian enemies; I suspect this statement reflects Magnusson's Viking instincts, for I recall no such use of the clacken in my time. The prefects were known as ephors, after a class of magistrates in the Doric states of ancient Greece, and the ephors used the clacken to beat erring boys. The punishment was administered in quasi-judicial fashion by the ephors in the room which they were allocated as part of their privileges. The victim, when found guilty (as he invariably was), had to place his head under the table so that his backside was elevated. The ephor chosen to administer the beating then ran at him from across the room and hit his bottom as

23

hard as he could. The relish with which this punishment was carried out left me with a permanent distaste for over-zealous authority. Giving boys the right to beat their juniors could not have other than a degrading effect. My offences, on the two occasions I was beaten, were trivial. I forgot to wear the school cap, then compulsory, and I refused to run round Fettes, an exercise imposed on us when rugby was impossible on frosty pitches.

For many years I puzzled why my father had sent us there, given his commitment to things Scottish. Apart from the strong English influences at the Academy, the fees were a very considerable burden. Scotland is not a highly remunerative environment for a professional writer and broadcaster. His achievement in educating his three sons and his daughter privately was considerable but his motives seemed enigmatic. The explanation turned out to be very simple, as I discovered when I discussed the matter with David while writing this chapter. As a bourgeois boy David was bullied at Wardie, the state school to which he had at first been sent. My mother found this intolerable. Nor did the choice of the Academy look so financially threatening at that time, for fees were still relatively modest. Given his hatred of the overweening claims of science, its classicism also appealed to my father.

One of the more ludicrous aspects of Academy life was the way in which some of the pupils aped the mannerisms of the upper class, sometimes adopting strangulated public-school accents which would occasionally dissolve, under emotional stress, into the refined speech of the Edinburgh bourgeoisie so beautifully lampooned by Maggie Smith in the movie *The Prime of Miss Jean Brodie*. In the debating society one evening the son of an Edinburgh turf accountant said memorably: 'Let's face it: we're members of the upper classes.' It was to the Academy's credit that this statement was greeted with hoots of mirth. There was another comforting incident. At cadet corps camp one summer, our leading platoon took part in a drill competition. They were comprehensively beaten by a choreographed group from an English school who lacked only the goose step in their repertoire of movements. Our mob sloped around in a positively shambolic fashion, a fact which gives pleasure when I look back on it though at the time we were a trifle embarrassed by our clear inadequacy. The Academy's aping of external models was never fully successful and always was on the point of degenerating into comedy.

When I passed my Highers at the age of 17 I did not wait the extra year to do A-levels but in the Scottish tradition went straight to the university of my home town. Had I had any academic gifts it would have been a mistake because I was not ready for the disciplines of study. But I had few such inclinations and was impatient to be getting on with life; I was stupid enough to think I could get through university on my wits. I left the Academy rejecting some of its attitudes and snobberies but in retrospect value much of the experience. It was a humane and decent institution. The masters who made us do so many précis (are they still done?), or who sweated with us over Latin, or who somehow miraculously contrived a pass for me in Higher Maths (in those kindlier days there was only a pass or a fail), unwittingly gave me a sound basis for a journalistic career, as indeed did my mother's incessant correcting of our grammar at table and my father's talk of the culture of newspapers and television. For all its sometimes ludicrous pretensions and delusions, the Academy was more or less free of the bullying and personal oppression that so often seems, according to their memoirs, to have made school an ordeal for generations of English young men.

There is an Academy 'voice' which sometimes puzzles those who try to place

24

it. It has a Scottish tinge but is soft and rounded so that people sometimes also think of it as Irish. Magnus Magnusson is the best known speaker of it. In 1992 I addressed a meeting in Ballina, an Irish town where Republican sentiment burns strongly. 'You haven't got a trace of a Scottish accent,' said an elderly woman afterwards, accusingly. 'It's the school I went to in Edinburgh,' I replied apologetically. 'I can't help it.' Like most other things at the Academy, it is the result of some kind of compromise.

In 1993 I went back to the school to talk to sixth-formers. It was Friday afternoon, they had been made to come and I fear I bored them. The old place looked much the same but it felt quite different. I told them about being beaten with a clacken by an ephor who ran at me across the room. They looked at me in incredulity. The past is another country.

CHAPTER THREE

Town and gown

Though I did not realise it at the time, Edinburgh University in 1957 was approaching a turning point in its long history (it was founded in 1583). It was still very much a product of its own long traditions. The course for the ordinary degree was designed to 'train the mind' and still resisted the separation of the arts and the sciences though the mushrooming science faculty was bringing the resistance to an end. Mathematics were not removed from the arts course until 1963. This was achieved with 'infinite difficulty'. After protracted negotiations arts managed to retain logic. Moral philosophy was at the heart of the arts course, reflecting the Aristotelean beginnings of the university, more influenced by contact with the Dutch university of Leiden than by connections with England.

In the eighteenth and nineteenth century the university's medical faculty had become internationally renowned. It invented the rational school of medicine (as opposed to London's emphasis on explorative anatomy). Professor William Cullen, who taught medicine and chemistry from 1755 to 1790, dazzled the American students in particular. He believed that medical theory could lead to dogmaticism and inappropriate prescribing. He thought rather that it should prompt empirical inquiry while providing a rational framework for diagnosis. Cullen and his successors were to inspire Conan Doyle's creation of Sherlock Holmes, and the late Professor Gordon Donaldson recorded, in a delightful essay, the lecturing technique of a later professor of chemistry, Sir John Fraser, holding court in one of the clinical lecture theatres at the infirmary. Enter the first patient, an elderly man with a walrus moustache:

Fraser: Your name? Ah yes, Mr Mackenzie. And what is wrong? Something at the back of your throat? (A quick look with a torch.) Yes indeed, there is a tumour there. (A pause for thought). What is your occupation, Mr Mackenzie?

Mackenzie: A bagpipe maker.

Faser gives a dissertation on the structure and function of bagpipes (he came from Tain).

Fraser: And the reeds, where do you insert them? And where do you keep the spare reeds handy? In your mouth, indeed? Show me how.

Fraser (turning triumphantly to the class): Just where the rear end impinges on the back of the throat at the tumour site. Thank you, Mr Mackenzie.

In the old days the professors were not paid by the university but by the students. This made the better ones rich: Cullen was able to build a country house. It encouraged squabbling among them and nepotism as they manoeuvred to hand down their lucrative posts to their offspring. To increase attendance they resorted to theatrical behaviour. The great chemist Joseph Black, who succeeded Cullen in the chair of chemistry, had great elegance, philosophical calmness and repose. Townspeople enrolled in his classes and chemical experimentation was an accomplishment to be expected in a gentleman.

J. B. Morrell described Black's theatrical gifts. He had extraordinary manual dexterity applied to ingenious experiments. 'These were performed not with the quackery of a showman but with an unparalleled fastidiousness and elegance.' But, like the high-wire man in a circus, he gripped the attention by conducting operations that were highly dangerous. A student recalled: 'I have seen him pour boiling water or boiling acid from a vessel that had no spout into a tube, holding it at such a distance as made the stream's diameter small, and so vertical that not a drop was spilt. While he poured he would mention this adaptation of the height to the diameter as a necessary condition of success.'

In those days Edinburgh was in Morrell's phrase a 'medical supermarket'. By the time I arrived the post-war expansion, caused first by returning servicemen and then by the offspring of the baby boom, had put some strains on the teaching capacity. The professors of the first ordinary classes still conducted lectures in the old way described by Professor Donaldson. Some still had a theatrical touch. But the traditions were beginning finally to go. The professors were of course now paid by the university. The students were no longer consumers in the old sense. The old humour seemed to be disappearing. We kept up the practice of foot-stamping, hissing and booing but without any understanding of its meaning; increasingly it seemed merely discourteous. In his essay, published in 1983, Professor Donaldson wrote:

> Students used to be far more demonstrative than they are now. According to all accounts the most rowdy scenes as a habitual way of behaviour; belonged to a period now receding into the forgotten past and few can now remember the type of disturbance that was once common . . .
>
> Until well after the Second World War teachers invariably received a welcome from stamping feet at the beginning, and applause from stamping feet at the end, of a lecture. It was not entirely conventional, because the stamping on one's entry could indicate the degree of welcome one received, and it was quite noticeable that there might be exceptional warmth when, for example, one returned after an illness or when one had achieved some promotion or there was some other reason for feeling on the part of the students.

One popular lecturer, after he received a doctorate, entered his classroom to find it decorated. By the Sixties all the traditional demonstrativeness went into sharp decline and in some cases stopped quite abruptly.

> It was a startling experience for a teacher when his peroration and his exit took place in a sepulchral silence, and he naturally thought, 'I don't believe it can have been as bad as all that.'

That the system had shortcomings had been recognised. The Oxbridge system was envied for its superior ability to set up personal relationships between teachers and undergraduates. The tutorial system had been introduced in 1907, but in my day it still floated uneasily on the mainstream of the university tradition. It also diluted the principle of the Oxbridge system, where the tutor's relationship with the undergraduate would be one-to-one or one-to-two. This system, according to a friend who had experienced it, actually gave protection to the shy and the dour by not exposing them to the judgment of their contemporaries. Edinburgh tutorials consisted of a group of about a dozen students sitting round the table. An air of embarrassment hung about them like a cloud. The tutor worked hard to stimulate discussion but it was always very difficult. Our native self-consciousness made us poor fodder for tutorials, which assume some sort of genuine social and intellectual interaction; this spirit is snuffed out by diffidence and reticence. Much has been written about this difference between English and Scottish students, which I am told persists to this day. Many explanations have been advanced for it. Scottish schools, it was said, taught too much by rote and did not encourage self-expression. The English students, having done A-levels, were a year older, more mature and self-confident, speaking the language of Shakespeare and the Bible. Whatever the explanation it still seems to be true that Scottish students are more likely to fail in the first year because they have not gone through the weeding-out process of A-levels; but those who survive the first year of their university courses do just as well as their English contemporaries. The Scot tends to be slower in the maturing, less precocious than many an English person of the same age. The Scot will think very carefully before committing himself to an opinion in public whereas the Englishman will talk cheerfully and eloquently without fear of mockery. This does not necessarily make his views more sensible but they are more likely to command attention. I noticed that this phenomenon persisted into later life. Editorial conferences on *The Guardian* were different from those on *The Scotsman,* just as Edinburgh tutorials must have differed from those at Oxford. The *Guardian* conferences were more expostulatory and declamatory, less inhibited, more politicised with factions pushing their point of view. That curiously English literary form – the self-revelatory autobiography, with a statutory confession of homosexual dalliance at public school – has no Scottish equivalent.

There is some cultural force at work here that is reflected in the lack of political certainty that Scotland has displayed since the Union. Scotland suffers from cultural confusion and has absorbed habits of deference against which it kicks from time to time. It produces individuals or those who ably serve others. It helped to build the Empire; indeed, without the Scots the Empire could scarcely have been built. But Scotland, perhaps inevitably because of its peripheral position and the historical weakness of central power in its experience, has shown nothing like the English gift for creating collective institutions.

William McIlvanney, in his novel *Docherty,* gave a list of the good old Scottish words outlawed by the local teacher. To be told that your natural speech is somehow unacceptable must be undermining but is an inevitable consequence of living on the edge of a more powerful culture. That reality was recognised by the decision of the Kirk to adopt the Authorised Version of the Bible. From that day on the old Scots tongue was in retreat. Today it largely survives in a slipshod urban caricature. After Burns revived it as a literary language it fell victim to the Kailyard. MacDiarmid's revival of Scots as a literary language was of course a reaction to infantile and self-conscious twaddle. But, like the bebop movement of the 1940s, it was rebarbative, exclusive and full of anger. In the poetry of Robert Garioch, perhaps, we hear the only successful assertion in our time of the tradition of Fergusson and Burns, free of sentimentality, unforced in its language and full of symbols prescient of the twentieth century, notably in his great poem, 'The Wire':

> On this dour mechanistic muir
> With nae land's end, and endless day,
> Whaur nae thing thraws a shadow, here
> The truth is clear, and it is wae.

By 1957 the university's transformation into a bigger and much different institution was beginning, and the old daft and rumbustious ways were dying out. The rectorial election campaigns used to be fought out riotously, with pitched fist and flour battles in the Old Quad, and one may assume that student misbehaviour had been a problem from the days of the university's foundation. Its first published regulations set out a formidable list of requirements. Attendance both at lectures and kirk was compulsory. Every student had to swear obedience. There was to be no physical competition for seats at lectures. Students were to speak Latin at all times. There was to be no use of Scots, no swearing, no blasphemy or fighting, no weapons, no ball games. So specific a set of prohibition is the clearest evidence one could have of the innately unruly nature of the student body. Because the university had no hostel accommodation until relatively recent times, the students were thrown on to the town and its taverns.

By the time I went to Edinburgh University in 1957, the rectorial and other campaigns had reached unacceptable levels of violence and the authorities had begun to feel very uneasy about them. My brother David was slightly injured in the Suez riots in the Old Quad in 1956. The most notorious rectorial of the period, in fact, was in Glasgow in 1958, when the installation of Lord Butler as rector was reduced to chaos. The platform party was drenched with flour thrown by the disrespectful student audience: John Mackay, *The Glasgow Herald*'s photographer whose classic set of pictures remains in the Outram archive, was knocked out by a flying cabbage. The authorities had had enough, disciplinary reprisals followed, and rectorial campaigns, with their flour fights among rival factions and a generalised air of anarchy, lost their political innocence and their quality of spontaneous and joyous exuberance. In our time at Edinburgh James Robertson Justice was the most colourful rector. Justice had begun to behave like one of the characters he played in films, the autocratic Sir Lancelot Sprat in *Doctor in the House*. He maintained the tradition of high theatre in his rectorial address (the playwright James Bridie had written Alistair Sim's celebrated rectorial address in 1948). Justice, in his oration, attributed the poem 'The Little White Rose' to 'my friend Compton Mackenzie'. This controversy is remembered by few people today but the poem appears in the standard MacDiarmid anthology:

> The rose of all the world is not for me.
> I want for my part
> Only the little white rose of Scotland
> That smells sharp and sweet and breaks the heart.

The end of the Fifties saw the university, at that time concentrated round the Old and New Quads and King's Buildings, begin the construction of a new campus.

It knocked down much of George Square, a treasure of Georgian Edinburgh, to the horror of conservationists. Many have not yet forgiven the university for this act of vandalism. In the next decade, as student numbers swelled and the university's native character began to be diluted by teachers and students from the south (bringing with them the English term 'undergraduate'), student energies became less robustly spontaneous, to be seen as a release from the constrictions of study or as a combustion of youthful adrenalin, and were canalised into organised protest. This reflected the rise of union influence in society at large. Professor Donaldson wrote:

> By a curious paradox, in a generation which has seen students become so much more vocal and aggressive in their criticisms of university policy and their demands for a share in decision-making, and so militant in some activities to press their claims, they have become incomparably more docile in the classroom.

The decade culminated in the sit-ins and riots of 1968 when it seemed that the very political order was under revolutionary threat. My colleague Harry Reid, who went to Oxford in the Sixties, believes that this period of protest was abruptly terminated by the self-immolation of Jan Palach in Wenceslas Square in 1969 in protest against the invasion of Czechoslovakia. This shocking event, prompted by a real deprivation of human rights rather than some minor grievance, made the agenda of the student protest movement seem intolerably trivial by comparison, and it fizzled out having reached its climax on the streets of Paris. Some of the student leaders of that generation have turned into comfortably superannuated pillars of society but they, and their predecessors in the Fifties, were blessed in one respect denied to contemporary students. They did not have to worry too much about finding employment; indeed, we did not much discuss careers so low was the level of anxiety about them. Today's student goes to university, as far as I can see, with a worried frown and an industrious heart, and the docility noted by Professor Donaldson as having emerged in the Sixties appears to have become even more pronounced.

By the Seventies students demanded working rectors and sustained representation rather than paternalistic goodwill from a figurehead. The first working student rector in Scotland was Dr Jonathan Wills, now an environmental expert and journalist in Shetland, elected after Malcolm Muggeridge's resignation because of a controversy over the contraceptive pill. When a year later, in 1972, Gordon Brown, later to be Shadow Chancellor, became the second student rector, he not only insisted on chairing the court but presumed to influence its business. This enraged the university authorities and the Edinburgh establishment. The devolutionary debates were in full swing. The universities in Scotland, now carrying large numbers of English teachers who had helped to enlarge them as a result of the Robbins expansion, came out against it. In insulting terms they denigrated the capacity of a Scottish parliament to protect their interests, implying that this little country which had given so much to education, and had so often been in advance of its more prosperous neighbour, would not fight for it any more. The experiences of the Thatcherite Eighties were to change the universities' minds. A Welshman, Alwyn Williams, principal of Glasgow, and an Englishman, Graham Hills, of Strathclyde, were among the more adventurous spirits pushing their colleagues towards the embrace of the Scottish Office. By one of those ironies which litter politics, the universities were devolved to the Scottish Office (unscrutinised, it is true, by any Scottish parliament) in 1992. What could not be achieved by political pressure in the 1970s was granted, almost absent-mindedly, in the Thatcher twilight, not out of generosity but because it was decided to end the 'binary line' between universities and centrally funded institutions such as technical colleges. Now the old universities must fight for resources against the host of new universities which the Government swiftly founded by upgrading the central institutions and polytechnics and funding them according to elaborate criteria of research effectiveness and relative unit cost.

I feel glad that my university life was in an age of innocence. My university education, in its haphazard way, contrived to be very useful. A perversity in my nature made me indolent in my own cause but good marks came when I toiled over an essay for a girl I was in love with. There was a reader in rhetoric called Dr Melville Clark about whom I thought often during later years in journalism. A grammarian and pedant, he brought the worst kind of legalism to the study of language and literature. T. S. Eliot had, in some essay, contemptuosly dismissed him in a footnote. Thereafter, Clark sneered at *The Waste Land* as 'waste paper'. One of his favourite remarks was that it was incomprehensible that someone who had attended a football game should want to read some paltry account of it in a newspaper. Experience in newspapers taught me that those who had been to the game were those who most wanted to read about it afterwards. He set a test in which the sentences in a passage of prose were jumbled. The students were asked to reassemble them. Somewhat to my surprise I managed this without error, and this facility was to prove itself useful later on the sub-editors' desk. This was about the only examination in which I did well. In the second year I failed honours in French and German but passed at ordinary level. This allowed me to go on to the third year, which would give me an ordinary MA if I passed. The four-years honours course, and the year in France which I had planned to spend in Grenoble, would be discarded. I accepted my fate meekly enough, although my mother was deeply disappointed in me, and did not attempt the autumn resit. In truth medieval French and German bored me. To complete my MA I had to take a science subject. I chose geology, a department in which Edinburgh enjoyed international eminence (and still does). The theory of mountain-building and river-formation was interesting and enjoyable; the practical side I found completely baffling. I was utterly unable to identify rocks. We had field trips, when we strode about Arthur's Seat with hammers, looking for fossils. While others in the party would give out periodic exclamations of delight, I could find nothing but bare rock. Many years later the professor of geology at Edinburgh told me that there were no fossils on Arthur's Seat, and so I may have been the victim of some elaborate joke. In the final exams I failed geology because of my practical myopia but was awarded a pass by some kindly examiner whose memory I bless. I graduated in the autumn, at a rather melancholy gathering of those who had had to try again, but by that time I was learning my trade, in the most unstructured way, on *The Scotsman*. In the traditional Scottish manner I had gone to university in immaturity. I do not regret that and I retain a strong sense of gratitude to those who helped me survive it.

In 1993 Sir William Kerr Fraser, who as president of the SRC in 1951 organised the flour-spattered installation of the nationalist John MacCormick as Lord Rector of Glasgow University, told me that rectorials weren't what they were in his day. I suspect he was quite pleased about that now that he was on the other side of the fence. His university is among those pressing the Government to remove the ancient rectorial claim of right to the chair of the court. But when the following evening one Johnny Ball, a television presenter, was elected to this historic office in preference to a woman poet and a campaigning female barrister, I felt entitled to ask: Johnny who? I was rebuked by a reader who pointed out that Johnny Ball through his skill and charm had led many a child on to the paths of knowledge. He is a rector of the television age.

PART II
ECONOMIC DECLINE

CHAPTER FOUR

Change, decay and renewal

A visitor to Edinburgh can scarcely miss *The Scotsman* building on North Bridge. The editor's bay window commands a noble view of Princes Street and that acme of Edinburgh refinement, Jenners. Today the careful security system in the august entrance hall is a reminder of a painful industrial dispute between the company and its journalists in the early 1980s, when those on strike were barred from the building. The managerial suite, with its walnut hall, is richly panelled in wood. In my time the managing director's room had a coal fire and a servitor would replenish it with the solemnity of ritual. One flight of the staircase was in marble and here was the war memorial, but the rest of the interior, constructed round a well, was sepulchral and secret, with dim mysterious corridors and back stairs. When Roy Thomson bought *The Scotsman* from Sir Edmund Findlay and his associates in 1953, he got it more or less for nothing because he immediately sold off the adjacent property in North Bridge. One evening in the Seventies – I must have been bored that night – I wandered through a forgotten entrance into the staircase of the surplus property next door. A disused lift shaft disappeared into the gloom above. There was dust everywhere and the marble tiles on the stair wall were grimy. I felt like a time traveller. The equity hidden in this adjacent property, containing shops and office suites, had been overlooked by the Findlay family's self-satisfied but somnolent professional advisers. The story of Scotland's decline as an industrial and mercantile nation might as well begin with this parable as with any other.

The Scotsman had been founded in 1817, as part of the Whigs' improving drive that had also produced The Edinburgh Academy; it had turned Tory after the Irish Home Rule Bill of 1886 and after the Second World War had sunk into genteel decline. A leader discussing a disappointing Edinburgh Festival of 1953, the year in which Roy Thomson bought the paper, gives an idea of its dullness at that time:

> It may be asked whether music and drama have not their lighter moments, and whether the Festival does enough to provide light relief ... The Tattoo, of course provides entertainment for a vast number of people, but there may be some unexplored territory between the field of Mars and the heights of Parnassus.

This is what used to be called pan loaf, pure pan loaf (a reference to the type of bread preferred by the better off and therefore an emblem of gentility). During my many years working on *The Scotsman* this was the authentic, fluting voice of a grey and conservative paper that served a business and professional class famous for its complacency and self-satisfaction. The classical references were designed to establish a bond with a small and literate readership and exclude the common folk who provided a ribald counter-melody to the stately but plodding march of the respectable middle classes. My father's lawyer was cut from this block of polite ice. 'Robert,' he said once, 'there is no such thing as a change for the better.' It was a proposition with which much of Edinburgh, and *The Scotsman*, all too obviously agreed. The Liberal belief in the need for renewal and improvement had evaporated; and the editor, Murray Watson, who served the last two years of his life under Thomson, resisted front-page news to the end.

The case of *The Scotsman* exemplified above all the failure of indigenous dynastic ownership. By the beginning of the post-war era its finances were in a terminally disastrous state, a situation shrouded in complacency. Even in my time, four years after Roy Thomson's acquisition of the paper, the composing room was a shambles, badly under-resourced. (Re-reading that sentence I am reminded that *The Scotsman* style book prohibited the use of the word 'shambles' except in the sense of a slaughterhouse.) Getting the paper out every night was a nightmare because of an enormous overset together with a perpetual famine of usable type.

The old composing room, with its smell of ink and lead, has gone from the industry now, but it was a place of genuine fascination. Surely no more beautiful or satisfying machine has ever been designed than the Linotype. Man and machine worked together in harmony and the machine's long arm, grasping the brass matrices from the pot where they had been used to mould the type and returning them to the magazine above, moved up and down in human rhythm. An often agitated wee man went round with a piece of tape measuring the set as it accumulated. On the hour, every hour, he would communicate the news that there was not nearly enough type to see the paper away in time, and some fairly desperate strategems, for example running the same picture on different pages or putting the results of *The Scotsman*'s own golf tournament on page one, were occasionally used.

The chief sub of the day would emerge from the composing room after the chaotic first edition carrying endless galleys of overmatter. This was type which had arrived too late for a first edition padded with material – often special foreign articles syndicated from *The Observer* – set in the small hours of the previous day. The capacity, in short, was there but it was not available at the appropriate time to meet the inevitable peaks of demand in the productive cycle of a morning paper. The task of the sub-editors was then to cut the overmatter into the second edition. In this harem-scarem manner I acquired an excellent training as a sub-editor, learning to work under pressure, to condense and rewrite. But I fear that the high fluting tone of the genteel and impenetrable editorials stayed with me for some time, and it was much later that I finally managed to rid my non-news style of it (or at least that is my delusion).

The Scotsman had an excellent reputation for picture reproduction, which it retains to this day, but in other parts of the process there was a marked lack of essential resources, whether in the advertising departments where dames who sat knitting took in the advertising business that walked in the door without prompt or salesman's canvass or in the composing room with its nightly panic (a recurring dream of mine at the time was of standing at the front page waiting for type I knew – because it was my fault – would never come).

Such inadequacies flowed from the financial feebleness that Thomson had inherited. Sir Edmund Findlay and his partners had allowed the business to drift into debt and death duties threatened to destroy it. The extraordinary complacency of the time is illustrated by the fact that Edinburgh, and the staff of *The Scotsman* itself, almost entirely ignored evidence given to the Royal Commission on the Press in 1948 which made the situation clear. When Sir Edmund had taken over his father's interest in *The Scotsman* he had also taken responsibility for future death duties on the assumption that profits would provide a basis for doing so. Slack management made such ambitions worthless. Profits did not materialise and the bank overdrafts grew.

There were in my time apocryphal stories that Sir Edmund liked a drink and would sometimes call into the counting house to pick up some petty cash before setting off for Monte Carlo. Whatever the truth of that, *The Scotsman*'s professional advisers determined that a sale was essential. Roy Thomson acquired his first newspaper in Britain and by releasing the equity of the surplus property immediately put the business on a sounder footing. This could presumably have been accomplished by the Findlay interests had they been more shrewdly advised. It took a brash young Canadian to show the Edinburgh professionals how such matters could be arranged; for this Roy Thomson was to pay a heavy price and he never took to Edinburgh. Polite society sneered at him; the doziness of Edinburgh professionals, so startlingly exposed, stoked their natural dislike of this Canadian parvenu. When Thomson flippantly said that he planned to introduce a page of comic strips, the town was aghast. It simply couldn't take the joke.

Immediately after Watson's death Roy Thomson appointed Alastair Dunnett as editor. Kemsley's sale of the *Daily Record,* which Dunnett edited from 1946 to 1955, had closed one door; Roy Thomson opened another and this small dark man, a humorous and lively journalist, revived the paper and brought to it and its editorial proceedings the wit and warmth of the West. The incumbent deputy editor, a frosty, unsociable and pedagogic man who had expected the job, was not easily reconciled to Dunnett. His response was a prolonged huff. One or two of the senior staff rallied to him and formed a disloyal opposition with which Dunnett had to cope for many years.

Some of them carried polite Edinburgh's distaste for sensationalism to the point of absurdity, at least when it occurs in a newspaperman. The dramatic critic, an Olympian and erudite Shakespearean, having completed a column on a poetry reading by T. S. Eliot which he had attended that evening, put on his hat and then, as an afterthought, informed the chief reporter that a lion had escaped at the circus playing in Waverley Market and mauled members of the audience. Yes, it was true, because he had observed it on his way to the poetry reading, having been commissioned (to his evident disgust) also to write a short review of the circus. On another occasion, sent to review Cliff Richard at the Empire, he devoted most of his piece to the jugglers who were second on the bill, making many scholarly references to the history of their art. Cliff Richard was mentioned in the last paragraph which, in the way of newspapers, was 'cut on the stone' (removed in the composing room to get the paper away). Another distinguished old boy, in the various specialisms which he covered, acquired the feathers of the flock in which he happened to be flying at the time. While dealing with religious affairs he adopted the mannerisms of a bishop; and during his stint of covering the Scottish Office, he strolled about like a senior civil servant carrying the latest White Paper on this or that; he once rebuked me for having published a scoop (by my brother David as it happened) prominently on Page One. 'We were most displeased,' he said, 'we' being the civil service.

The Scotsman survived this inherited torpor. Thomson went on to acquire Scottish Television. This investment opportunity was shunned by the Scottish financial community. It became, in Thomson's typically candid phrase, a licence to print money and funded his emergence as Britain's most significant post-war newspaper proprietor, at least until the advent of Murdoch. He acquired the Kemsley chain, including *The Sunday Times*. He played a leading part in rationalising the declining market for evening papers. He revolutionised revenue-raising techniques; the Thomson methods of telephone canvassing have now become standard. The pinnacle of his career was his acquisition of *The Times* but this happiness was wrecked by persistent labour troubles. Sometimes on *The Scotsman* we were stupidly suspicious of Thomson, or at least of the organisation which he put in place when he moved to London, and our desire to maintain our independence partly explained why *The Scotsman* in the Seventies so enthusiastically endorsed devolution, to the point that it irritated and even alienated many of its Conservative and Unionist readers.

The episode of *The Scotsman* showed dynastic failure but also that the arrival of new proprietorial energies and management skills could be re-invigorating. Newspapers, however, are not like other businesses. They have a resistance to import penetration. It is fortunate for us all that Japanese newspapers have no appeal in Sauchiehall Street and that the geographical rationalisation of their production is possible only to a limited degree. In Lanarkshire, for example, the Wishaw local paper is now printed in nearby Hamilton, much to the regret of older locals.

CHAPTER FIVE

A *dissipated patrimony*

The next step in Thomson's career with *The Scotsman* leads into an episode of more general application to Scotland's experience of industrial decline. By 1963 he had concluded a deal with Westminster Press which created a series of evening newspaper monopolies. As a result the successful *Edinburgh Evening News* was absorbed by The Scotsman Publications, which closed its own evening paper, *The Evening Dispatch*.

The following year he turned his attention to the morning paper scene, and made a bid for *The Glasgow Herald*. Although the pledge was made to maintain the distinctive nature of the paper, some amalgamation, at least of printing and newsgathering activities, would inevitably have resulted. A white knight appeared in the form of the draper (if so significant a capitalist can be so called), Sir Hugh Fraser. He was the third in a dynastic line of drapers, all of them called Hugh. The first sold cloth round the doors. His mother kept a pub and ran a Clyde ferry at Cardross. In 1849 the first Hugh opened a shop at the cheap end of Buchanan Street. From such origins the third Sir Hugh (later Lord Fraser of Allander) became by far the most significant capitalist to emerge in post-war Scotland. The dissipation of his empire after his death was the classic cautionary tale of rags to riches and back again; the part played by predatory capitalism was typical also of its time when enterprises were being accumulated into conglomerates.

Scottish and Universal Investments (SUITs) had been incorporated in 1948 as a private limited company wholly owned by the Fraser family. The main aim in establishing the company had been to acquire part of the family interest in House of Fraser Ltd, which became a public company in the same year, and protect it from bids. SUITs became a public company in 1960. At that point its holding in House of Fraser still represented more than 90 per cent of its net assets and the Fraser family had more than 70 per cent of the share capital.

George Outram, named after a former editor of *The Herald* (an advocate who has a residual fame as a writer of light verse, *Legal Lyrics*), had become a public company in 1919. By 1964 it had a wide spread of private and institutional shareholders and Sir Hugh was its deputy chairman. He had built up the House of Fraser into a national chain of department stores and shown himself to be a master of public takeover battles by successfully outbidding Debenhams for the control of Harrods.

In September 1964 Lord Thomson mounted a hostile bid, of £5.25 million, for Outram. Over 52 days, interrupted by Harold Wilson's general election victory, a classic, indeed notorious, takeover battle was waged between Fraser and Thomson. When the two found themselves on the same flight to London Fraser told Thomson: 'If it's a fight you want, Roy, then I'm your man.' The business editor of *The Herald*, R. E. Dundas, wrote in 1992 of what followed:

And so, indeed, it proved. Fraser soon decided Outram's independence could not be preserved. Having been made chairman for a brief period he resigned from the Outram board and used SUITs . . . to mount a counter offer. Five times Thomson bid, Fraser only twice. The second Fraser bid valuing Outram at £7,343,644, won the day, although too late in the struggle Thomson made his final offer which valued the company at £8,294,383.

The tactics employed, especially by the Fraser side, were ruthless, as they had been in the battle for Harrods. Many of them are no longer permitted by the City code on takeovers and mergers. Fraser's financial adviser, Mr John B. Kinross, organised an orgy of share-buying in Outram through friendly stock-brokers which swept Fraser to victory with the lower offer.

Hugh Fraser was everybody's favourite tycoon in the Sixties, and West of Scotland families who owned Outram shares were flattered to receive phone calls from the great man asking them to sell out to him. More than once a round of golf was interrupted to make a crucial call. Elderly women were told their fathers would have wanted their shares to go to the Fraser camp.

I had only just joined *The Herald* staff, and I remember my grandfather, who had a modest holding and who, it must be said, had himself been part of the Fraser empire as advertising manager at Pettigrew and Stephens in Sauchie-hall Street, railing against the impertinence of Thomson. Local loyalties and a distrust of Thomson's bid to add yet more newspapers to his pile were decisive factors in the battle. The Fraser interests ensured, too, that the SUITs terms were always attractive by assiduously supporting its share price in the market.

Some close to the scene were sure that Fraser claimed victory before he had bought 50 per cent of the shares. Thomson went on buying in the market, believing Fraser had not yet won the day. The then editor of *The Herald*, Mr James Holburn, himself an Outram director, penned a controversial leader deploring the public auction of 'a famous organ of information and opinion – part of the political machinery of our country – like a beast in the ring'.

SUITs now began its transformation into an industrial holding company. In the years after securing the ownership of *The Herald* and *Evening Times*, it acquired a number of Scottish weekly papers and various other interests. By the middle of the Seventies its assets reflected a wide spread of interests in printing, publishing and bookselling; the drinks trade; engineering; textiles and insurance broking.

The group turnover in the year to March 1976 was £49 million, with profits before tax and before internal interest of £4 million. SUITs therefore was now much more than a Fraser bulwark against predators. It was one of the few significant industrial holding companies registered in and operating from Scotland. At this time great concern was being expressed, notably by the Scottish Council (Development and Industry) about the external ownership of companies in Scotland and the development of the 'branch' economy.

Fraser died in 1966 and was succeeded by his son, Sir Hugh, with consequences that can without exaggeration be called tragic. This amiable figure exemplified the penalties of birth with a silver spoon in the mouth. Sir Hugh had come young to office, and for a while dazzled an admiring public. He was made Young

Businessman of the Year. His marriage was the social event of 1962. Despite all his misfortunes he somehow contrived to remain both popular and prominent. From the start he showed little aptitude for business but with this lack of ability, as is so often the case, came a lack of self-knowledge. It is not given to every man to go to Corinth; had he recognised that he was not a chip off the old block, had he lived quietly on his investments, he might have died a happy man. In the Seventies he was one of a group of businessmen who flirted with the Scottish National Party in the hope that the opportunities of North Sea oil could revive the native tradition of entrepreneurial capitalism. He renounced his father's peerage, on the grounds that there could be only one Lord Fraser of Allander, but he was driven throughout his life by a desire to emulate his father. As his business judgment was consistently poor, as his amenable nature was forever exploited by unscrupulous or incompetent associates, this could have only one result. He was to prove, if proof were needed, that a fool and his money are soon parted, but there is a genuinely Faustian quality to the story of his friendship with R. W. (Tiny) Rowland.

By 1975 he was in deep trouble because his lack of business judgment was compounded by an addiction to gambling. He told Murray Ritchie of *The Herald* in 1978, the year SUITs fell into the clutches of Lonrho despite spirited resistance by most of its directors, that he had accumulated gambling debts of more than £3 million. Tom Bower put them at £4 million in his 1993 biography of Rowland. He wrote:

> The unpublicised cause of Hugh Fraser's decline was his irrepresssible addiction to gambling on the roulette wheel. As a regular and welcome visitor to London's casinos, Fraser frequently played two wheels simultaneously and, betting on 32, his 'lucky' number, was known to lose £500,000 in an evening. To John Patterson, his friend and personal assistant, Fraser mentioned his nightly misfortunes in the third person . . . Patterson could see that his friend was excited by gambling, actually enjoyed losing, and was unrepentant about the forced sale of shares to settle his debts . . . The amounts were staggering and the flow continued unabated.

The SUITs accounts for the year to March 1975 had begun to signal that all was not well. They recorded without comment one of Sir Hugh's major lapses of judgment. He paid Beaverbrook Newspapers, which ceased printing his titles in Scotland in 1974, the staggering sum of £2.76 million for the title and goodwill of the *Evening Citizen,* which then closed. There is a phrase used in the West of Scotland to describe someone who is lucky at somebody else's expense: Lord Beaverbrook truly 'won a watch' and Sir Hugh unwittingly helped foot the redundancy bill. The largest extraordinary item in these accounts, however, was the writing off of £13.8 million, being the excess of the purchase price of subsidiaries over net assets acquired, i.e. 'goodwill on acquisition'. This expensive goodwill – or premium – was deducted from shareholders' funds. Given the state of the accounts the self-satisfaction of the chairman's remarks, and his gratuituous advice to the government of the day on various matters, still have the power to startle.

In October 1974 SUITs sold 21.3 million of its holdings of House of Fraser ordinary shares to Carter Hawley Hale Stores of the United States. By 1978 its holding was between 10 and 11 per cent of the House of Fraser issued share capital. For the 1975 sale SUITs received £25.8 million, and in his chairman's statement in the 1975 report and accounts Sir Hugh explained what had happened to the money. More than £9m was used to repay existing borrowings and of the remainder, he said, approximately one third had been invested in the equity market; one third had been used to build up whisky stocks, a claim about which there was continuing scepticism among insiders; and the final one third, he stated, had been held as short and medium term loans. He added: 'The effect upon the parent company finances has been worthwhile as will be seen from the profit and loss account.' In fact the accounts showed the exact opposite and a profit after tax of £2.9 million had been achieved only after the transfer of capital reserves of £7.25 million.

The next year's report and accounts showed there had been a lack of frankness, or worse, in the 1975 statement. What Sir Hugh had concealed was a disastrous property speculation. In October 1974 he made a loan of £4.35 million to Amalgamated Caledonian Ltd (Amcal) for the redevelopment of the property in Westminster acquired by Amcal following House of Fraser's acquisition of the Army & Navy store. It subsequently became apparent that because of the depressed state of the property market it was unlikely that Amcal would be able to repay the loan and related interest and it was eventually provided for in the March 1976 accounts.

The failure to disclose the loan in the 1975 accounts and to report dealings by certain directors in SUITs shares was the subject of a Stock Exchange inquiry and subsequent proceedings under the Companies Act. Sir Hugh said that the cash for the loan had come from the proceeds of the share sale to Carter Hawley Hale and that its omission from the 1975 report had been an 'accounting error'. I was told in 1993 by a senior banker that this was almost certainly truthful as far as it went: an accountant in the company had a love affair with the bottle.

Sir Hugh told the annual general meeting in September 1976: 'I hope shareholders will accept my assurance that this was a genuine mistake and was not in any way an attempt to present the financial position of the company as being stronger than in fact it was.' He added with the optimism of the gambler who never knows when to quit: 'It is clear with hindsight that this was a bad investment, although I hope – and I maintain this hope – that it may eventually prove not to be as bad as prudence now compels us to regard it.' In the event the company recovered £700,000 of the £4.3 million loan in 1978.

When Sir Hugh came to court, Sheriff Irvine Smith took a lenient view. Sir Hugh and three directors were convicted of failing to disclose the Amcal loan in the accounts. Sir Hugh was fined £600, William Forgie £110, Nicholas Redmayne £100 and Angus Grossart £75. The sheriff said he found it 'incredible that this balance-sheet went through with an elementary error undetected.' Forgie, Redmayne and Grossart all resigned from the board. Charges relating to massive undisclosed sharedealings by Sir Hugh were not proven.

By the time the report and accounts were presented for the year ended March 1977 much had changed. Four directors had resigned and Tiny Rowland was in the chair with Sir Hugh as his deputy. Sir Hugh had had at March 1975 the beneficial interest in 4.5 million SUITs shares. Now he had none; this part of his patrimony was squandered. Although the transaction was not recorded in this set of accounts, the Monopolies and Mergers Commission in its report of 1979 into the proposed merger between Lonrho and SUITs noted that in March 1977 Lonrho had acquired a 24 per cent interest in SUITs from Sir Hugh, members of his family and family trusts. A further holding of 5 per cent was acquired in the market between March and July.

How had it come about? Rowland had come galloping to the rescue as Sir Hugh searched with increasing desperation for a way out of his gambling debts. Rowland was still smarting from various encounters with the regulatory authorities and was beginning his assault on bastions of the Establishment. Sir Hugh was to be his tool.

The maverick boss of Lonrho had formed an ambition to gain control of Harrods but his motivations remained enigmatic. For 11 years of my editorship, he was my proprietor. We never met. Lonrho made few attempts to interfere editorially, except for one suggestion that *The Herald* should carry material unfavourable to the Fayed Brothers, whose success in gaining control of Harrods, after his own bid had been refused, was to embitter Rowland. 'Never mind the libel' came the message along with a bundle of defamatory material for our use. Our position was that, as proprietor, Lonrho had every right to insert statements in *The Herald* but these must not purport to have been freely and independently reported. This message was given; it was received with evident displeasure.

My anxieties were greatly eased by the staunch support of the then managing director, Terry Cassidy, who to his ultimate cost loved nothing better than telling the bosses where they were going wrong. A classic instance of this was the occasion on which we lunched George Younger, then Secretary of State and now Lord Younger. The purpose was to lobby against the imposition of VAT on newspapers. George came in cheerily and announced it was clearly a nonsense to think of it. Throughout lunch Terry lectured him on the incompetence of 'you bunglers' in government. As he left, now rather icy, George remarked that since Terry was so supremely competent he would be easily able to take VAT in his stride. Terry's lack of tact was to ensure that his spell at Celtic Park where he later became chief executive was brief but colourful. To nobody's surprise he rapidly fell out with the board.

There was another outburst of seigneurial anger when *The Herald*, after Cassidy's departure, ran a sympathetic profile of him. This did not go down at all well, and Rowland's wrath could be heard like distant thunder through the agitation of his subordinates. Luckily for *The Herald*, Rowland had *The Observer* to assist him in the prosecution of his sense of injustice over Harrods, at some expense to that newspaper's reputation, and so we were spared his closer persuasion. The only other, and slightly ludicrous, example of proprietorial interest, though not from Rowland himself, came early in my editorship when one of our reporters discovered that an African prince was staying at a Glasgow hotel called the White House. For a while he toyed with the idea of a diary paragraph headed 'Black prince at White House', made some inquiries and then, sensibly given its crassness, abandoned the notion. I had an apprehensive phone call from a Lonrho executive. The prince was visiting Scotland at Lonrho's expense and apparently had a habit of going on the town and making indecent advances to waitresses ('putting a hand up their skirt,' was the indelicate phrase used).

The prince was one of Rowland's many connections in black Africa. He himself had emerged from Africa in 1961. Lonrho had been incorporated in the UK in 1909 as a mining company operating in Southern Rhodesia. Over the next 50 years it expanded into property, ranching, agriculture and asbestos. It also dealt in shares, mostly mining shares. In 1961 it entered into an agreement with Rowland, then a director of Rio Tinto companies in Central Africa. Rowland became joint managing director of Lonrho which acquired the majority of the assets of a company he owned called Shepton Estates. This reverse takeover was financed by

Lonrho shares and share options. Great difficulties were caused in 1965 when the Rhodesian Government made its unilateral declaration of independence (UDI). By now Lonrho's turnover had increased eightfold to £32 million and it was operating not only in Rhodesia but also in Zambia, Malawi and South Africa. Sanctions placed on trade with Rhodesia were a setback but in 1967 Lonrho resumed its policy of development in the newly independent African states. A period of acquisition followed and during the next five years Lonrho expanded into the United Kingdom and Europe in the wine trade, textiles, construction, engineering, shipping and motor distribution. In 1975 it began a second wave of sustained expansion in the United Kingdom but by this time a large shadow had fallen across it.

In 1971 its finance director and other executives were arrested in South Africa on charges relating to an abortive takeover bid. The charges were subsequently withdrawn. Later that year Lonrho's financial advisers and two of its non-executive directors resigned. The cumulative effect was a loss of confidence. Lonrho took various restorative steps and in 1972 felt able to make a £10 million rights issue. A year later it was in trouble again. The group accounts raised certain matters, which together with disagreements on policy, caused eight of the directors to seek Rowland's removal from executive office. The dispute was put to the shareholders who strongly supported Rowland and dismissed the eight directors opposed to him. That May the Secretary of State for Trade and Industry appointed inspectors to investigate Lonrho's affairs. The report recognised Rowland's abilities and that Lonrho was very much his creation. But it was in some cases extremely critical of his actions. In 1973 Edward Heath issued his famous denunciation of Lonrho as the unpleasant and unacceptable face of capitalism. The report was examined by the Director of Public Prosecutions who decided that further action was not justified.

These events left a powerful impression and helped to shape Rowland's attitudes thereafter. Other influences were noted by Tom Bower in his 1993 biography of Rowland:

> Even his oldest colleagues could only speculate that the source of his vitriol dated back to the 1940s when, as a suspected Nazi sympathiser, he had been interned by the British Government. Having buried that legacy, he was later pursued for avoiding payment of taxes. Twenty-five years afterwards, he was outlawed as a pariah by the City. Like a woman, Tiny wanted to be admired and, by the same token, loathed his critics.

These attitudes expressed themselves as a dislike of the Establishment (which became obsessive after his takeover of Harrods was blocked in 1981) and a desire to acquire some of its ripest plums. In the mid-1970s his wish to own a UK national paper became explicit and in his pursuit of Harrods he chose the ripest English plum of all. If Jenners was the acme of Edinburgh gentility, Harrods was the very symbol of English taste and quality.

In 1975 Rowland seemed to young Sir Hugh as the purest white knight. His gambling debts were being called in (they had mutated into loans from financial institutions and were thus recoverable at law). He had to sell some of his SUITs shares, about six or seven per cent of his holding. His problem was that he could not place them on the market in a bundle without seriously damaging confidence and the share price. He therefore turned to Rowland. According to SUITs insider lore, Rowland took his shares off him, but Fraser's friends were left in no doubt that if Rowland wished to extend his holding in SUITs Sir Hugh would support him.

By 1979 Lonrho had gained control of SUITs when the Monopolies and Mergers Commission found a merger not to be against the public interest. Immediately the SUITs directors were ordered to transfer the SUITs shareholding in House of Fraser to Lonrho headquarters in Cheapside, London. At middle market price? they asked. No, came the answer: at original purchase price. When the transfer formally took place SUITs was given a credit of £8.7 million for shares carrying a market value of £20 million at the time. Lonrho could congratulate itself on a major coup. From the first the SUITs acquisition made a positive contribution to its cash flow. The total outlay by Lonrho had been almost £57 million. By 1982 it was estimated, after taking into account cash transfers and the costs of acquisitions loaded on to SUITs, that the true cost of the acquisition to Lonrho had been a paltry £5.72 million. Truly had Sir Hugh sold his patrimony for a song and Tiny 'won a watch'.

It was a sorry story but it had not happened without dogged resistance. From the moment of Lonrho's involvement on the board it had become apparent to the SUITs directors, now under the able chairmanship of Hugh Laughland, that Rowland had bigger fish to fry than the affairs of a Scottish holding company. In transactions in 1975 and 1976, SUITs had purchased shares bringing its holding in House of Fraser to 10.3 per cent. Since 1960 SUITs had greatly changed. By 1978 it was no longer an investment company first and foremost. Now 90 per cent of its profits were derived from its direct operating subsidiaries. In 1977 the SUITs board, on the advice of its then merchant bankers Robert Fleming & Co Ltd, decided in principle to sell its total shareholding in House of Fraser and to concentrate its activities on industrial trading. This was opposed by the Lonrho directors on the SUITs board and no more was heard of it, an eloquent omen. Hugh Laughland, when we conversed in 1993, had a slightly different recollection. His idea had been to retain the House of Fraser holdings and use them as collateral to finance expansion and acquisition.

The threatened disposal prompted Rowland to make a more substantial acquisition in February of that year. In March he told the SUITs board of his 24.5 per cent holding, acquired from Sir Hugh, his family and certain family trusts. As a result he was appointed chairman of SUITs, though he was usually represented at board meetings by an alternate. Sir Hugh continued as deputy chairman. Lonrho went on buying SUITs shares in the market and by July 1977 held 29.3 per cent of the issued capital. It also built up its holding in House of Fraser and during this period floated the idea of a wide merger embracing Lonrho, SUITs, House of Fraser and Carter Hawley Hale. Eventually Lonrho told Sir Hugh that it would make a direct offer for SUITs not involving the House of Fraser. On 19 April 1978 Lonrho made a public offer for the issued share capital of SUITs which it did not already own. With Sir Hugh and James Gossman (a loyal aide of Sir Hugh's father) dissenting, the SUITs board felt unable to recommend acceptance, and in May it was referred to the Monopolies and Mergers Commission. The bid lapsed during the inquiry.

Murray Ritchie, at that time a bright young investigative journalist on *The Herald* (in 1992 he was appointed its European Editor based in Brussels), looked into the affair. His article was shown by the editor of the day to Lonrho and encountered its displeasure. He finally got to publish it, with an explanatory preamble, after Lonrho disposed of *The Herald* in 1992, but it is worth quoting:

> After six weeks, during which Lord Fraser's late son, Sir Hugh, proved helpful, I produced 6000 words describing what was a fascinating and sometimes farcical fight among some of big business's most illustrious names. The only part missing was Tiny Rowland's side of the story. I spoke to Rowland on the telephone. At least I think I did. He had a colleague, a Mr Spicer, who often intercepted Rowland's calls and who gave me this advice: 'When you speak to Mr Rowland, you speak to me. And when you speak to me, you are speaking to Mr Rowland. We are interchangeable.'
>
> I explained to Rowland, or his alter ego, that I would like his own account of the SUITs takeover battle. 'Let me see what you have written so far,' I was told. Submitting copy for vetting by a proprietor is foreign to the journalist's nature unless you happen to work for the maniacal type like a Maxwell or Beaverbrook. But there seemed no choice. *The Herald* was, after all, his property. Our editor agreed to send the story to Tiny Rowland.
>
> Some days later, the message came back (and I can remember the conversation clearly): 'Mr Rowland doesn't like this story. In fact, he doesn't like it at all. He suggests you stick to reporting world news.' The Rowland/Spicer voice added, as though by way of an afterthought: 'And some Scottish news . . .'
>
> The story never appeared because it was inevitably one-sided. Most of it is irrelevant now although some of the detail remains illuminating. Tiny Rowland won his battle to take over from the vacillating Sir Hugh – who had warned me the story would never appear because Tiny had promised him it wouldn't – and until last week it remained locked away in a forgotten file, a type-written relic of old technology.

Sir Hugh admitted to Ritchie that he had suffered gambling losses of £3.5 million. He was introduced, at the suggestion of management consultants, to Rowland. 'Tiny's an exciting guy,' Sir Hugh said admiringly. He proved susceptible to his charm and malleable in his hands. (Bower described how Rowland cajoled him over lunch with flattery, feeding his self-delusion. 'He's a fantastic guy, just like my father,' Sir Hugh told Patterson.) In the SUITs board there had been frequent confusion about the initials on internal memos for directors. Laughland was known as HL and Fraser was known as HF. But a typist, presumably a Cockney, had misheard an instruction to type HF on a memo for Fraser and typed 'I. Jeff.' From that moment on Fraser was nicknamed Jeff.

At one point in the battle Sir Hugh changed his mind, saying that Rowland's latest offer was insufficient. He fell back in line with the dissenters, saying there was 'no personal disagreement'. Rowland invited Fraser to dinner at a hotel in Knightsbridge. The dissenters were terrified that Fraser would be beguiled, change his mind again and part with the vital 8.94 per cent of SUITs shares held by the Fraser Trustees. A City cynic said: 'SUITs were scared stiff that Jeff would gaze into Tiny's big blue eyes and turn.' The fears were justified. That night the late Robert Martin, City Editor of *The Herald*, was telephoned by a contact and told: 'Jeff has turned.' Fraser had changed sides again, this time for an extra 15p. Fraser had clinched the deal over dinner and telephoned from his car with details of his agreement. Messages of sympathy came into Laughland in the SUITs office in Park Gardens. When one caller expressed congratulations for the stand SUITs had taken, Laughland replied: 'It was worth the candle.' He told me in 1993 that in a way he was glad to have been pushed out of the small pond of West of Scotland to survive in deeper waters, as he did. When he got his next job he was told that Rowland had given him an enthusiastic reference, an interesting revelation: Tiny respected those who fought him honourably.

In their objections to the merger, the majority of the SUITs directors told the MMC they believed it would be against the public interest because SUITs was strong and its management now effective. Lonrho on the other hand was financially over-strained as a result of its numerous acquisitions. There was consequently a like-lihood that SUITs funds would be diverted to other Lonrho purposes. It was important to Scottish interests that the control of one of the few remaining signifi-cant public companies in Scotland should not be removed from that country.

For its part Lonrho had made various promises. Its management structure of autonomous regions retained a great deal of independence and regional identity. SUITs would become a regional centre headquartered in Glasgow. SUITs as part of Lonrho would build up its existing activities. It would become a vehicle for Scottish projects and acquisitions which in themselves would be too small for Lonrho. It promised 'large potential' markets overseas through its connections for SUITs whisky, educational publicatons and engineering services.

The commission gave Lonrho the benefit of the doubt. Events quickly proved it wrong, as it acknowledged in the report two years later which decided that a Lonrho takeover of House of Fraser would be against the public interest. To his stupefaction Sir Hugh found himself under bitter attack from his old patron and benefactor, the man he had worshipped. His weakness for gambling, from which Rowland had given him respite, was now turned against him when he was removed from the chairmanship of House of Fraser during the period immediately before Rowland's bid for it in 1981.

At a House of Fraser board meeting Rowland attacked Sir Hugh's fitness to be a director of any public company and invited him to vacate the office of chairman. Rowland and Lord Duncan-Sandys (the Lonrho chairman) had written to Sir Hugh about his gambling debts and his cheques in payment for gaming tokens being dishonoured on presentation. They claimed this implied his insolvency.

Sir Hugh's explanation was if anything more pathetic than the problem. He explained that his cheques had been dishonoured under a long-standing arrange-ment with his bankers designed to inhibit his urge to gamble. He told the MMC that this arrangement was known to the casinos concerned, who had instructions not to grant him credit and accepted that if they did so they would be paid when it suited him.

Lonrho did not develop SUITs as a Scottish holding company. It used it as a cash cow and a vehicle for acquisitions that made no sense to SUITs. It put no new equity into the companies but milked them until disposal became the prudent option. In its report on the House of Fraser bid, the MMC recognised the rapid deterioration in the position of a company that had been cash rich and with unused borrowing capacity. In the 1975 accounts it was shown as having net assets of £30.9 million. Among its liabilities were long-term loans of £770,000 but there was no overdraft.

We now know, of course, that this set of accounts concealed an important liability but with the new directorate that took over after the boardroom purge and energetic management the company made a strong resurgence. By 1979 its net assets had reached the very substantial figure of £60.5 million and, on acquisition in September of that year, it had shareholders' funds of £51.7 million and borrowings of only £6.8 million.

So strong an industrial holding company could with judicious leadership have played a leading role in regenerating and reorganising key sectors of the Scottish economy and sustaining its tradition of native entrepreneurial capitalism. But by September 1990, its net assets had slumped to £48.4 million and its bank loans and overdrafts now totalled a staggering £72.2 million, an increase of £66.8 million since takeover.

The increase arose partly from borrowings to finance acquisitions dictated by Lonrho and partly from the borrowings of acquired companies. SUITs acting for Lonrho had acquired the motor distributors Dutton-Forshaw and the security printers Harrisons in 1980. Both were debt-laden. In neither would the old board of SUITs have been remotely interested. The price of Dutton-Forshaw was £23.2 million which SUITs financed through loans from the Bank of Montreal and the Swiss Bank Corporation. What Rowland appeared to want from Dutton-Forshaw was the Jack Barclay Rolls-Royce franchise, another supreme symbol of England. Harrisons had the prestigious contract for the Post Office.

The usefulness of SUITs, apart from its stake in House of Fraser, was as a means of externalising liabilities from the Lonrho balance sheet. When SUITs was in danger of breaching its banking covenants, cash would flow from Lonrho on the right side of the year end and various adjustments were made to the balance sheet. Outrams, the SUITs subsidiary, was used to acquire *The Observer* in 1981, and when it launched *The Sunday Standard* the same year, in response to a gap in the market for a Scottish quality Sunday newspaper, it received no new input of equity, had to finance the paper out of borrowing, had to service the borrowing out of revenue, and had to work off the £5 million debt when *The Sunday Standard* closed, not surprisingly in these unfavourable circumstances, after two years. *The Observer* was in the end excluded from the SUITs accounts but not before the Lonrho financial bosses had accepted the unfairness with which SUITs was being treated.

In the four years between 1979, the year of acquisition, and 1983 there was an effective transfer of cash or assets from SUITs to Lonrho of more than £69 million. Despite the enormous debt burdens, SUITs under its new chief executive Kenneth Graham restored profitability; but Lonrho broke the last of its many promises to the MMC in 1986 when SUITs ceased to be an employing company. The chief executives of the operating companies became employees of their own companies. Long-serving directors were declared redundant. By now the empire had shrunk; by 1992 the printing company Holmes McDougall, the whisky distillers Whyte & Mackay, and the chain of Scottish local newspapers, Scottish and Universal, had been sold. Outram, shorn of the £8 million it received when it realised its Reuter shares, was among the last to go as Lonrho moved to placate a City increasingly critical of its high gearing. It had been savaged in the *Financial Times* Lex column for a lack of frankness about the extent of its liabilities.

Outram was acquired from Lonrho in a management buyout with the support of Flemings (a throwback to the old days) and other banks and institutions, a premium was extracted, and to the purchase price was added the residual debts on the presses and other equipment. The exhausting business of the buyout had been conducted by our managing director, Liam Kane, his deputy Iain M. Forbes and our finance director Ron MacDonald. They were a magnificent trio. For my part I carried on with a long-planned holiday with French friends in Burgundy. There was no phone in the cottage but the neighbouring farmer, who spoke no English, had been taking the incomprehensible messages. He summoned me to the phone and Liam told me that we now (with the help of others) were paddling our own canoe. Before we got down to the hard work we allowed a certain euphoria to break out. My deputy Harry Reid wrote a leader on the day the buy-out was announced, in May. I suppose we might have been accused of naivety; but from an editorial point of view we had been left in benign neglect and we had been greatly amused by Rowland's jousts against the Fayed Borthers (conducted in exceptionally well pro-duced volumes of sustained vituperation, such as Hero from Zero), and for us Harry's leader carried the mood of the moment:

> The management buy-out at George Outram is good news for ourselves, and good news for Scotland. *The Herald* and our sister paper, the *Evening Times*, are returning to Scottish ownership. There is a real sense of homecoming in the news. A great Scottish institution is once again just that, in every sense. This development will be unreservedly welcomed by the Scottish business community and indeed by the Scottish community at large. More important still, it will be welcomed by *The Herald*'s hundreds of thousands of readers. There are many challenges ahead, but today we can simply rejoice that what is perhaps the most exciting change in the 209-year history of *The Herald*, the oldest paper of its kind in the entire world, has been successfully accomplished ... It would be churlish not to mention our former owner, Lonrho. The international trading conglomerate, under the ever-controversial but often inspired guidance of Tiny Rowland, has never been a favourite of the British establishment. But Lonrho never interfered with *The Herald*'s editorial content and it was essentially a benign rather than a hostile proprietor.

When he was shown the leader, we were told that Tiny looked puzzled and said: 'Did we ask for this?' Such was the instinctive response of a man whose representa-tives on several occasions had pledged to the Monopolies and Mergers Commission fidelity to the principles of editorial freedom!

I have given this story in some depth because it touched on my personal experience and I hope will add to an understanding of what happened to a major Scottish company. It is sobering to think that the Scottish interest, so ably argued in front of the MMC by the SUITs directors who resisted the bid, was not judged to be of sufficient importance to justify a ruling against it. But Lonrho's broken promises, and its rape of the SUITs treasure chest, together with its uninhibited harassment of the House of Fraser board as it softened it up for takeover, must have influenced the MMC a year later when it rejected the bid that would have given Rowland the pinnacle of his ambition – Harrods. The MMC was too polite to say so. In the end it placed more value on the autonomy of the House of Fraser, the issue on which it ruled against the merger, than on the Scottish interest. In the context of this book, that is perhaps the point of greatest significance. Scotland was powerless to prevent the dissipation of an important resource because it had no political means of doing so. It had, and indeed has, no power of veto.

SUITs was also a victim of its time. On the day after the buy-out was announced, R. E. Dundas wrote:

The history of Outram mirrors the history of British commerce over the last 30 years. Companies lost their independence and found themselves members of huge, often illogical conglomerates. Times have changed and big is not always beautiful. Financial institutions have become hugely innovative in finding the means to give local management ownership and control of their own businesses when the opportunity has arisen. George Outram is the latest beneficiary of this well established process through one of the biggest-ever management buy-outs in Scotland.

Rowland could never have got hold of SUITs had it not been for the weakness, of temperament and judgment, of Sir Hugh. Thus the failure of Scottish dynastic capitalism must hold primary responsibility for the company's eventual disappearance, except in the most residual of functions, and the dissipation of its resources. Now we have come full circle, and the future of *The Herald* (as it has been called since 1992) again rests on indigenous energies. When Caledonian Newspapers, under the chairmanship of Ian Macpherson, emerges from its indebtedness by means of a flotation, I hope there will be a diffused shareholding among institutions and individuals so that its long-term future, as one of Scotland's leading newspapers, will be secure and that it will be beyond the reach of predators. In going the rounds talking to groups of readers I find this suggestion receives a warm response.

When Sir Hugh died in 1987, a small funeral service was held in his mother's house. About 20 people attended, among them Tiny Rowland. Afterwards the coffin was taken to a country churchyard where Sir Hugh was to lie beside his father. One of those who held the cords as it was lowered into the waiting grave was Tiny. For some of those present, that was the final irony.

CHAPTER SIX

The price of war

One sunny evening in May of 1993 the trim figure of Matthew Neil appeared in my office. At the age of 75 the former secretary and chief executive of the Glasgow Chamber of Commerce looked youthful in his retirement. He is one of only three secretaries or chief executives to have served the Chamber in the twentieth century. He took over after the war and was succeeded by Ewan Marwick in 1983. (Ten years later Marwick died tragically in a road accident in Moscow while on a mission to Russia under the British Government's 'know-how' scheme.) I poured Neil a dram and we fell to talking of industrial change and decline in the West of Scotland, the engine-room of the old Scottish economy and a forcing house for ships and munitions in both world wars.

There could be no more eloquent or knowledgeable witness. Neil's career, first as a lawyer and then in the Chamber, spanned the Second World War. When he was growing up in Paisley memories were still vivid of the round of industrial failures that followed the first war. Through his study of the Chamber archives and academic works, he has an exceptional grasp of events and trends and is in no doubt that the two wars were chief causes of the West of Scotland's decline.

As the First World War began, an era of extraordinary industrial achievement was nearing its end. Argyll Motors in Alexandria once had the ambition to challenge Henry Ford. It had the capacity for 3,000 cars a year. Once or twice output reached 1,000, which put it second only to Ford. The company collapsed in 1914 and there were two theories for its demise. One held that it had spent extravagantly on the offices and factory still standing today (used as a torpedo factory during the Second World War). The other preferred to believe that the death at the age of 38 of Alexander Govan, the founder and managing director, robbed the company of its dynamism. He died of food poisoning after eating in a well-known Glasgow restaurant. So completely is he forgotten today that he does not rate a mention in Chambers lamentable *Scottish Biographical Dictionary* (I should declare an interest since it omits my father, too).

Neil wrote in 1990 of the many men 'whose energies and abilities made them legends in their lifetimes, who made vast sums of money (a large part of it not infrequently disbursed in the public interest), who built up great companies and whole industries, industries which, a generation later, had sunk without trace or become so attenuated as to be only of minor significance in the economy'.

William Beardmore Jnr, later Lord Invernairn, despite having a wealthy and successful father, left school to be apprenticed at Parkhead Forge and go to night school. At the end of the first war he planned, in vain, to manufacture passenger vessels, tankers, locomotives, marine engines, buses, trucks and taxis, aeroplanes, airships and much more. At least he tried. Many sons of the big magnates were sent to England or the Continent for their education. Edward Priaulx Tennant, Lord Glenconner, son of Sir Charles Tennant and great-grandson of the Charles Tennant who established the chemical works at St Rollox in 1800, went to Eton and Trinity. Sir Maurice Denny, of the shipbuilding family, went to Lausanne, Heidelberg, and Massachussetts Institute of Technology.

The dynastic principle saw the scions of the industrial barons migrate to politer professions or to no profession at all. Sir William Burrell, who sold his shipping fleet on a boom and invested the proceeds in the collection now housed in the Burrell Gallery in Glasgow, was an example of capital mutating into unproductive use. (The storing of surplus economic value in works of art had been started by, among others, by J. P. Morgan and Andrew Carnegie. Burrell tried to emulate them, and collectors like Henry Clay Frick, but there was little consistency in his taste, a fact that gives the Burrell Collection a curiously appealing magpie quality.)

Both wars had similar effects. The requirements of war, and their delusive booms, masked underlying stagnation. On the part of capital there was a failure to re-invest or to respond to market change. Demand for ships and munitions soared, providing a false market. As Glasgow and its industrial district poured out guns, ships and other armaments, new industries, like motor and aircraft production, were being established in the south. This happened in the first war and then 'blow me', said Neil, it happened again in the second.

In the first war exceptional stresses were also placed on the social fabric. The housing system, already inadequate, was savagely distorted. Rents soared; women whose men were fighting were evicted and public anger grew. There was a series of rent strikes, often led by women. Joseph Melling, in *Scottish Housing in the Twentieth Century*, wrote:

> The actual events of these turbulent months suggest that the key to victory in the battle against the house owners was found in the active support given by a range of distinctive organisations and groups, many of whom were radicalised by their direct experience of the conflict. Drawing on these diverse, largely apolitical, bodies for the conduct of the campaign, rent strike-leaders developed a particular kind of urban politics which took both landlords and Government by surprise.

The Rent and Mortgage Interest (War Restriction) Act of 1915, put through by Lloyd George in response to public unrest, fixed rents for the duration of the war. The legislation was renewed with only slight modifications in 1919 and rent restriction stayed on the statute book until long after the Second World War. The last tenement of the traditional kind was built in Glasgow in 1915, an official of the city architect's department told me in conversation in 1993.

Neil gave me an account of the social importance of tenement housing, of which he became aware when he was doing conveyancing in Paisley, when still a practising lawyer, before the Second World War. The tenement was for its builder often a shield against retirement, in the days before unit and investment trusts. A well-to-do tradesman would build the tenement and often occupy the ground-floor flat himself. He undertook the repairs and collected the rents. As long as the housing market was in equilibrium, reasonable rents could be secured. However, this may be the recollection of an exception rather than a norm. Richard Rodger, also in *Scottish Housing in the Twentieth Century*, wrote that in Glasgow in 1900 private individuals constituted 64.4 per cent of landlords and that many of them delegated the management of their properties to factors. The system attracted many complaints and much resentment.

The war sucked in labour to Glasgow and, after the Act had frozen rents, new landlords did not come forward; the supply of rented homes dried up, the properties deteriorated and the result was the appalling slums which shocked Baldwin on a visit to Glasgow in 1925. Melling wrote:

> The Labour Governments of 1924 and 1929 were committed to the continuance of rent controls and the improvement of working-class housing, but the Wheatley Act [the Housing (Financial Provisions) Act of 1924] did little to alleviate the slum problem. Rent restrictions in fact created a safe ghetto of older, poorly maintained and frequently over-crowded dwellings that could be rented for well under ten shillings a week. Their occupants were reluctant – especially in the climate of the 1920s and the early 1930s – to abandon these controlled houses and venture into the free market.

To local authorites fell the task of providing subsidised housing at cheap rents. The Housing (Scotland) Act of 1935 for the first time fixed standards of overcrowding and placed the responsibility of remedying them on local authorities. The council housing urgently put up after the war was a response to the slums, and therefore many of the post-war problems of housing in Scotland, a major preoccupation of governments, could be traced to the 1915 Act. A chronic shortage of rented accommodation at reasonable prices remains a characteristic of our housing market. Owner-occupation has also been the choice of relatively few. After a decade of Thatcherism it finally rose above 50 per cent of housing as classified by forms of tenure. Politically, housing policy produced the post-war Labour fiefdoms in which, in Sir Teddy Taylor's view, the working classes were imprisoned and which skewed election results to the disadvantage of the Conservatives.

From these social difficulties many of the dynastic inheritors simply migrated, physically or socially. Lamentably weak management is identified by Neil, and most academic commentators, as another reason for decline. The hated gaffers or foremen ruled with an arbitrary hand, often discriminating on grounds of religion. On the side of labour, exclusive and nepotistical craft labour unions – in the steelworks, in shipyards, in some docks, in engineering – controlled recruitment and were left to be autonomous arbiters of much of the industrial process. In Clyde shipbuilding, it was an extraordinary fact, recorded by the historian W. Knox, quoting a Department of Trade and Industry report of 1973, that 'except in yards building warships, control of quality and dimensional accuracy is provided by the workplace.' Neil recalled that on the Clyde, where the shipyards directly employed 55,000 men at the end of the second war, each part of a ship would be 'chalked out' by the craftsmen on an enormous floor so that its dimensions could be determined. They had drawings but they interpreted them. Each ship was a unique artefact. It was magnificent in a way but it was madness; system and module building spread through the industries of competitors. Much less magnificent were the lunatic restrictive practices recorded by Correlli Barnett in *The Audit of War*.

Against these trends, of decline, change and rationalisation, Scotland and its politicians kicked for quite a long time. But in the end they could not halt them. The old industries have disappeared and industrial de-skilling has taken place. The control of capital has largely moved elsewhere. The application of technology was for a long time retarded and, even when installed, resisted by the powerful craft unions who refused to apply it properly. It is now shifting the demand for human resources.

The changes in the labour market can be seen from the decline in employment in the older sectors. Apart from shipbuilding, Neil reminded me that before the war Glasgow had a pottery industry employing about 3,000. Templetons, in their replica of the Doge's Palace beside Glasgow Green (known locally as 'Dougie's Palace'), were a powerful carpet-maker. After the war there were still four companies making locomotives. According to an account of Scottish Capitalism edited by Tony Dickson, Scotland's share of world shipbuilding averaged 12 per cent between 1951 and 1954. The railway engineering industry employed more than 10,000 men in the early 1950s, and with 5,000 workers in three plants the North British Locomotive Company was a world giant. By 1960 it was moribund. Neil recalled that it was closed overnight and the workers arrived to find their jobs had gone.

Only traces of this greatness remain. Gone is dear dirty old Glasgow which knocked down its tenements with enthusiasm and smashed up Charing Cross with a motorway. Only two shipyards remain on the Upper Clyde, one working for the Navy and the other manufacturing liquefied gas carriers. In 1993 Clydeport, the privatised child of the old port authority, stopped dredging the Clyde beyond Meadowpark and HMS Glasgow was unable to tie up at its customary berth, Yorkhill Quay, because the water was by now too shallow there. I am fond of a poem by Iain Crichton Smith written in 1972, entitled 'You lived in Glasgow', which goes in part:

> You were happier here than anywhere, you said.
> Such fine good neighbours helping when your child
> almost died of croup. Those pleasant Wildes
> removed with the fallen rubble have now gone
> in the building programme which renews each stone.
> I stand in a cleaner city, better fed,
> in my diced coat, brown hat, my paler hands
> leafing a copy of the latest book.
> Dear ghosts, I love you, haunting sunlit winds,
> dear happy dented ghosts, dear prodigal folk.

The Scottish Economic Bulletin for the winter of 1992/93 reported that the number of employees in manufacturing had fallen from 444,000 to 368,000 in a decade and was exceeded by the number in the services (1.4 million in 1992 compared with 1.2 million in 1983). The composition of the workforce had changed, also, with a continuing rise in the employment of women, many on a part-time basis, and a fall in the male labour force.

The response of both government and labour to the forces of change was to retard them. Three examples make the point – the attempt to save jobs represented by the work-in at Upper Clyde Shipbuilders in 1971, the workers' co-operative that tried to save jobs from the closure of the Scottish Daily Express in 1975, and the attempts by successive governments to retain strip steel-making at Ravenscraig.

A belief in central planning had permeated Whitehall after the war as a result of its success in mobilising national resources, a process encouraged by Churchill's delegation of home affairs to Attlee. Throughout the Fifties and the Sixties Scotland's relative economic performance was poor. Governments responded by subsidising industrial investment and wooing foreign capital. A whole series of major investments took place, many of which put down shallow roots. The Highlands and Islands Development Board, created by the Labour Secretary of State William (later Lord) Ross in 1965, adopted an industrial policy that now, with hindsight, seems inappropriate. An aluminium smelter and a paper mill were the fruits of this period of Highland investment. To the Lowlands came the Ravenscraig strip steel works, opened in 1958, British Leyland's truck factory at Bathgate, opened in 1961, and the Linwood car plant of 1963. All were hailed as miracle restoratives; all have now closed.

Linwood failed because of an inadequate product and a lack of industrial discipline. Men raised in the autonomous craft traditions of shipbuilding and other heavy industries could not take to the production lines, and years of inadequate management control had weakened industrial discipline to the point that excessive drinking and absenteeism were endemic problems in many of the West of Scotland's heavy industries. The machine rooms of some newspapers, for example, were 'no-go' areas for the managements on pay night and out-of-work compositors used to wait at the back door of the old *Herald* building in Mitchell Street in the hope that a few staff men would be sent home drunk and casuals would be hired in their place. There was a famous *Herald* story about the celebrated Harry Moyes, a photographer known for his permanent insobriety. As he came in to the office one day, the managing director, coming out and meeting him by chance, rebuked him. 'Drunk again?' he said. 'Yes,' the photographer replied cheerfully, 'so am I!'

Edward Heath was the first post-war Conservative leader to attempt to accept the consequences of industrial change. In Opposition he had decided that Selsdon Man should bury Butskellism. The market would be liberalised and union power would be curbed. In a phrase that would return to haunt the Conservatives, 'lame duck' industries would be allowed to die.

He was soon thwarted by, among other things, the remarkable episode of the work-in at Upper Clyde Shipbuilders. This was a consortium which had been created by the Wilson Government to save an industry which, as Neil pointed out, was supremely well equipped to build passenger liners for which the market had collapsed. The combine, formed in 1968, pulled together the yards of John Brown of Clydebank, Charles Connell of Scotstoun, Fairfields of Govan, Alex Stephen of Linthouse and Yarrows of Scotstoun. It carried the debts of the old yards and the costs of compensation to the old owners, and was soon in difficulty. In June 1971, Yarrows returned to independent work, mainly for the Navy, and a liquidator was appointed for the rest of the business. Eight-and-a-half thousand jobs were to go. The yards faced a distinctly unfriendly hearing from the Heath Government, elected in 1970.

The men voted to refuse redundancy and began a work-in at the yards. Led by communist shop stewards Jimmy Reid, Jimmy Airlie and Sammy Barr, they presented a direct challenge to the Government. Reid addressed a mass meeting and made the famous incantation that there would be 'no bevvying'. On 18 August about 200,000 workers downed tools around the country and as many as 80,000 people marched for UCS. Jimmy Airlie later recalled:

It was an atmosphere I had never experienced; it was an expression of the Scottish people, a sense that the decline of Scotland's manufacturing base and its industrial heritage must stop. There was a feeling that the Scottish people were once again on the move to claim what was theirs . . .

Support came from businessmen resentful of the loss of indigenous control and from UCS creditors. Money came in from churches, old age pensioners and Conservative Women's Associations. Jimmy Reid recalled that a bunch of red roses arrived with a donation of £1,000 and a card. The message on the card was read out, including the signature, 'Lennon'. Gerry Ross, an old communist shop steward, shouted out, 'Lenin's deid!' It was of course from John Lennon and Yoko Ono.

The Government was already in retreat from its own policies. In 1971 when Ted Heath rescued Rolls-Royce, Gordon (later Lord) Campbell (of Croy), then Secretary of State for Scotland, said: 'Rolls-Royce was like Buckingham Palace, a major part of Britain, and the decision was taken that Rolls-Royce could not be allowed to close. I was determined that UCS should not be treated any worse than Rolls-Royce.'

The yards and all the jobs were for the moment saved. The new Govan Shipbuilders received £35 million of Government aid. Marathon (the oil-rig manufacturer persuaded to take over Clydebank) was awarded a series of incentives including 30 per cent of the wage bill for the first three years. The U-turn was complete.

Teddy Taylor, who had worked in the yards and was then MP for Cathcart, said in 1991:

We could probably have achieved more by sending an aeroplane to drop £10 notes over the area.

Little was done to reform antiquated working practices and craft in-fighting continued unabated. But in the short-term the successful resistance to the Government fed the nationalism which was to dominate Scottish politics and preoccupy Parliament between 1974 and 1979.

Similar feelings drove the workers' co-operative that attempted to save jobs when the *Scottish Daily Express* pulled out of its Scottish publishing centre at Albion Street, Glasgow. Allister Mackie, the leader of the workers' co-operative set up to publish the *Scottish Daily News,* which appeared for six months in 1975, has given us a remarkable account of this period, and of the workers' uneasy alliance with the tycoon Robert Maxwell, in his book *The Trade Unionist and the Tycoon,* which I had the pleasure of editing. In the foreword Tony Benn described the pressures on the Wilson Government, in which he, as an interventionist Secretary of State for Industry, worked against the grain of civil service thinking. He expressed his personal support for the co-operative, 'knowing how hostile my own colleagues, my civil servants and the Treasury would be to what was proposed'. He continued:

We had taken over from the Heath Government after the miners' strike which he had precipitated, and almost immediately I discovered that several huge companies like Ferranti, Alfred Herbert and British Leyland were on the point of collapse, and we never knew from day to day whether we would survive, as a minority Government in a hung Parliament. There was also a major internal battle going on inside the Labour Party between those of us who were committed to the radical manifesto upon which we had been elected and the majority of the Cabinet who had no intention whatever of implementing our election policies and wanted to damp down all such expectations . . .

Never in my long political and ministerial life have I encountered such violent opposition as there was against the co-operatives. The Treasury, which had happily provided enormous sums of money to bale out private companies, was resolute in arguing against even the smallest grants to the co-operatives, and the City saw that if they were allowed to develop then the ultimate sanction against trade unions and workers – which was the sack – would lose its sting and the bosses would lose their most powerful disciplinary weapon . . .

The trade union leaders were equally unhelpful because trade unionists – as they saw it – were there to bargain with management, and not to set up some new management structure of their own . . .

But so strong was the public support, at that time, for the policy which I was following that those who wanted to prevent it had to set up absurd legal and financial hurdles which they hoped would prevent these new enterprises from getting off the ground . . .

In the event, when the paper did appear, though it had dropped the right-wing Beaverbrook bias, it lacked the sharp political cutting edge that Benn had hoped to see. Its life was short and it closed after a bruising experience at the hands of Maxwell.

The Scottish Office, even during the first two Thatcher administrations between 1979 and 1987, continued to placate and delay. The death of Ravenscraig was long retarded by political pressure. There was an all-party struggle to prolong its life, and many Conservative politicians worked earnestly to persuade British Steel to retain it. But once it was privatised in 1988, its death was inevitable.

The Conservative politician Michael Ancram was one of the victims of the 1987 election when Scotland gave Thatcherism a bloody nose. He was already in trouble with his constituency party in South Edinburgh for being insufficiently Thatcherite. In a conversation in 1992, he described to me also the sense of betrayal he felt when the voters of South Edinburgh rejected him despite all his best efforts to save jobs. In November 1982, then Conservative chairman in Scotland, he went to an STUC conference in Motherwell and committed the party to fight for Ravenscraig's survival. Its closure, he said, would be unacceptable to any party.

When he made this statement he was going out on a limb. He did have the endorsement of George (now Lord) Younger, Secretary of State for Scotland from 1979 to 1986, but Mrs Thatcher had not been consulted. She subsequently asked him to justify his action, accepted his explanation and supported him (though not to the point of halting the privatisation of British Steel).

In 1983 Ancram became a Minister in the Scottish Office. I have heard senior civil servants speak highly of his ability, to get money out of the Treasury among other things. He himself says that, quite against the national trend, he managed during his tenure to increase public spending on housing in Scotland.

He and the party got no thanks for that either, he said ruefully. When he lost his seat he decided to rebuild his political career in England. He was selected as Conservative candidate for Devizes in Wiltshire and was returned with a majority of almost 20,000. As a constituency MP be became involved in the struggle between Devonport and Rosyth for survival as naval dockyards. In Wiltshire he felt a pretty strong local tug in favour of Devonport. As a Scot he had some sentimental interest in Rosyth. But his disillusion with Scottish political attitudes influenced his thinking. The Prime Minister, Mr Major, was advised that if Rosyth were saved he should expect no political dividend; after all, the struggles to save Ravenscraig had yielded none. In 1993 Devonport duly won the contract for refitting the Trident nuclear submarines despite many Government promises in previous years that Rosyth would be awarded the work. The consolation, of work on surface ships, was regarded in Rosyth with some suspicion, and was not felt to be sufficient to secure the yard's future. Earlier in 1993, in the reshuffle following Norman Lamont's resignation as Chancellor, Ancram returned to the Government, bringing his skills — and his religion, for he is one of Scotland's leading Roman Catholics — to the Northern Ireland Office.

These struggles against change by governments of both parties and by the labour movement were ultimately fruitless. They are not over yet, because reductions in defence expenditure have put at risk not only the Rosyth naval dockyard, in the short term, but also in the longer term the Yarrow naval shipyard; Barr & Stroud, which gave up civil manufacture to concentrate on military optics; and Ferranti, the electronics company which took a similar strategic decision. Out of such choices has grown the Japanese dominance of civil manufactures for consumers.

With the advantage of hindsight we can see that Government and Labour were struggling against international forces and could hope only to delay their impact. Capital had become rapidly less capable of control by national governments, just as extra-terrestrial television began to evade government regulation. The advent of tough American managements, for example at IBM at Greenock, hastened the decline of trade union militancy, already under attack from labour laws which removed the right of secondary picketing and made it possible for striking workers to be dismissed after 90 days.

During the Thatcher years the slogan 'Scotland's Oil' came back to haunt the nationalist mind. The removal of the last exchange controls by Sir Geoffrey Howe in 1982 had permitted the overseas investment of revenues (a move long advocated by the economist Donald MacKay, who in 1993 became chairman of Scottish Enterprise). The oil wealth drove up the exchange rate, which hastened the end of many of the older industries: the list enumerated by the political scientist James Mitchell, in his book *Conservatives and the Union,* included Singers in Clydebank, Goodyear in Glasgow, Monsanto in Ayrshire, BSR in East Kilbride, the Wiggins Teape pulp mill in Fort William, the Invergordon aluminium smelter, Caterpillar in Uddingston, Burroughs in Cumbernauld, Plessey in Bathgate, Rowntree Mackintosh in Edinburgh, and the Gartcosh steel mill.

The feelings that inspired successive governments to delay or avoid the consequences of change were eloquently expressed to me in 1993 by George Younger. During a chat in the chief London office of the Royal Bank, of which he was now chairman, he said he thought there had been two distinct periods during his years in government. By the time of the Heath Government of 1970–74, the post-war boom which had protected the heavy industries had ended. He continued:

> That had come to an end by then, or was rapidly coming to an end. We then had things like the problem of UCS, which came from there. I think it was premature. The Government didn't deal with it, it retreated. The whole thing was just too early. It was before its time.

People were buying time, trying to retard the impact of change?

> Yes, or it may have been, and this turned out later to be correct, that you had to
> sort out the trade union problem before you could sort the industrial problem.
> Heath made a shot at that which got bogged down, massively. He then retreated
> on UCS and the miners came after that, and so all that effort was aborted. You
> then had to go through this catharsis of the Labour Party having its chance.
> They made a fearful balls-up of it and ended up with the winter of discontent [in
> 1978/79]. Then you had a radical regime which came and sorted out the trade
> union movement at the same time as dealing with the industrial problem which
> by then was further down the tubes. And of course what was aimed at in the late
> Sixties and early Seventies happened effectively after the 1981 recession, and we
> see the completely transformed Scottish economy as a result.

Ravenscraig? Was it a resignation matter?

> Yes. I don't recall actually ever saying that to Mrs Thatcher's face but it was
> pretty clear to everybody. Everybody knew. I felt very strongly that the reasons
> then for the closure of Ravenscraig were wrong and I would say the subsequent
> events proved that to be the case, because they couldn't have done without
> Ravenscraig in 1987–89. So I believe that was right. I also felt very strongly that
> this was the last bit of the true west of Scotland indigenous home-based industry
> and it had to be preserved if possible. I did think it was preservable. We bought
> some time and they would have been in a pickle without it.

The Scottish economy that has emerged is open. It is probable that we can never
again expect industries to generate employment on a large scale. The control of
industrial investment decisions, except those on a medium or small scale and
therefore unlikely to be richly productive of employment, has passed elsewhere.
The feeble performance of indigenous entrepreneurship has become a major preoccupation of Scottish Enterprise, which has taken over from the Scottish Development Agency. Scotland's rate of company formation continues to be low, and its
intellectual capital, in its 25 universities, rarely makes a meaningful alliance with
venture capital.

The relationship between capital and industry, and in particular the short-
term pressures generated for profits and dividends, may lie at the root of a more
general British industrial decline of a gravity which persuaded Mr Major, in 1993,
to confess that while in Mrs Thatcher's Government he had always been opposed
to the policy which discounted as unimportant the loss of manufacturing. To the
question of why he did not say so at the time, there is no satisfactory answer!

Ravenscraig enjoyed a brief Indian summer. Productivity achieved record
levels. When it was finally closed in 1992, there was much ritual gnashing of teeth
and vilification of the British Steel chairman and former chief executive, Sir Robert
'Black Bob' Scholey, who was widely believed to have been bent on closure for
many years.

Union officials and politicians like Ancram were convinced that Sir Robert
wanted Ravenscraig to go, both as a punishment for its involvement in the 1980
steel strike and to justify his support for huge investment in the Welsh steelworks at
Port Talbot and Llanwern. He opposed upgrading the Ravenscraig blast furnaces
and coke ovens and was once said to have ordered management in Wales to 'get

their fingers out' if they were not to undermine his entire strategy for steel. It is human to look for a scapegoat, and the hard truth was that rationalisation of steel capacity had to hurt someone. But for Scotland Ravenscraig had become a symbol of its traditional industrial virility. Its closure marked a death, but it was now accepted with resignation as an inevitable dispensation of nature. A rueful reflection was that if Scotland had been, like Ireland, an independent state within the EC, it would have retained at least some steel capacity.

CHAPTER SEVEN

A salvage job

Two cases, in which I was marginally involved, illustrate the forces of change working on the Scottish economy and show how little importance was attached to the Scottish interest, either by government or Scottish institutions, as a specific factor in decisions determining the future of important indigenous companies. I begin with the strange case of Ernest Saunders, the disgraced Guinness chairman. The story of how he led Guinness into the takeover first of Arthur Bell, the whisky distillers, and then of the mighty Distillers Company itself, is familiar to most people and I shall concern myself with some of the related issues as they touched on Scottish attitudes.

In 1992 Alan MacDermid reported in *The Herald* that three leading psychiatrists had attacked the diagnosis of dementia which helped to free Saunders. They feared that his remarkable recovery since being released the previous June could make it difficult to convince courts in future of genuine cases of Alzheimer's disease. Saunders, aged 55 at the time MacDermid's story was written, received a five-year sentence over an illegal share-support plot during the Guinness battle for Distillers Company in 1986. But he was freed on parole after ten months. The Appeal Court halved the sentence after hearing evidence from three doctors that he was suffering from progressive pre-senile dementia (Alzheimer's disease). Since his release Saunders had amazed observers with his recovery, playing tennis. He was to receive a pension reported to be £75,000 a year.

During the first takeover battle for Bell's in 1985, Saunders came to see me, as did the defending chief executive of Bell's, Raymond Miguel. This was no great distinction in the case of Saunders, as he was going round Scotland telling anybody who would listen how wonderful he was, but I can claim that I fell out with him more or less on sight. The defeat of Miguel in his defence of Bell's, however, leaves some sour reflections. Here was a reasonably well managed Scottish company, with a good product and plant and a big share of the UK market. Analysts did question its ability to sustain and increase its performance, particularly abroad. Doubts had also grown about Miguel's management style, which was described as idiosyncratic but less euphemistically would be called autocratic. He obliged his executives to go jogging and set many pettifogging rules for them. He seemed to have convinced himself that he owned the company. In fact it was owned by institutions, led by its Perth neighbour General Accident. The autocrat found that he had few friends when he needed them. Many who began by supporting him were seduced by the attractive price offered. Saunders, by contrast, had the advantage of being relatively unknown and he skilfully exploited the City's doubts about Bell's.

Saunders breezed round Scotland, an elegant figure exuding confidence and charm, the big marketing genius who had restored the Guinness family fortune by putting pep back into the company share price and restoring the famous stout to its rightful place. He took some senior *Herald* business writers, and myself, to dinner in a Glasgow hotel. It started amicably, with a Saunders monologue. Eventually, I tried a question. I'll take that at the end, he said. After he had given the next six questions the same treatment, I said rather rattily that if he didn't want a genuine discussion then I had work to do. He took a few questions and the evening proceeded rather uneasily.

Chaps who suddenly buy you dinner, pump your hand and say how much they admire your paper are unlikely to have disinterested motives. Saunders was 'working' the press to get good coverage. He succeeded notably in some cases. Some of the uncritical support he secured in London papers included sneering and unpleasant attacks on the Scots. However, beyond a certain distaste for his style, I cannot claim to have suspected anything worse. Nor did the rest of the Scottish financial community; but when James Gulliver bid for DCL the company's reaction was, to say the least, curious. DCL were horrified.

Sir Charles Fraser, a leading figure in Scotland's corporate life, had, as senior partner in the legal firm of W.J. Burness, acted for Guinness during the Bell's takeover. When it was rumoured that Gulliver was contemplating a bid for DCL, he was approached by Saunders. Like everyone else in Scotland he had no reason to think that Saunders was other than he seemed, and was delighted to act for him.

DCL was organised as a confederation, or an episcopal church. Each company operated independently, some successfully like Johnnie Walker, some not. There were famous brands like Buchanan and White Horse. It was helpful to your career prospects if you had a military record and a low handicap (with the good sense not to beat the chairman). If you were promoted on to the main board then, in the words of one intimate observer of the company, you disappeared. You were a great gentleman who did not really sully your hands with commerce. You flew around the world a bit inspecting market opportunities, but since most of the distribution was in the hands of third parties, and since you let them set your brands against each other in competition, your duties were largely ambassadorial and honorific. And if you were the chairman then you were the pope, at least. It was misleading to think of Distillers as being under Scottish control. Not only were its headquarters in London but so were those of its component companies. Federalism ruled and the giant slept. It was also a company not free of snobbery. In the Seventies I once visited the White Horse distilleries in Islay. We had a splendid time. We watched a puffer unload its barley and with the skipper shared a dram of the distillery manager's malt. We were flown back to Edinburgh in the company plane. The company chauffeur who took me back to our modest terrace house in Newhaven dropped me with a sneer.

Gulliver was, in the dismissive phrase put about by supporters of the Guinness bid, a grocer's boy from Campbeltown. He had built up Argyll Foods into a major player. As early as 1981 he had identified the fact that DCL was seriously undervalued. 'It was a vast under-used asset,' he told me when we talked in 1993. The opinion in the City was that John Connell, who had just taken over as chairman, should be given a chance, and Gulliver was advised to wait. He did so, but came back to it in 1985 by which time it was clear that the company was incapable of reforming itself.

The DCL board reacted to his bid as if the chauffeur or gardener had proposed that he should sup with them rather than in the kitchen. Gulliver still gets a wry amusement from the insults that went around: he was the 'ghastly grocer'. At the height of the battle, the Guinness department of 'dirty tricks' made much of the fact that his entry in *Who's Who* implied, misleadingly, that he was a graduate of Harvard Business School. Social death, in the form of rule by Gulliver, seemed to have descended on the mandarins of DCL. A senior banker close to the events, however, discounted the idea that DCL were motivated by snobbery in its reaction to the Gulliver bid. He commented drily that 'fierce' would have been too dynamic a word to describe their response. He continued:

> Within Distillers there was no doubt shock and, I guess, outrage. But if what you are getting at is a suggestion that it was the fact that the bidder was Jimmy Gulliver that provoked the resistance, you are over-simplifying. I am afraid that any bid for the mighty and, I'm afraid, complacent DCL would have been a shock and affront to those running it.

This authoritative source was 'pretty confident' that the idea for a bid from Guinness did not come from DCL who were 'all too sure' that they didn't need a bid at all. It was possible, he thought, that a bid for DCL, once Bell's had been digested, had been part of the Guinness strategy all along. This was also the view of Sir Charles Fraser. Having won the battle for Bell's, Saunders was riding high. His reputation as a marketeer of rare talent was unquestioned. He was ultimately endorsed, not without doubts, by Sir Thomas Risk, Governor of the Bank of Scotland since 1981. Saunders made various promises to Scotland during the bid. These were designed to match or trump commitments by Gulliver who said that he would base the company headquarters in Scotland and that he himself would live in Edinburgh, where he has a house in Heriot Row. There was a ludicrous photocall during this period when Saunders and his wife were snapped by the hacks one day in the New Town of Edinburgh; they were 'looking for a house' to be 'upsides' with Gulliver.

Some people told me that Sir Thomas, now retired, had not recovered from the shock of finding out what kind of man Saunders was. I think it more probable that Sir Thomas experiences a sense of irritation that, in the context of a long and distinguished career, the Guinness affair attracts disproportionate attention from journalists and chroniclers. For him at the time the analysis would have been rational rather than personalised in the manner of the press coverage. What brought Guinness out ahead in his mind, apart from issues of management and the crucially important question of price, would no doubt have been the nature of the Guinness business, international and brand-related. By contrast, Argyll's experience and expertise were in the domestic sector and retailing. Guinness seemed better qualified to bring about the revolution in attitudes, organisation and marketing that DCL so clearly needed and were incapable themselves of engineering.

The directors of Guinness and DCL, and their merchant bankers, agreed to invite Sir Thomas to be the chairman of the merged company. Saunders personally pledged that this would be so. This gave Sir Thomas influence rather than power. At the time he did not know Saunders and had to make his own assessment of his character and abilities. Friends recall that he perceived strengths and at least some of the weaknesses. But he gave Saunders the benefit of the doubt and I recall meeting Sir Thomas at a dinner around this time when he expressed confidence in the various assurances given.

When it became clear that Saunders was much less than the full shilling, Sir Thomas and Sir Charles suffered a considerable amount of adverse publicity. Indeed, Sir Thomas's friends believe, there was a campaign to discredit and replace him. He found this, they recalled, 'moderately uncomfortable'; but discomfort gave way to worry that people might be misled, irritation at the distraction from his main occupation, and relief that he would not have to work with people for whom he had lost respect.

After Guinness had won the battle for DCL, it became clear that Saunders would not fulfil his promises to make Sir Thomas independent chairman and to locate the company headquarters in Edinburgh. Sir Charles was incensed but could find little support in the City or in Government for his view that there had been a breach of faith and contract. Indeed, at a disgraceful AGM, the City endorsed Saunders. An eloquent advocate on his behalf was the late Robert Maxwell. Only one dissentient Scottish voice spoke against him. In disgust Sir Charles terminated professional contact with Guinness and severed the relationship between it and his law firm. When Morgan Grenfell refused to follow his example, he resigned as its Scottish chairman. Some senior bankers became convinced that Saunders enjoyed the endorsement of Government at the highest level. At that time, as will become clear later in the book, there was growing hostility to the Scottish interest in Downing Street; and Sir Charles, senior civil servants and others who cried 'foul!' were ignored as tartan trouble-makers who deserved their fate. I was reliably informed that the Scottish Office pressed for a public inquiry but was overruled.

Then Ivan Boesky sang in Manhattan and the extent of the illegal share-support operations, which puffed the value of the Guinness bid and brought it victory, began to emerge. The confessions by the king of the arbitrageurs were described as the biggest event on Wall Street since the crash of 1929 and were to inspire Oliver Stone's movie, also called *Wall Street*, in which the anti-hero, Gordon Gekko, spoke the line that summed up the age: Greed is good. Here was a Byzantine network of greed and criminality, of share 'parking' and illegal price support. The essentially fraudulent nature of the bid for DCL became clear to the whole world.

Even then, Saunders hung on for a time. There were some who felt he should stay as Guinness chairman but be 'black-balled' from his clubs in the hope of forcing him to fulfil his promises. As his deeds came to light, this idea became impossible to sustain. For the first time in British mercantile history non-executive directors were imposed on an industrial company. Norman (Lord) Macfarlane, chief of Macfarlane Group Clansman, Sir David Plastow (Vickers), Ian MacLaurin (Tesco), Tony Greener (Dunhill), and the publisher Ian Chapman did not think social leprosy a sanction of sufficient force. The deal was that Saunders stayed on as chairman but the non-executives could remove him and his deputy. This they did. Lord Macfarlane became chairman of the non-executive directors on 1 December 1986, the same day that the Department of Trade and Industry inquiry was announced as a result of evidence supplied by the Guinness finance director Olivier Roux. Lord Macfarlane arrived in the Guinness boardroom to find two men from the department sitting there. They told him they had sealed Saunders's office to preserve the evidence. On 14 January 1987 Saunders, who had received a letter of dismissal, stepped down from the chair. In the book he subsequently wrote he cheekily suggested a certain betrayal; after all, he said, he had appointed the non-executives (which in a literal sense he had).

At a Sunday night meeting in the Vickers office Lord Macfarlane agreed to be

The funeral of John Maclean (1923)

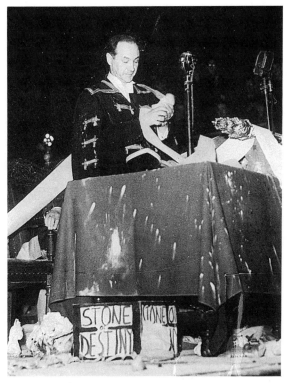

John MacCormick makes his rectorial address in Glasgow's St Andrew's Halls amid flour and toilet rolls (1950)

*The escapade of the Coronation Stone. From left: Ian Hamilton,
Dr John MacCormick and Gavin Vernon (1951)*

*The Very Revd Charles L. Warr with the Queen and the Duke of
Edinburgh as they leave St Giles Cathedral (1953)*

*R. E. Muirhead, the veteran Scottish nationalist, makes a lonely
protest (1960)*

The wedding of Sir Hugh Fraser in St Mary's Cathedral (1962)

Mr Macmillan and Lord Fraser at Glasgow Central Station (1964)

Robert Kemp (right), with (from left) Tom Fleming, producer Colin Chandler and actress Lennox Milne: at a Gateway Theatre conference on Kemp's new play, Conspirators *(1965)*

Greeted by piper Robert Hill and carried shoulder high by her supporters, Winnie Ewing arrives at London's King's Cross Station to take up her seat in the House of Commons (1967)

Willie Ross, Secretary of State for Scotland, holds hands with Harold Wilson (1970)

From left: Douglas Young, with C. M. Grieve (Hugh MacDiarmid) and Eoin O'Mahoney, seen at Charing Cross where Young was addressing an open-air election meeting on behalf of Grieve (1973)

William Wolfe and Margo MacDonald at an SNP press conference
(1973)

SUITs annual general meeting. Tiny Rowland (chairman) and Sir
Hugh Fraser (deputy chairman) talk to the press after the meeting
(1978)

Jim and Margo: Mr and Mrs Sillars after their wedding (1981)

Anti-Thatcherism: Ron Brown, MP, is led away from the Holiday Inn, Glasgow, after protesting against a visit by Mrs Thatcher (1982)

chairman. Next day he went to the office and found a demoralised and confused workforce. On a sheet of paper he wrote out a list of things to do. At its head was the need for a new chief executive. He then went to see the Sun Prudential, the biggest shareholder in Guinness, and later gave a full damage report to a meeting of about 40 medium-sized shareholders. This was apparently something of a culture shock and afterwards one of them said: 'This is the first time we've heard the truth about Guinness for five years.' Saunders exemplified in a British setting a trend that was worrying analysts in America – the assumption of excessive power and rewards by a cadre of senior executives out of the control of shareholders. The non-executive directors found that Saunders had treated the people who owned Guinness with contempt. Board meetings were irregularly held. Sometimes the directors, who included members of the Guinness family, would assemble and hang around for a couple of hours. Then Saunders would unilaterally announce that there was to be no meeting and send them away.

The board was lucky enough to find a suitable chief executive, (Sir) Anthony Tennant, who was between jobs. Lord Macfarlane then went to Robin Leigh-Pemberton, Governor of the Bank of England, and explained that he wanted to recruit Michael Julien as financial director. This highly abrasive man was a financial engineer of genius. He had resolved the Midland Bank's disastrous relationship with its Californian subsidiary Crocker by selling it off to Wells Fargo and was now up to his armpits in Eurotunnel. The Governor agreed that Guinness's needs were greater even than Eurotunnel and Julien joined the team. He and Tennant started work on the same day. With their help Lord Macfarlane addressed the burden that had been hung round his neck – the various promises that had been made during the battle that Guinness would locate its headquarters in Scotland. He was there to placate outraged Scottish sentiment. During and after the takeover battle many pubs had stopped taking Guinness, substituting Murphy's, the rival stout from Cork. Lord Macfarlane was chosen because he was a trusted and successful Scottish businessman, having built up a commercial stationery and packaging business from scratch and because as a supplier he knew the whisky trade well.

He rapidly came to the conclusion that the promise given to move the Guinness headquarters to Scotland was untenable. He believed it would have destroyed the company. The DCL headquarters in London and the offices of the various brands were closed. They ceased to be fiefdoms, and everything was brought into Lamark House, Hammersmith, the Guinness headquarters. The leading brands were given a floor each but integrated into the management and marketing structure. They ceased to compete with each other in world markets. Instead the brand that did best locally was given the support. At the same time the new company moved to assert control of its overseas marketing and distribution. By 1993 it had transformed the system. At the time of the takeover about 25 per cent of overseas distribution and marketing was in the hands of DCL. Guinness now controlled 90 per cent.

The influence of Lord Macfarlane was seen in the decision to locate the international export centre at Port Dundas in Glasgow and the headquarters of UK sales at Perth. The new subsidiary company, United Distillers, was registered in Edinburgh. Lord Macfarlane worked hard for the next few years restoring the company's reputation. There was a great deal of sponsorship and much skilful public relations. Then, in 1992, the company moved to rationalise and modernise its operations with a £100 million programme of investment. Seven bottling (or packaging) plants were to to be replaced by three state-of-the-art centres. There were 700 job losses but the company had taken the unions with it. Campbell Christie, of the STUC, was even invited on to the board but had to decline so hostile a reaction did he get from fellow trade unionists; but there was in Scotland generally a reluctant acceptance that such changes were necessary and inevitable if the company's future was to be secured.

As an exercise in damage limitation it was impressive. But Scotland's loss could not be concealed. Despite Miguel's idiosyncracies, Bell's was a powerful brand, locally managed. In the long term it would have been worth more, to the economy and the community, as an independently run company. In the case of DCL, the outcome was again a loss of discretion and control from Scotland. Although the DCL board had been based in London and the board had behaved like distant potentates, their very remoteness and the company's balkanised structure had left some autonomy in the individual brands. The takeover resulted in the centralisation of control. Scottish banks lost the brand accounts and the hope that the company would move its main account to a Scottish bank was not fulfilled. Buying of goods and services was centralised. Lord Macfarlane's response to the location of power at the headquarters was to get as much as possible for Scotland but he could not reverse an inevitable rationalisation. Scotland's most famous industry had been put on a sound footing. But not even it had been able to escape the branch economy syndrome. He stepped down from the chairmanship in 1989.

When we had breakfast together in 1993 I found Gulliver remarkably free of rancour. He did not believe he had been the victim of snobbery, of the New Club 'mafia'. He believed that at the beginning he had been given a fair hearing by the Scottish financial institutions, who were well known for taking an unsentimental view and not allowing questions of Scottish interest to cloud their judgment. What defeated him was the illegal share support scheme launched by Saunders. The rival bids were of roughly even value. Indeed, his bid had a higher cash element. But the share rigging inflated the paper value of the Guinness bid. He became aware that something suspicious was going on when a pattern of persistent share dealing in the afternoon emerged. This suggested American purchasers, but when he complained to the authorities they blandly told them they had received an assurance that the buyers were acting independently. We now know, of course, that they were not.

Gulliver endorsed the marketing strategy pursued by Guinness since the acquisition of DCL but said that he would indeed have based the company HQ in Edinburgh, creating a valuable nexus of senior management skills and culture. Nor is his commitment to Scotland spurious. He spends most weekends in his house in Heriot Row, Edinburgh, and has been active in the counsels of the Scottish Conservative Party. In the context of this book, the salient episode was Gulliver's visit to Michael Howard, a junior minister at Trade and Industry and a devotee of free-market principles. (He became Home Secretary in 1993.) It was made very clear, said Gulliver, that the Scottish interest was not a factor; as with SUITs, as with DCL. That stuck in Gulliver's craw, and it sticks in mine.

The failure of the Crocker Bank, which became apparent in 1985, and the crisis it brought for the Midland, created another set of stresses in Scotland where the Clydesdale Bank was a Midland subsidiary. Richard Cole-Hamilton was chief general manager of the Clydesdale at the time and is now a non-executive director on the board of Caledonian Newspapers, the company set up to run Outrams after the management buyout. When he joined the bank in 1967 he did not even know it was owned by the Midland so quiet had the relationship been kept. The Clydesdale had at one time been the biggest of numerous Scottish banks.

The Midland was very highly regarded and its slogan was *The Great British Bank*. It had bought family banks all over England and in the Twenties had acquired the Clydesdale and the North of Scotland. The Midland was thus a confederation of local banks and had very close ties with the local communities. It therefore left the Clydesdale alone. There was also a strong personal bond between Len Mather, the chief general manager of the Midland, and Robert Fairbairn, his equivalent at the Clydesdale. Fairbairn had gone from Perth to work in the Midland and at a branch in Bolton had been Mather's accountant.

There was no sign of any ambition to corral the Clydesdale but there was one small sign of things to come in the early Seventies when Cole-Hamilton was money-market manager. Mather came up to see Fairbairn and Alex Macmillan, later to succeed to the general managership. Mather proposed that there should be a group treasury. He made the obvious point that the Clydesdale might be putting out overnight funds and that the Midland might be looking for them; it seemed a bit silly to pay brokers to undertake such transactions. Fairbairn and Macmillan resisted the idea but as a concession moved Cole-Hamilton to Lombard Street so that he could attend the Midland money-market meetings. Cole-Hamilton began to golf with the senior members of the Midland management. They were all, he recalled, 'very good fellows' and not at all interested in interfering with the Clydesdale.

Changes in legislation, as part of the Heath-Barber reforms to liberalise the markets and strengthen competition, meant that banks had to disclose their reserves. The Midland was now discovered to be a high-cost bank and pressures began from shareholders and analysts. Macmillan was now chief general manager at the Clydesdale and was so strongly resistant to Midland interference that he began to be regarded as something of an obstacle to change. Some thought that had he not retired he would have been pushed aside.

Cole-Hamilton succeeded him in 1982. Some pressure developed, mostly on agricultural lending where the Midland showed some desire to co-ordinate its activities; but at this point Cole-Hamilton was fairly relaxed because there were evident advantages in having a strong local personality with group products to sell. It was the Crocker crisis, of 1985, which marked the next stage in the Clydesdale's loss of autonomy. The Midland's venture into California was a disaster. The Crocker loan book collapsed along with a slump in local property prices.

The crisis put the Midland's ratios under enormous pressure. The deterioration in the capital ratio seriously curtailed the normal banking activities of lending. The cost ratio focused attention on the potential areas of economy and rationalisation, and that brought the Clydesdale into the harsh light of central scrutiny. It had its own head office, a substantial target, and the obvious thing was to turn it into a region controlled from the centre. At this point Sir Kit McMahon came in to sort out the Midland's balance sheet and it became clear that the infrastructure was a serious problem.

Consultants presented their report at a meeting in Chewton Glen, a hotel near Bournemouth, in 1985. Cole-Hamilton was in the 20-strong group of executives, consultants and members of the working parties who attended the meeting. It took about two-and-a-half days. On the last day the consultants presented a structure plan and put up an organisation chart. It was on UK lines. There was a retail side, a corporate side, a support side and a travel group to look after Thomas Cook.

Cole-Hamilton immediately spotted a big hole in it – his job. The structure represented a group philosophy. There was nowhere in it for a chief executive of the Clydesdale. Cole-Hamilton swallowed hard and raised the matter. They said that they would always need a chief executive. He told me in conversation in 1993:

> Then they used this expression which I never quite understand: 'It will be transparent to the customers.' And I said, there's no way it will be transparent to our customers because there's no way it's going to be transparent to our staff. The staff in Glasgow are waiting to hear from me what we've decided to do. If we decide they're not going to have a chief executive and are all going to have to report to London then the customers will very quickly find out. I said if you want to do this you must not flannel; you must put the Midland sign up over all the Clydesdale branches.

In Cole-Hamilton's response, which was immediate and instinctive, there was a certain irritation. He was fed up with the playing of games. He was particularly incensed by the phrase 'transparent to the customers'. He said: 'I think it means the customer doesn't know, but I've always thought transparent means you can see through it! . . . We were all trying to work towards something but we weren't being true to ourselves.' In the garden, as they strolled after the meeting, a colleague who had been on the working party turned to him and remarked, 'Christ, what have you said?'

The party broke up, and discussions carried on for about two years. It became clear that they weren't going to put up the Midland bank sign over the Clydesdale network. The expectation was that custom would bleed if this step were taken, although some bold souls argued that it would be worth losing 30 per cent of your business if you lost 60 per cent of your cost. 'But we were faced with the demise of a bank. To be fair to them, once that was put to them they were never going to do it.' Some people still think that they should have taken the pain of making the Clydesdale a region of the Midland. They pointed out that the Royal Bank of Scotland had put its name over the William Glyn network in England, a bold decision no doubt resented but without the motor of national sentiment to make it truly embarrassing. In Cole-Hamilton's mind the important thing was that the Midland should 'stop pussy-footing and come up front'.

Internal audit and international operations began to emerge as obvious candidates for centralisation. The question of combining treasury functions came up again. There was pressure to introduce a standard approach to corporate accounts. A slow death of the Clydesdale's independence began to be in prospect. Information technology presented acute difficulties. Alex Macmillan had made sure that the Clydesdale's system was incompatible with that of the Midland. Now the fear was that the Clydesdale system would be starved of development capital.

At that time Cole-Hamilton was being as co-operative as he could. He tried to convince the staff that the Midland connection was good for them. But whatever he gave, it was never enough. The pressure to reduce costs was continuous and inescapable. Even the note issue was questioned; and so was the necessity to publish a separate balance sheet. At that time Cole-Hamilton drew strength from the support he had on the Clydesdale board, from the chairman Sir Eric Yarrow and directors like Norman Macfarlane who realised the importance of the branded identity.

In 1988 the Clydesdale was rescued from this creeping absorption by the

National Australia Bank which acquired it from the Midland. One day Sir Eric and Cole-Hamilton came into my office to tell me of this *deus ex machina*. An editor has to beware of what are called 'snow jobs' – propaganda exercises designed to convince him that black is white – but I sensed their genuine relief and excitement. Cole-Hamilton had been playing golf with Scottish Television and while on the course had to take a phone call. The message was that Sir Kit would like to meet Sir Eric and himself the following morning. Sir Eric was at Wimbledon and Cole-Hamilton had him paged on the Centre Court. Cole-Hamilton went down on the sleeper and they met for breakfast. 'Who's your money on?' asked Sir Eric. 'Who are they going to sell?' Cole-Hamilton replied: 'It might be Thomas Cook, it might be Forward Trust, but it won't be us because we're part of the UK business sector.'

At the meeting chaired by Sir Kit they were told that the Clydesdale, the Ulster-based Northern Bank and the National Irish Bank had been sold to the National Australia Bank. Sir Eric, asked for his reaction, said, quick as a flash: 'When can I meet my chairman and my chief executive?' Sir Kit said they'd be over on Sunday and asked Cole-Hamilton for his reaction. He replied: 'I have to confess to a great sense of relief.' Brian Goldthorpe, to whom Cole-Hamilton reported, said: 'I quite agree with you. You and I have always got on well and more and more we were going to have to corral you into the group.' NAB bought the three banks for a total of £420 million with the Clydesdale believed to have cost around £320 million. Two years later it acquired the Yorkshire Bank for about £1,000 million.

Apart from removing the ambivalence of its relationship with the Midland, the acquisition went down well in Scotland. At the press conference Sir Eric and Cole-Hamilton were asked how the customers would react to being owned by a foreign bank and Cole-Hamilton replied, in typically humorous fashion: 'A lot of them think we have been owned by a foreign bank for years!' But, to be fair, he acknowledged the Midland's goodwill down the years and its recognition of the Scottish dimension. Since then the Clydesdale has got on well with the Australians. It has not escaped pressures to reduce costs of staff and infrastructure. But the Australians were traditional bankers and appreciated the value of the Clydesdale's deep roots in the community through its branch network. At times of takeover or acquisition, inflated promises are often made, and the idea put around that the Clydesdale would move aggressively into the North of England has come to nothing. It remains very much a local Scottish bank and NAB was operating as a confederation. It had 48 per cent of its assets in Australia, 33 per cent in Europe and Britain, ten per cent in New Zealand and nine per cent in the rest of the world. The centralising tendencies would continue to be present but there was no dispute about the importance of local identity.

The Guinness and Clydesdale experiences have many dissimilarities. One was criminal in content, the other a slow and friendly osmosis driven by external commercial forces. Both amounted to the same thing – a loss of economic autonomy from which men of goodwill salvaged what they could.

PART III
THE FAILURE OF DEVOLUTION

CHAPTER EIGHT

The rise of nationalism

Through my years of journalism no question has puzzled me more than that of Scotland's political identity and consciousness. My parents cared deeply about it; I have lived and worked through the excitements of various nationalist surges. In the Seventies home rule seemed almost to be with us. North Sea oil and its abundant revenues had created optimism about how Scotland might prosper on its own. But its people's failure to endorse with sufficient enthusiasm the Scotland Act of 1979 (51.6 per cent for, 48.4 per cent against, with 36.4 per cent of the electorate abstaining) destroyed some naive assumptions about how they might view the future. In those days, as deputy editor of *The Scotsman*, I was one of those members of Edinburgh's chattering classes who deluded themselves that Scotland was impatient for change; journalists and political scientists, keen to create a polity to enrich their own lives, were accused of inventing the devolutionary movement of the time, although they were merely the descendants of a long line of campaigners.

The truth was that Scotland was confused, uncertain and deeply divided. The politics of grievance, skilfully developed by civil servants and politicians of both parties to enhance Scotland's financial advantages within the Union, came back to punish us. We were inured to the idea of failure and relative disadvantage; indeed it had become central to our rhetoric in dealing with the state. We had acquired the sour tastes of dissatisfaction but we were not at all united in our view of how they might be dispersed. The Scottish public was offered more of what it had been told to dislike – government. Not surprisingly it was less than enthusiastic.

In Edinburgh, surrounded as one is by the mementos and monuments of Scottish statehood, it is easy to fall into a nostalgic dream of lost glories; it is easy to resent the provincial status foisted on Scotland by the British government machine and the London press; it is easy, and human, to respond to the anglicising and standardising values peddled by the establishment, the educational system and the electronic media. Early in 1993 I met an intelligent young woman working in television who told me that at her school in a polite suburb of Glasgow they had been taught no Scottish history.

In Glasgow these last dozen years, by contrast to my days in Edinburgh, I have been exposed to an almost universal and adamantine Unionism among the business classes: people do not talk about independence or devolution as much as they did – and do – in Edinburgh. The Labour movement, which runs so much of local government, is much more interested in hard questions of power and resources than in those of constitutional change; like the Tories the Labour Party has since the 1970s used placatory concessions as a shield against nationalism, without compelling conviction if with some success, and the leading Scottish Labour politicians of the age see their careers at Westminster rather than in any devolved parliament in Edinburgh. In Aberdeen and the North suspicion of the central belt is a more powerful sentiment than resentment of London. Indeed, the northern cities, and those in the islands, would probably prefer London rule to governance from Edinburgh, although the asperities of Thatcherism in the Eighties changed that at least for a time. Even in the north it is a presumptuous commentator who assumes a common interest between Aberdeen and Peterhead, or Aberdeen and Inverness.

It is something of a miracle that this disparate, quarrelsome and individualistic country has retained so strong a sense of its own identity. Scotland is, as David McCrone has said, a stateless nation or, in the phrase of Tom Nairn, a decapitated nation. It is unusual among the small stateless nations because it was not conquered by a more powerful neighbour. Through its own sovereign parliament, admittedly after some English cajoling and bullying, it subscribed to political union. For most Scots its sovereignty remains entrenched in the Treaty of Union, though that principle has not always been honoured by the state. Revisionist historians, lawyers and politicians have claimed that the Scottish parliament was merely absorbed into the English parliament continuing. This, indeed, has been the orthodox view of the British Government which refers to the 'Act' rather than the 'Treaty' of Union, implying that all of it is open to parliamentary revision. This attitude has been reflected in its official publications; and, during the 1992 election campaign, it underlay Mr Major's claim that if Scotland seceded from the Union it would not be a successor state with automatic EC membership. Mr Major and his Secretary of State for Scotland, Ian Lang, later softened this position. Their document 'taking stock' of the Union in 1993 specifically acknowledged Scotland's reality as a nation though persisted in calling the Treaty an Act. Like many Scots I adhere to the opinion classically enunciated by Lord Cooper in 1954. The Treaty of Union is not an Act of the English Parliament capable of revision at its whim: it is an entrenched constitutional guarantee embodying Scottish sovereignty.

Scotland is a nation so divided by regional jealousies and so tortured by self-doubt, in which radical or socialist politics have never been able to form an enduring alliance with bourgeois or romantic nationalism, that it is easy for the UK ruling party to govern it without a majority of Scottish seats and to introduce legislation which is unpopular in Scotland. The 'magic circle' of those enjoying power and patronage in Scotland is deeply committed to the Union, as is the business class and the financial community (with only a few exceptions). Since the war Scotland's universities have been enlarged and extensively anglicised, continuing a process begun by the Whigs in the nineteenth century when they saw that traditionalism would consign Scotland to a backwater of mediocrity. Westminster statutes are eroding its body of distinctive law. Its true capital, London, is outside its borders. Most Scottish businessmen or civil servants go more often to London than to other Scottish cities. It is not an uncommon experience, for example, to meet a Glasgow businessman and frequent shuttle traveller who says that he has just taken the family and the children for the first time to Edinburgh and, yes, they really enjoyed the Castle and the Royal Mile.

To visitors and sympathetic English observers, Scotland's acquiescence in the Union can be puzzling. In an article in *The Times* in 1993 Jan Morris expressed her astonishment that a country so full of history and with two of the most interesting cities in Europe should be largely content to be ruled from London. Perhaps, she quoted one jaundiced Scot as saying, we no longer have fire in our bellies. But at least part of the answer is that for Scotland the Union has until now been a practical success and an external capital has moderated internal jealousies and tensions. The British state has given Scots access to the English mercantile and imperial system and to its frameworks of influence and patronage; indeed the Scots have been notably successful in penetrating them. It has provided an outlet for Scottish energies, given careers to graduates and technicians. The Irish have recently emerged from the De Valeran isolationism in which they immured themselves for so long after 1922 and are beginning to operate successfully from the platform of a sovereign state with a seat on the EC Council of Ministers. With their abundant harvest of young graduates, they are probably penetrating the European political culture with more success than the Scots for whom the outside world still begins in London.

The history of Scottish nationalist and devolutionary agitation over the last century shows a remarkable continuity, both in the cyclical pattern of actions and responses, and the arguments deployed by the parties. There is some dispute among historians about the modern movement's roots. This is not surprising: the question is of the 'how long is a piece of string' variety. H. H. Hanham's standard work convincingly traces them to the long line of Scottish patriotic icons like Wallace and Bruce. In 1559, after an English army sent by Queen Elizabeth had ejected the French from Edinburgh, John Knox decreed the presbyterian system which entrusted poor relief and education to the Kirk. His vision of a minister and a dominie in every parish was genuinely revolutionary and the Kirk's democratic system of organisation, and its perception that it had no human leader but that God was its Head, was to influence the secular thinking of the Scottish National Party after the Second World War.

In the seventeenth century the covenanting wars made presbyterianism synonymous with nationalism and the Kirk imposed its parochial authority with particular cruelty with a bout of witch-killing believed to have been in excess of anything experienced in Europe. John Buchan's novel *Witch Wood* suggests that satanic orgies were a popular reaction to the excessive social restraints developed by the presbysterian orthodoxy. Feminist historians like Elspeth King have suggested that male chauvinism lay at the root of the persecution of women who may sometimes have been dottled but were rarely more than nuisances or gossips.

In the eighteenth century, in the years following the Union, Scots patriotism was subjected to two conflicting pressures. First, their need for acceptance within the English polity made leading Scots uncomfortable about their own Scottishness of speech and manners. The long process of anglicisation began that was to persuade many of the gentry and propertied classes to give their offspring an English education. The bourgeoisie developed the strangulated compromise which we today call Morningside or Kelvinside speech, the very essence of gentility: sex is what you put the coal in. The tortured accents of the conforming Scot is the theme of Robert McLellan's play *The Flowers o' Edinburgh*; Robert Burns struggled to please Edinburgh society by writing in English, with vapid results, and reverted to Scots in which he worked with assurance, the descendant of a literary line going back to Dunbar. The result was that the many Scots who moved within the English political system at the highest level became so completely anglicised that it was impossible to distinguish any peculiarly Scottish qualities about them at all, Ramsay Macdonald being an obvious exception. At the same time the closer encounter with England set up a contrary force which made other Scots cling to their Scottish-ness with stubborn pride. Hanham wrote that David Hume the philosopher found it easier to be liked in France than in England. Such Scots became anti-English, covertly or openly. Anti-Englishness was to be an enduring theme of later nation-alist agitation just as English dislike of Scots is an enduring feature of our political landscape. We girn and whinge and take up too much parliamentary time.

For a full historical review of Scottish nationalism readers should turn to Hanham or Andrew Marr's useful paperback *The Battle for Scotland*. The briefest of sketches will suffice here. Cultural nationalism underpins most contemporary forms even if it is often disguised as rational economic analysis. Few nationalists are as ready as Douglas Henderson, an SNP Member of Parliament from 1974 to 1979, to acknowledge its emotional content. Indeed, specifically nationalist agitation of a recognisably modern kind began in the nineteenth century at a time when the Union was yielding clear economic benefits. The archives of the Glasgow Chamber of Commerce show little evidence of unhappiness among commercial interests but elsewhere we do find two important strands of discontent that have come down to the present day – emotional dissatisfaction involving the idea that Scotland's dignity as a nation had been slighted and the claim that Westminster had neither the interest nor the time to legislate on Scottish matters.

In the eighteenth century the first concern of all intelligent Scots was with national development. Scotland's poverty, its failing economy and its exclusion from the English mercantile system had driven it into the Union in the first place. Now they were aware that Scotland could not survive as an impoverished back-water. The 1745 rising drove the Lowlands unequivocally into support for the Union. It tainted nationalism with Jacobitism, and the powerful legal establishment in Edinburgh, to which the management of Scotland was so largely entrusted, spent much time living 1745 down, as did the merchant classes of Glasgow. Both groups rallied to the volunteer militias to help put down popular unrest after the French Revolution and the courts dealt cruelly with Radical agitators. A former editor of *The Glasgow Herald*, Samuel Hunter, a keen member of the Volunteers, had the distinction of being burned not once but twice in effigy.

In the nineteenth century, in a country now empty of its own political institutions, the Whig and Liberal supremacy made Scotland dance to an inevitably anglicising tune. From 1745 to 1828 Scotland's managers, of whom Henry Dundas, the first Viscount Melville, was the supreme example, were given a free hand by the Government. But by the 1820s it was becoming difficult to run Scotland simply by judicious attention to patronage and the management of elections. When the second Lord Melville refused to serve under Canning in 1828 no Scottish 'manager' could be found to replace him. The old system quietly came to an end and Scotland was placed under English ministers at Whitehall.

The Reform Act of 1832 created the Whig and Liberal hegemony of Scotland that lasted until Gladstone espoused Irish Home Rule in 1886. For the first time Scotland had a system of free elections. The bad old days were associated with the Tories. The Whigs also enjoyed intellectual ascendancy. Even Tory administrations had to appoint Whig lawyers to the Bench. For more than 50 years after 1832 the Scottish MPs were almost entirely Whig or Liberal.

Hanham argued that Liberal supremacy coincided with a bout of enthusiasm for the Union 'which even the Disruption did little to modify'. Yet the Disruption, if it much diminished the influence and power of the Church of Scotland which survived as a rump, released a remarkable explosion of energy, a hectic round of church-building which also reflected a general growth in prosperity, and an intellectual ferment. The role of ministers, or their offspring, in the subsequent nationalist movements is again a constant theme. Nor was the Disruption a sudden event; it was the culmination of a long period of unrest after the restoration of Kirk patronage to the landed classes. Callum G. Brown, in his work on this period published in 1990, believed that historians have largely failed to grasp the significance of schism between 1733 and 1843. By 1800, he wrote, a quarter of Lowland Scots adhered to presbyterian dissent and arguably more. By 1826 the figure was upwards of one third, and by 1851 the figure for Scotland as a whole was over a half. The Church of Scotland for a time consisted of less than a third of all church-goers.

Modern historians perhaps underestimate the spiritual energy behind the Disruption, and look too much for political and economic explanations. Contemporary accounts show that there had been a religious revival in many parts of Scotland, and the traditions of the covenanting days were very much alive in the popular mind. It is also true, of course, that the development of tenant farming as a result of the agricultural revolution set tenant farmers naturally in an adversarial position against the landowners exercising Kirk and other forms of patronage. After the Disruption this was to associate the Free Church with the Liberal Party, although Michael Lynch thought that such radicalism did not persist until the end of the century.

The General Assembly's Claim of Right of 1842 which preceded the Disruption of 1843 specifically rejected the state's authority to legislate on spiritual matters on which the Church was held to be the supreme court. It asserted that:

> All and whatsoever Acts of the Parliament of Great Britain, passed without the consent of this Church and nation, in alteration of or derogation to the . . . government, discipline, rights and privileges of this Church . . . inserted in the Treaty of Union, as an unalterable and fundamental condition thereof, and so reserved from the cognisance and power of the federal legislature created by the said treaty . . . shall be, in themselves, void and null and of no legal force or effect.

This statement contains at least three important ideas. It says that the interests of the Church and the nation (Scotland) are the same. It claims that the Treaty of Union is entrenched and inalterable. It asserts that the UK constitution is 'federal', meaning that it is not the English Constitution continuing but a new Constitution dating from 1707. It amounts to a rejection of the English doctrine of parliamentary sovereignty. This confrontation with the state demonstrated the legality and inflexibility of presbyterians. Scotland lacked the English gifts of compromise and as a result was less successful in creating enduring indigenous institutions. The Disruption gravely weakened the Church's influence: the English secular state, wrote Michael Fry, was made more powerful. At least part of Scotland's subsequent chronic disunity must stem from this act of self-destructive stubborness, yet it flowed inescapably from the attitudes of a legalistic religious tradition. All the ideas expressed in the Claim of Right have cropped up time and again in the 'declarations' which have been so favoured a device of modern nationalism, echoing as they do the Declaration of Abroath of 1320.

Edwin Muir summed up the enduring dilemma of Scottish Toryism, felt keenly by Sir Walter Scott. It sanctified the established order and tradition, of which the Treaty of Union was part. Therefore, in John Buchan's phrase, all Conservatives were Scottish nationalists – because they must honour and preserve Scottish traditions. The peculiar pain caused by this position was that the Union – to which the Conservatives were committed – would itself undermine and dilute the old Scottish verities. This insight does much to explain the repeated response of Conservative administrations to nationalist and devolutionary agititation. The Conservatives have played a leading part in creating administrative devolution and, in the Scottish Office, a Government department uniquely (until the creation of the Welsh Office in 1964) removed from direct London control.

There thus began, in the latter decades of the century, a period of all-party agitation for administrative devolution or home rule. In 1880 the young fifth Earl of Rosebery, who was Gladstone's host during the Midlothian campaign and had gained influence with him, proposed a Secretaryship. Gladstone responded by creating an Under-Secretaryship at the Home Office and making Rosebery its first incumbent. He was frozen out by the London civil servants and resigned in disgust after two years. In 1884 the Convention of Royal Burghs organised an all-party rally in Edinburgh; leading Scots Tories backed the mainly Liberal demand for a Secretaryship. This coalition secured quick results: a Liberal Bill of 1884 was put through in August 1885 by the Tory Prime Minister Lord Salisbury. The first Secretary of Scotland was the Tory Duke of Richmond and Gordon, accepting the commission somewhat cynically offered by Lord Salisbury. The exchange, in summary, went like this:

Lord Salisbury: The work is not very heavy
Duke of Richmond: The office is quite unnecessary.

Around this time a series of boards was set up – on prisons, poor law, lunacy. The Scotch Education Department was founded in 1872 and the Crofters Commission in 1886. A formula for apportioning British revenues on the basis of national populations, the Goschen formula (named after the Chancellor of the day, George Goschen), was introduced in 1888. The first motion for Scottish home rule was moved in the Commons in 1889. By 1966, Dr Jack Brand calculated, 13 motions or Bills had been introduced. None was carried into law.

Developing Irish nationalism, and British concessions to it, were to act as a powerful stimulus to the home rule movement. If the Irish could get concessions from London, why not the Scots? The desire of the state not to be seen to be giving favourable treatment to Ireland under duress, but proceeding towards constitutional change on a rational basis, explained much of the all-party support for Scottish home rule which evaporated when the Anglo-Irish Treaty of 1922 removed this thorn from the flesh of the state.

Anti-Catholic sentiment was also an important influence in the creation of Unionism. When the Irish issue began to dominate Westminster in the 1880s, fundamental realignments took place in politics. The Irish issue, and that of disestablishment, let the Conservatives in from the cold and the emerging industrial electorate gave them a new power base. The Liberals were to have an Indian summer in the elections of 1906 and 1910, but winter was imminent. The Conservatives forged close links with the Ulster Unionists and the Grand Orange Order. In 1912 the Conservative Party had given up the unpopular name of Conservative and became the Scottish Unionist Party. This endured until 1965 when the word Conservative was reintroduced. James Mitchell noted that from the outset the Union in question was that with Ireland. The party was exploiting intellectual and theological fears of Catholicism and the potent alliance they formed with working-class resentment of the economic threat posed by Irish immigration.

To the Scottish Secretaryship was added, in 1897, a Scottish Grand Committee, consisting of Scots MPs with ten to 15 others recruited to ensure a fair reflection of the balance of parties in the whole House. The Tory Governments of 1895 to 1905 let it lapse, but the Liberals revived it in 1907 permanently, to deal with the committee stage of Bills pronounced non-controversial.

Historians regard 1913 as the highwater mark of Liberal agitation for home rule. Sir W. H. Cowan's Scottish Home Rule Bill was passed not only on the first but on the crucial second reading, by 204–159, with a Scots majority of 45–8. A. J. Balfour, for the Unionists (as the Conservatives were now called), countered with a scheme for all four UK nations on the basis of a 'glorified county council'. In May 1913 Asquith announced that his Liberal Government would put through an act for Scottish home rule in the current session of Parliament. But a scheme for Ireland was running into serious opposition in the Lords, who would probably have blocked any parallel scheme for Scotland. Douglas Young wrote:

> At any rate it was shelved, and with the outbreak of war in 1914 most Scots nationalist activists betook themselves to securing independence for Serbia and Belgium, many of them being killed.

CHAPTER NINE

A *painful evolution*

The Scottish Labour movement emerged from the First World War with a commitment to home rule which was intact but not as solid as it seemed. It came above all from the conviction that it would take much longer to achieve socialism in England than in Scotland. Glasgow had been radicalised during the war. The needs of its industries had placed enormous strains on the social fabric. Bourgeois Scotland, and the British Government, went in mortal fear of Red Clydeside. The city was full of Highlanders. Their hatred of landlordism merged with the industrial grievances of the Lowland and Irish working classes. In this fertile soil grew the more exotic blooms, too, of Celtic revivalism and the Scottish literary renaissance. The air was heady with the scents of Ireland's Easter Rising and the Bolshevik revolution.

Labour's hopes of home rule by the parliamentary route petered out by 1924. The Red Clydesiders who went to Westminster in 1922 were sincere enough. But they found that the real power lay at Westminster; there they could pursue social legislation, on housing and poverty, with some prospect of success. In 1924 the home rule Bill brought forward by one of the Clydesiders, George Buchanan, fell with the first Ramsay MacDonald Government. In 1925, at the Scottish Labour Party conference, home rule was not mentioned during the proceedings. The closing of the parliamentary route stimulated Labour home rulers to look for new alliances. Douglas Young identified four main groups that were to cohere into the National Party of 1928. There was the Scots National League, largely activated around 1918 by Thomas H. Gibson, with its monthly publication *The Scots Independent;* the Scottish National Movement, led by the poet and anthropologist Lewis Spence as a breakaway from the league in 1926; the Glasgow University Scottish Nationalist Association, largely the creation of John MacCormick in 1927; and the Home Rule Association, which had been revived in 1917 by Roland Muirhead, a wealthy owner of a tannery and like MacCormick with an ILP background. Among its activists were Tom Johnston, later to have a profound influence on the development of Scottish politics as the war-time Secretary of State, James Maxton and Hugh MacDiarmid.

The curious and eccentric figure of Muirhead, so influential in the development of modern Scottish nationalism, has been largely forgotten today. One day in 1993 there arrived in my office a slim volume called *Scotland's Constitution*. It was dedicated 'to the memory of Roland Eugene Muirhead (1868–1964) who for 75 years relentlessly campaigned for an independent Scottish parliament'.

The publication of this constitution was an act of piety by a small band of faithful followers. Muirhead was one of a group which formed the Young Scots League around 1900. It sought home rule through the Liberal Party and began Muirhead's lifetime of propaganda for home rule. Muirhead, by now a Fabian, helped Johnston launch his newspaper *Forward* in 1906. In his autobiography, Johnston wrote fondly of Muirhead. He recalled that from the society's foundation in 1900 Muirhead 'got the set of his life, from which there has never been any deviation.' Despite his wealth he dressed shabbily, his suit pockets stuffed with press cuttings. He stored the numerous pledges and pronouncements from success-ive governments promising home rule, including one from Winston Churchill in 1911 supporting a Scottish parliament within the Union.

After turning to the ILP, he practised what he preached in 1914 by transform-ing his family business, the Gryffe Tannery in Bridge of Weir, into a co-partnership with model conditions and a 40-hour week. Johnston continued:

> Half a century ago he packed his bag and walked out of the family tannery business in Renfrewshire to live the free life, first in an Owenite colony in the State of Washington (USA) and then in a non-violent anarchist colony in the same state.
>
> I never rightly got the hang of what happened during his brief sojourn in these oases in the wicked world, but he was soon back in London organising a co-operative tannery, and shortly thereafter he was engaged managing the old family business in Renfrewshire, which – lest you think he is simply a starry-eyed dreamer! – he has managed for years and still does with conspicuous success.

Matthew Neil, later to become secretary of Glasgow Chamber of Commerce and at the time an apprentice lawyer in Paisley with a first in philosophy from Glasgow University, remembered Muirhead in action. Muirhead lived in the farmhouse of Meikle Cloak in the Calder Valley above Lochwinnoch. Every Whitsunday and Martinmas Neil had to sue him on behalf of the Church of Scotland for non-payment of teinds on his farm. He was not a member of a church, and indeed an atheist. He did not see why he should support the Kirk. Neil wrote in 1990:

> He appeared in Paisley Sheriff Court in kilt and a long cloak down to his ankles, and, after I had moved for decree, he would invariably attempt to make a speech about the evils of church government, English rule and the like. Sheriff Hamil-ton, of blessed memory, had heard it all before and cut him off sharply.

When the Second World War broke out, Johnston wrote, there was an energetic police round-up of the few – if any – subversive pro-Nazi and Mosleyite elements.

> At the time somebody took it upon himself to hint to the police that Roland might be a sympathiser with Hitler, or at any rate was sufficiently anti-English to warrant a raid upon his house. A raid duly took place and after some locks had been forced there was borne off in triumph a sporting rifle of last-century vintage which had belonged to an uncle or a brother, plus a few rounds of revolver ammunition, but no revolver.
>
> Fortunately there existed at the time in the offices of the Crown prosecu-tor and the Lord Advocate a sense of humour, and the engines of war referred to were hurriedly ordered to be returned, so that Roland Muirhead was deprived of

a martyr's crown. But he complains that he has never yet been compensated for the damage to his locks.

After the Second World War Muirhead came to the conclusion that the parliamentary route would not bring independence. In 1950 he formed a group called the Scottish National Congress to pursue independence Gandhi-style, by non-violence and non-co-operation, but he could not accept the rule, introduced under the chairmanship of Dr John McIntyre, banning dual membership of the SNP and other parties (the rule which also saw the departure from the party of Douglas Young).

He revived the Scottish Secretariat at Elmbank Crescent, Glasgow, under whose auspices *The Scots Independent* had for a time been published before the war. Here would meet the Committee of Articles. It examined the constitutions of the world and prepared a Scottish constitution. Noted lawyers helped. They included Andrew Dewar Gibb, professor of Scots law at Glasgow, a founder of the Scottish (Self-Government) Party in 1932 and the Saltire Society in 1936.

The proliferation of groups and parties before 1928 was clearly a nonsense, wrote Hanham. Not until a catalyst was found in the form of the Glasgow University Scottish Nationalist Association were the rival groups prepared to come together to form the National Party of Scotland. The university association was formed in 1927, more or less on the back of an envelope in a café in Byres Road, by John MacCormick and two other students with labour and nationalist sympathies. MacCormick had been born in Glasgow in 1904 but was the son of a Mull sea captain and his mother was a MacDonald from Glenurquhart, Inverness-shire: she was the first Queen's District Nurse for the Western Isles. His nationalism and socialism both had an inherited tinge of Gaelic romanticism. MacCormick and his associates persuaded the durable and colourful R.B. Cunninghame Graham to contest the 1928 rectorial campaign. After a brilliant campaign he finished, to the amazement of the nation, only 66 votes behind the Prime Minister, Stanley Baldwin.

MacCormick's talent as a speaker had blossomed into genuine eloquence. His fervour for home rule led a heckler to ask whether Scotland would have not only independence but her own 'King John', a nickname that stuck. During the rectorial campaign the then Secretary of State, Sir John Gilmour, was hustled off the Union platform to the cry of 'Get off, Sir John, and give King John a chance.'

Cunninghame Graham's achievement invested the nationalist movement with a new credibility and the National Party was formed in the same year, 1928. MacCormick was its first chairman and later its secretary. It emphasised its reasonableness and moderation. Two years later its membership approached 4,000. MacCormick was less successful in his long career of contesting parliamentary elections and by-elections. He mustered 1,600 votes in Camlachie in 1929 and 4,000 in Inverness in 1931. He was beaten again in Inverness in 1935 and in Hillhead in 1937. By the end of the Second World War he had joined the Liberals. He was beaten once more at Inverness in 1945. His most significant achievement was in the Paisley by-election of 1948, when he rattled the Unionist Establishment.

For the general election of 1931 MacCormick for the first time used the propagandist idea of The Covenant, a name rich in historical meaning. It promised the pursuit of an independent parliament. But MacCormick was anxious to secure a broader front and to rid the party of people like MacDiarmid, whose group was regarded by the public as a lunatic and dangerous fringe. His aims were dramatically advanced with the Cathcart Unionist breakaway of 1932. This brought into the nationalist front the right-wing or moderate figures of the Duke of Montrose, Professor Dewar Gibb and Sir Alexander McEwen.

In 1937 Professor Dewar Gibb wrote a book called *Scottish Empire*. It was an account of how Scotland had reacted to the conception of Empire and of the part it had played in promoting it. Dewar Gibb argued that the Scots had made a conspicous contribution to the Empire. They were on the whole hard workers. They were less class conscious than the English. (On this last point I had some confirmation in 1992 when the Indian High Commissioner told me that the Scots had been better regarded in India than the English.) Dewar Gibb then delivered what is still a classic statement of Scottish dissatisfaction with the consequences of the Union, which, he wrote, had turned London into a great imperial capital and made Edinburgh and Glasgow no more than Newcastle or Bradford:

> Both countries helped to make the Empire, but in doing her part Scotland was contributing to the greatness of England, as distinguished from the Empire, since the empire founded by England could not, as it grew, fail to rebound to the credit of the founder ... In doing *her* part in empire-making, England was certainly *not* contributing to the greatness of Scotland either deliberately or incidentally.

James Mitchell, in *Conservatives and the Union*, called the Cathcart Breakaway of 1932 one of the most intriguing episodes in the history of the home rule movement. No matter how ephemeral or even quixotic the episode now appeared, it had been treated seriously by the Unionists at the time. In 1931 Compton Mackenzie had been elected rector of Glagow on a nationalist platform. MacCormick regarded it as a pyrrhic victory because opponents exploited Mackenzie's Catholicism as a liability. But it was also of considerable propaganda value because his defeated opponent was Sir Robert Horne, one of the most prominent Unionist advocates against home rule.

Newspaper polls, an early example of the genre, showed considerable support for devolution. A newspaper war had broken out in Glasgow with the arrival of the *Scottish Daily Express*, which commenced Scottish publication in the Albion Street building now occupied by *The Herald* and *Evening Times*. Lord Beaverbrook mischievously published a front-page endorsement of home rule. The *Daily Record* responded by giving home rule enormous and enthusiastic coverage. Mrs Pat Baird, the librarian of the *Daily Record* and *Sunday Mail*, kindly sent me, in 1993, voluminous cuttings from the papers of the period. They included a guide to the various nationalist factions:

1. Anti-loyalist direct action. Anglophobe. On extreme left, negligible in number. It comprises two groups. One demands complete sovereignty for Scotland, which would join up with some unspecified part of Europe. The other is a group called the Democratic Scottish Self-Government Organisation, a breakaway from the National Party in protest against a telegram of loyalty sent to the King.

2. Separatist home rule. The National Party of Scotland. Fought four seats at the general election with percentages ranging from 10 to 14. Stands for complete separatism within Empire. Separate fiscal policies, ambassadors, army etc. Some people such as Compton Mackenzie move between Groups 1 and 2. He endorsed the direct actionists who, led by

Wendy Wood, replaced the Stirling Castle Union Jack with the Lion Rampant. [This extemporaneous action was led by Wendy Wood after a Bannockburn Rally in 1932.]

3.   Internal home rule. This 'Moderate' group, not yet formalised, wants independence for home interests such as education, agriculture and fisheries. It contends that if the Empire is to remain it must have a strong British nucleus. Among the leaders are the Duke of Montrose and other members of the Imperial Committee of the Cathcart Unionist Association [the leaders of the Cathcart Breakaway]. They warmly support the Scottish National Development Council [a body set up to fight recession, the precursor of the post-war Scottish Council Development and Industry]. Endorsed by the *Daily Record*.

4.   Limited devolution or the 'half-loaf' school. A number of Conservatives said to be in favour of a scheme, stopping short of federalism, proposed by Lieutentant-Colonel D.C. Moore, Conservative member for Ayr Burghs. 'Many devolutionists have schemes of their own.'

5.   The All's Well opposition. Led by *The Glasgow Herald,* suspected of being the official Unionist organ. Blamed for being 'Anglophile'. Sir Patrick Ford was trying to bridge the gap with devolutionists but did not believe a Parliament would halt the southward movement of industry.

The Cathcart Breakaway was organised by Kevan McDowell, a Glasgow solicitor. Acting with the authority of his constituency party council, he set up a home rule front, arranged meetings and made statements. He was expelled from the party. The rebellion provoked the offical Scottish Unionists, under Sir Robert Horne's leadership, into a denunciation of parliamentary devolution, which was impossible and undesirable. Administrative devolution, on the other hand, was not ruled out, an attitude that has remained typical of modern Conservativism apart from the Thatcher interregnum. The Cathcart Breakaway provoked fury in Protestant, mercantile Glasgow: a well-attended meeting at the Merchants House issued a statement denouncing 'exaggerated nationalism' and endorsing the Union as in Scotland's best interests. This position was adopted that November at the Scottish Unionists' conference when Sir Robert denounced separatism as an affront to commonsense. His speech, dutifully and amply reported in *The Glasgow Herald*, was a statement of the connection between imperial greatness and Scotland's place in its sun, a rebuttal of the Dewar Gibb critique:

> One of the things that appealed to his heart more than anything else about this whole matter was that to set up the kind of parliament the Duke of Montrose and his people would wish, so far from making Scotland prouder or nobler, would immediately demonstrate to the world that we were a people of a small population, that we were only something like one-eighth of the population of England, that our wealth was immeasurably less, and that the business which we could have to conduct in Parliament was something infinitesimal as compared with the great business which the Scottish members in the Imperial Parliament had been conducting now for 200 years.

Fear of exclusion from a larger economic and political system was to be a theme of opposition to devolution in the Seventies and beyond. *The Glasgow Herald* of 27 October congratulated the Unionists MPs on their strong opposition to the proposal to set up a separate parliament for Scotland. Written in Olympian extended periods, it was a classic, if pompous, exposition of the mercantile class's anxieties:

> Being, many of them, men of business experience and in touch with affairs, they (the Unionist MPs) are in a position far better than the academic theorists who play such a prominent part in the Nationalist Party to judge the intimacy and economic links which bind Scotland and England and the closeness of the ties which have formed in the past two centuries of expansion and development. They too, of any people, have the first-hand knowledge of the detailed working of the present system of government on which to base a correct opinion as to its fairness and equity. It surely stands to reason that if, as the nationalists allege, the Scottish members at Westminster are constantly over-ruled by an English majority, Scottish affairs are neglected, and wanton injustice is done to Scottish interests, the 50 Unionist MPs from north of the Tweed would be acutely aware of the situation and would be ready to take whatever steps were necessary to provide a remedy. But what do we find? The Scottish Unionists certainly do not suggest that the existing system is perfect – like ourselves, they believe that improvements might be effected by the introduction of a greater degree of decentralisation and by the more effective use of the Scottish Grand Committee – but they are unanimously of the opinion that it is in essentials sound and equitable and that any substantial departure from it would be disastrous. Their opinion, in fact, is that the maintenance of the parliamentary Union is vital to Scottish prosperity . . .

At the conference the Cathcart rebels proposed a counter-motion to the official line and then backed down. A day later the home rulers held a meeting in an Edinburgh hotel where they founded the Scottish (Self-Government) Party, with the Duke of Montrose as chairman. The Scottish Party fought no seats: that was not its significance or purpose. MacCormick moved with the ruthless determination which marked him out as a political operator of superior ability though in the end empty of achievement. His idea that the National Party and the Scottish Party should sink their differences of policy was fiercely opposed. But in 1933, after a purge which saw the expulsion of about a fifth of the National Party membership, he pushed it through. In April 1934 the parties merged to become the Scottish National Party. Michael Lynch called it a 'glittering array of irreconcilable talents'. Its first president was Cunninghame Graham, its chairman Muirhead, and its secretary MacCormick.

The literary men were now in the wilderness. With some bitterness they watched the Kailyard recover all its old luxuriance, particularly in the Scottish newspaper press. They resumed a flirtation with fascism and communism. Edwin Muir argued that Scots writers should abandon the use of Scots. MacDiarmid was by now using English but felt betrayed and decamped to Shetland.

Nor did the SNP find peace. Splits and controversies continued to bedevil it. Now the issue was pacifism in the shadow of war. After 1935, according to Young's account, the SNP participated to some extent in the 'popular front' against fascism led by Sir Stafford Cripps. In 1937 the party at its annual conference voted that members of military age should refuse to be conscripted by any non-Scottish

Government. In the same year Wendy Wood set up the Anti-Conscription League. A new Convention organised for 1939 did not take place because of the war. In the event most nationalist young men did fight but some refused.

The SNP was not bound by the wartime electoral truce and its decision to fight by-elections caused internal tension as well as external resentment. It fought a by-election in Argyll in 1940. Tempers rose even higher over the decision to contest Glasgow Cathcart in 1942. But its candidate William Whyte mustered only 1,000 votes, well behind the 3,807 secured by William Douglas Home who, together with an ILP candidate, had split the anti-Government vote and took second place.

Protests continued against industrial conscription, particularly of Scottish girls sent to work in the armaments factories of England, and criticism of the leadership's feeble attitude to it. *The Scots Independent* attacked the pacifism of Douglas Young, one of those who had refused to fight. Young was then a lecturer in Greek at Aberdeen University. As a boy I have a memory of a tall, lean and bearded figure coming to the house (he was 6ft 7in, I learn from the obituary in *The Herald* library): my father, I recall, was fond of him. He was born in Fife in 1912, educated at Merchiston, St Andrews and New College, Oxford, where at the end of the interview he was asked if there was anything he did not know; he was a scholar, a translator of Aristophanes, and my father admired the disciplined way he read the newspapers – going through them, marking items of interest, and cutting them out for future reference. Once, as they were travelling together to Glasgow by train, Young pointed through the window in the direction of Saughton Prison and alarmed their respectable companions in the compartment by recalling, with apparently pleasurable nostalgia, the time he had spent inside.

In April 1942 he was sentenced to 12 months' imprisonment for resistance to the National Service Act as contrary to the Treaty of Union. While released on bail pending appeal, he was elected chairman by the SNP annual conference of May 1942. Dissidents rejected MacCormick's placatory offer of resignation from the secretaryship and Young defeated MacCormick's nominee for the chair, the journalist William Power, by 33 votes to 29. MacCormick and his allies seceded and formed a non-party pressure group, eventually called the Scottish Convention. After the war Young himself was to be extruded from the party when it refused to let him, or anybody else, be a member of the Labour Party too.

The SNP acquired Dr Robert McIntyre as its secretary, 'revived remarkably' in Hanham's phrase, cleared its debts and in by-elections exploited the electoral truce. In 1944 Young was almost elected for Kirkcaldy Burghs, taking 45 per cent of the poll (the authorities responded by again imprisoning him, because of his non-compliance with industrial conscription). In 1945 Dr McIntyre won Motherwell, giving the SNP its first parliamentary seat, though he lost it at the general election six weeks later when the SNP no longer enjoyed a near-monopoly as the anti-government party.

MacCormick's Scottish Union was soon renamed the Scottish Convention. It had strong similarities to the old Scottish Home Rule Association, aiming to build a consensus for home rule. Its activities were to dominate the headlines after the war. Meanwhile the SNP, under Dr McIntyre's efficient chairmanship, was acquiring a Poujadiste quality, with elaborate ideas about the role of the state and the individual heavily influenced by Scotland's tradition of presbyterian church government. But the SNP was about to enter the shadows while most of Scotland marched to the beat of the Covenant's drum. And this is where I came in.

CHAPTER TEN

Below the salt

After the war, while Dr Robert McIntyre was busily writing a new party constitution and cleansing the SNP of its ambidextrous members like Douglas
Young, a new wave of offended national sentiment gripped Scotland – and the SNP
had little to do with it. As it was nearing its height, about 1950, I had reached the
age of 11 and I have reasonably vivid memories of the atmosphere that imbued
Scotland at the time. That it was a universal mood I did not doubt until, in
conversation in 1993, John Smith told me that while growing up around this time
in Ardrishaig, the son of a radical schoolteacher who raised his family on the *New
Statesman,* he had not been aware of the Covenant at all.

In our house there was particular resentment over the decision, confirmed by
Winston Churchill with a certain arrogant hypocrisy given his willingness to exploit
Scottish national sentiment as a means of attacking Labour, that the new Queen,
who was crowned in 1953, should be known as Queen Elizabeth II (she was the
first since the Union created the United Kingdom). This caused widespread and
genuine outrage. I remember my parents' fulminations very well. They went on
about it for years.

They were also greatly put out when after her coronation the Queen came to
Edinburgh to receive the Honours of Scotland (the regalia restored to public
acknowledgement and display thanks to the efforts of Sir Walter Scott) wearing not
her sovereign robes but a coat and carrying a handbag. Later Scotland was to have
a more painful experience of a lady with a handbag.

The heightened feeling found a focus in John MacCormick's creation, the
Covenant. Then, on Christmas Day of 1950, four enterprising students, supporters
of MacCormick, liberated from Westminster Abbey the Stone of Scone, the Coronation Stone of Scottish kings and the symbol of Scottish sovereignty. The episode
caused great public excitement. It is still widely believed that the Stone eventually
restored to the Abbey is not authentic but merely an imitation (since it is symbolic
this scarcely seems to matter) and that the real stone is in the care of the Knights
Templar.

One of the leaders of the raid, one of the 'reivers' as they romantically styled
themselves, was Ian Hamilton. He is now a senior QC and is from time to time an
adornment not only of the Bar but also of Babbity Bowster, the inn in Glasgow's
Merchant City where he delights his friends with the conversation of an unquen-
chably irreverent and independent spirit and arrives in full leathers from his Argyll
home on a powerful motor-cycle to begin a few days' stint at the High Court down
the road. He travels also by this means to the northern circuit. When I asked him

whether he found it dangerous, he agreed that it was but added that, at the age of 68, he would prefer death by motor-cycle accident to some other ways of dying. He felt he was ahead of his time, and others in the Faculty of Advocates were following his example and taking up an exhilarating sport. From time to time he stirs things up in the Faculty to the ineffable pleasure of the press and the discomfiture of the great and the good. He has given us a warm portrait of MacCormick in his delightful book, *A Touch of Treason*.

The idea of liberating the Stone had been made by Muirhead in a letter to Wendy Wood in 1937 and it had been used fictionally by Compton Mackenzie. Hamilton was unaware of such a provenance. He told me in 1993 that the mission had been his idea and it had come to him afresh. It had, he said, been extraordinarily easy, so relaxed was the British state at the time. It was still an age of innocence. The ploy amused the nation. The plodding embarrassment of the police was much enjoyed. And it adroitly made the point that Scottish sovereignty still resided north of the border.

There was sympathy for the reivers even at the highest levels of the Scottish establishment, though not from Charles L. Warr, minister of St Giles' Cathedral and Dean of the Thistle and of the Chapel Royal of Scotland; he dealt with the episode in memoirs, *The Glimmering Landscape*, imbued with a reverence for the noble traditions of Scotland, a reverence that to the modern mind may seem odd. His national sentiments were subordinated to his much greater respect for law and order. He described with unconscious humour his horror when it was suggested by Nigel Tranter (the author of many popular historical novels on Scottish themes) that he should take the Stone into 'direct custody' in St Giles':

> I replied with an emphatic negative. Putting all sentiment aside, the plain fact remained that the Stone fell into the category of stolen property. I would be in duty bound to inform the police.

This is not the stuff of which successful nationalist movements are made. He went on in the same windy way:

> Whether or not a plea on behalf of the Scottish Nation were made to the Government to return the Stone to Scotland, it was obvious that no such negotiations could possibly be entered into until the Stone had been returned to the place from which it was stolen.
>
> John (later Lord) Cameron now entered the discussion with a 'brilliant suggestion' that the Stone should be taken to the Abbey of Arbroath, left there before the high altar, and the authorities informed as to its whereabouts. St Giles' being out of it, we all agreed this would be an excellent solution, and later that night Mr Tranter motored through to Glasgow to see Dr MacCormick and asked him to convey this advice to all concerned. The following day a mystery party turned up in a covered van at Arbroath Abbey. They placed the Stone, covered with the St Andrew's flag, before the high altar. Then they informed the custodian who they were and what they had done and drove away. The ham-fisted indignities to which the Stone was then subjected by the police, as by stages it was taken back to London, did nothing to help the highly inflammable atmosphere that prevailed in Scotland.

More insults were to come from the authorities as preparations were completed for the Coronation of Elizabeth. A special committee had been appointed by the General Assembly and much thought, wrote Warr, had been given to its due recognition in Scotland. There was, he said, 'widespread rejoicing' when a statement from Buckingham Palace announced that the Queen wanted a national service to be held in St Giles' in June 1953 during her Coronation visit. It was her desire that the Honours of Scotland (Crown, Sceptre and Sword) should be carried to the cathedral. 'This was thrilling news indeed,' burbled Warr. The Sword of State, presented by Pope Julius II to King James IV in 1507, had been carried once before in St Giles', in 1911 at the inauguration of the Chapel of the Order of the Thistle. But the Crown, believed to incorporate that worn by King Robert the Bruce, and the Sceptre, presented by Pope Alexander VI to King James IV in 1494, had never been in the cathedral before.

While Warr was assiduously engaged on this 'very delicate matter', the preparations for the Coronation itself in London were going on, and it rapidly became clear that the place reserved for the Church of Scotland in the proceedings was very far below the salt. As a concession to the surging nationalism, the Moderator had for the first time been given a place in the ceremony at Westminster Abbey. The first idea was that he should receive the Bible at the altar from the Dean of Westminster and carry it to the Archbishop, who would then present it to the Queen. 'This I strongly opposed. It was the sort of thing that could be done by an acolyte,' wrote Warr.

Finally it was agreed at the Anglican end that the Moderator should carry the Bible and himself present it to the Queen, the Archbishop beginning the traditional admonition and the Moderator concluding it with the words: 'Here is wisdom; this is the Royal Law; these are the lively oracles of God.' From the Anglican point of view, wrote Warr, this inclusion of the Moderator did not mean as much as Scotland thought it did. The presentation of the Bible was at an early stage of the proceedings before the real Coronation office, the act of Consecration embodied in the Anglican rite of Holy Communion, had begun. The Moderator did not receive Holy Communion with the Anglican dignitaries who communicated together with the Queen.

Back in Edinburgh, Warr's great day duly dawned but on its eve he had been afflicted by panic.

> Late that night I went up to St Giles' just to see that everything was in order. Workmen were still moving in and out of the church finishing various odd jobs, when suddenly a thought struck me. Pillar-boxes had recently been tampered with in protest at the Queen's designation. With all this coming and going of workmen and officials, who might not have slipped into St Giles' and concealed themselves? It was quite possible that some fanatics of extreme Nationalist views might have done so and be waiting till the church was finally closed to come out and wreck and disarrange the whole interior. I sent a message to police headquarters and an inspector came round. I told him of my apprehension and asked if he could supply men to search the cathedral. He considered this a very sensible precaution. So until the early hours of the morning every nook and cranny of St Giles' was scrupulously investigated.

The next day brought, he reported with a touching myopia, 'scenes of romantic pomp and splendour which had not been witnessed for centuries'. The television lights beat down on the 'breath-taking brilliancy and colour', on the 'sumptuous uniforms, on the velvet and ermine, on silk and gold braid. Looking back on moments of high emotional excitement in my life, none equalled that when I took in my hands the ancient Crown of Scotland and placed it on the Holy Table.' If Warr noticed the royal attire, of raincoat and handbag, he was too wrapped up in his happiness to mention it. This was pure old Toryism of the Walter Scott variety. (There is an old *Glasgow Herald* anecdote about the Service of State in St Giles'. Its reporter was waiting in the queue for admission. The befeathered and richly garbed man in front identified himself as the *Marchmont Herald* and was admitted. Our man, of course, then said: I am *The Glasgow Herald*.) Sir Stanley Cursiter, the Queen's Limner, recorded the great event. From his painting, which hangs today in Holyroodhouse, he tactfully expunged the handbag.

Hamilton and MacCormick had some consolation when two years later they went to the Court of Session to contest the legality of the royal style Elizabeth II. They failed in their case against H.M. Advocate but on appeal Lord Cooper of Culross held that certain articles of the Treaty of Union were incapable of subsequent modification and that the English doctrine of parliamentary sovereignty had no equivalent in Scots constitutional law. Lord Cooper's judgment is a last great cry of the Scottish judicial mind against the process of assimilation, written with elegance; but it also recognises that such matters are questions not so much of law as of power:

> Considering that the Union legislation extinguished the Parliaments of Scotland and England and replaced them by a new Parliament, I have difficulty in seeing why it should have been supposed that the new Parliament of Great Britain must inherit all the peculiar characteristics of the English but none of the Scottish Parliament, as if all that happened in 1707 was that Scottish representatives were admitted to the Parliament of England. That is not what was done. Further, the Treaty and the associated legislation by which the Parliament of Great Britain was brought into being as the successor of the separate Parliaments of Scotland and England, contain some clauses which expressly reserve to the Parliament of Great Britain powers of subsequent modification, and other clauses which either contain no such power or emphatically exclude subsequent alteration by declarations that the provision shall be fundamental and unalterable in all time coming, or declarations of a like effect . . . I have not found in the Union legislation any provision that the Parliament of Great Britain should be 'absolutely sovereign' in the sense that that Parliament should be free to alter the Treaty at will.

However, Lord Cooper acknowledged also that there was little point in asking if Parliament could 'do this thing or that' without also enquiring who could stop it if it did. In an interview in 1993 John Smith, the Leader of the Opposition, acknowledged the spirit of the Cooper judgment – that Scotland was a nation – but accepted that in terms of realpolitik it would have to take its place in the evolving institutions of Europe, with its four layers of government, at the level of nation/region, like Catalonia or Bavaria.

The episode of the Stone comes from an age of innocence, before the horrors of modern terrorism. The occasional Scottish attempts at more extreme forms of protest have always had an amateurish and bungling quality which no one can regret. The first pillar-box to carry the ERII crest was put up in Edinburgh in 1952.

90

It was tarred and then a small but crude bomb was put into it; it did not go off. Later, in the Seventies, when an 'Army of Provisional Government' on the Irish model was created by some extremists, a team sent in to rob a bank found the branch closed. The authorities have taken the intermittent terrorist activities seriously enough, and by the use of agents provocateurs and informers have kept them in check. However, the extremists lack the sustenance of popular support.

By the time the Attlee Government took office after the war, home rule had slipped out of Labour's portfolio. There were more important things to be done. Hugh Gaitskell's Diaries for 1949 show that Labour was concerned about the communist leadership of the miners' union in Scotland; home rule gets nary a mention. Douglas Young, that assiduous chronicler of broken Labour promises on home rule, noted that it was not mentioned in the UK Labour manifesto in 1945 but a manifesto put out by the party's Scottish office gave a Scottish parliament a priority second only to the defeat of Japan. Twenty-four out of the Labour MPs returned from Scotland personally undertook to promote such a parliament.

This promise was soon submerged. Labour's response to the agitation of this period, which cohered round MacCormick's Scottish Convention, was a series of adjustments to the way Scottish business was conducted at Westminster. A 1948 White Paper proposed a slight enlargement of the Scottish Grand Committee's deliberative province (never in its long career as a palliative has the committee been allowed to vote on matters of principle). Later the two Scottish Standing Committees were set up to deal with the committee stage of Scottish Bills but their membership was adjusted to reflect the balance of the House.

In the inevitable way of home-rule politics, MacCormick's movement offended the Labour Party because its rhetoric was rich in attacks on 'London government'. The Secretary of State for Scotland, Arthur Woodburn, regarded it with justice as a front aimed at overturning the Attlee Government.

Attlee wanted to know the economics of home rule and a committee under Lord Catto was appointed at the height of the Covenant movement in 1950. By the time it reported feeling had ebbed and its report was inconclusive. But it was the beginning of a more elaborate examination of the underlying economic relationship between Scotland and England which was to occupy a central position in the debate in later decades, and John S. Gibson traces in it the start of a more sophisticated economic intelligence in the Scottish Office. The Treasury's portrait of Scotland as being the recipient of English generosity is now a fixed myth of political life, although it requires considerable qualification.

Labour's manifestly unenthusiastic responses allowed the Unionists in Scotland to exploit the patriotic mood. James Mitchell was in no doubt in his study of Conservative responses of the post-war period that they were motivated by short-term considerations of political advantage. He wrote that they played the Scottish card as a means of embarrassing their opponents in Government. This approach led to a period of severe difficulty and disunity later.

But both major parties were badly split eventually, and the Tories did have a long history of Unionism that honoured Scottish traditions; within this framework their flirtation with national sentiment must have seemed perfectly natural though it conveniently coincided with a more passionate dislike of socialism. James Stuart (later Lord Findhorn), chairman of the Scottish Unionist MPs and Secretary of State from 1951 to 1957, masterminded a Unionist policy document in 1947, *Scottish Control of Scottish Affairs*, which attempted to resolve the essential ambivalence of the party. Union was strength, but Union was not amalgamation. 'Scotland is a nation.'

The death in that year of Stanley Baldwin is regarded as the beginning of this period of Conservative 'nationalism'. In the same year the Convention convoked a national assembly attended by 600 delegates from local authorites, the Church of Scotland, every trade union, chamber of commerce and trade association, and a variety of other bodies as well. The blueprint for Scotland demanding a Scottish parliament, adopted the following year, attracted a fair measure of Conservative support and tied the Liberal Party to its home-rule traditions.

MacCormick had declared himself a Liberal after the war, unsuccessfully contesting Inverness in 1945. He stood again as a Liberal parliamentary candidate in the Paisley by-election of 1948 and for a time he greatly alarmed the mercantile establishment. The Conservatives did not oppose him, supporting him as a 'national' candidate against Labour; but the decision was not universally popular in the party. *The Glasgow Herald,* still at that time the authentic voice of mercantile Unionism, advised its Paisley readers not to vote for the 'national candidate'. This was an early indication of how the issue of devolution was later to cause bitter divisions among Scottish Conservatives. Two senior Liberals also denounced the pact. In the event MacCormick hurt both the Unionist establishment and the Labour interest. He polled 20,668 votes, cutting the Labour majority from 10,330 in 1945 to 6,545. *The Glasgow Herald* dourly said the result was 'disappointing but not altogether surprising'.

The third assembly met in October 1949 in the Church of Scotland Assembly Hall on the Mound in Edinburgh. Here, a year before, *The Three Estates* had been revived at the second Edinburgh Festival, and to Scotland's great surprise and delight it discovered that all these years it had been harbouring a dramatic master-piece. From the assembly came the Scottish Covenant demanding a Scottish parliament with adequate legislative authority. Within a week 50,000 had signed it, and within six months a million signatures were within sight. Eventually a total of two million was claimed but many were forged or spurious.

For the Conservatives Walter Elliot, who had been Secretary of State for Scotland between 1936 and 1938, played the Scottish card with considerable skill. The centralisation of power under Attlee was a major theme of Tory rhetoric. Elliot vigorously attacked Labour's forgotten promises of home rule; they had 'gone with the wind'. He even attacked Labour for having three English-born MPs in Scottish seats. Mitchell viewed Elliot's nationalism as 'insubstantial, cosmetic and ugly'.

In 1950 Winston Churchill came to Edinburgh, a week before the general election, and continued the theme. He said Scotland should not be forced into the serfdom of socialism as a result of a vote in the House of Commons, an interesting anticipation of the arguments used against the poll tax in the Eighties – that a Government without a majority of Scottish seats had no mandate to impose contro-versial legislation on Scotland.

By the following year the Conservatives were back in office and, in by what was now recognisably a pattern of agitation and placation, Churchill's enthusiasm for Scotland's rights evaporated. In any case the Conservatives had done well in Scotland and could regard the vote as an endorsement. In the 1951 election they got 49 per cent of the popular vote and 35 seats (one point more than Labour and the same number of seats). Mitchell cites, in support of his view that the Tory flirtation with national sentiment was merely cynical, Churchill's remark to Lord Home when he appointed him the first Minister of State at the Scottish Office: 'Go and quell these turbulent Scots and don't come back until you've done it.' However, there seems no doubt that the Covenant years left a strong impression on Lord Home and explained his endorsement of devolution in the Sixties and the Seventies, though not in the form that eventually emerged as the Scotland Act of 1979.

The creation of the post of Minister of State for Scotland was itself one of the ways in which the new Government attempted some sort of fulfilment of the promises it had made in opposition. It also set up, in 1953, the Balfour Royal Commission on Scottish Affairs but excluded home rule from its remit. In its report it nevertheless recognised that the relationship between England and Scotland had deteriorated. It cited fears that Scotland would be treated merely as a province, and resentment of economic decline. Some administrative devolution resulted, the classic palliative. Responsibility for roads and bridges was moved from the Ministry of Transport to the Scottish Home Department. Gibson argued that the changes were not as minimal as they might appear. Without the shift in responsibility, he argued, the Forth Road Bridge would not have been the first estuarine crossing in Britain.

Thus the Covenant faded away. It disappeared, almost like a puff of smoke, because it had no significant location in parliamentary politics. The Conservatives had been its fair-weather friends. They insisted that any change must be by the parliamentary route. There was, *The Glasgow Herald* noted, a tacit compact between the major parties not to seek an alliance with the home rulers which 'might have baffled a wiser leader' than MacCormick. He had his swan songs: he was elected rector of Glasgow University in 1950 where all those years ago he had helped to create modern Scottish nationalism. It was a small but precious triumph and he was an assiduous 'working' rector (in the ancient universities the rector chairs the court, a duty which if carried out with enthusiasm is guaranteed to irritate the university authorities intensely). John Smith was one of a brilliant group of student debaters at Glasgow later in the Fifties – others included Donald Dewar, Neil MacCormick (a son of John and now regius professor of public law at Edinburgh University), Teddy Taylor and James Gordon (said by Smith to be the best of them all and now managing director of Radio Clyde). Smith remembers MacCormick as a genial but faded figure, wizened and with a sardonic wit but not very dominant. In 1959 he fought his final election campaign as Liberal candidate for Roxburgh, Selkirk and Peebles. When he died in 1961 *The Glasgow Herald's* obituary summed up his life thus:

> MacCormick was a man of great talent who had little opportunity in politics to put it to constructive purposes. For a brief moment he caught the ear of a good part of Scotland as no one else has done since the Second World War. His critics accused him of being a sentimentalist and glorifying a Scotland which belonged to his imagination rather than to his own times. His attitude to politics and history was certainly dictated by his romantic vision of the Celtic past and what he himself called his sense of 'dispossession' as a Highlander. He drew political conclusions from theories about Celtic influence which might have been better left to scholars.

By the middle of the decade Conservative or Unionist power in Scotland reached its apogee. In 1955 the Tories secured a majority of popular votes, with 50.1 per cent and 36 seats. Labour, with 47 per cent, had 34. Thus the policy of playing to

Scottish sentiment seemed to have been amply justified. But if this was the high point it was also the start of the party's decline which reached a level where, in 1992, it was even expected that it might lose all its Scottish seats. Conservative explanations for the decline have not been perceptive. They have sought scapegoats, in the Scottish press, the local government establishment or the Scottish Office and its offshoots. Yet the decline sprang from social and economic changes which could hardly be resisted. The new housing schemes created new and sometimes alienated communities. The Kirk lost members rapidly, at a rate comparable to the decline of the Conserative vote. For the Tories this was a serious matter because the Church of Scotland was long closely associated with Conservative voting, as James Kellas pointed out. After the war the Church had a period of rapid recruitment and growth. Then began what Callum Brown called 'catastrophic' decline from the middle 1950s. Secularisation, new moral attitudes, the new materialism and the distractions of the age of television and the car loosened the Kirk's grip on society. Meanwhile the older industries were beginning to disappear. Along with them went their cadre of skilled working-class (and Protestant) Tory voters. A new Labour power base was constructed out of the rapid expansion in the duties and finances of local government. The collapse of the Progressive coalition compounded the effect.

One of the last exponents of the old urban Unionism in Scotland was (Sir) Teddy Taylor. When we talked in 1993 he told me that the reasons for the Conservative decline in Scotland were the party's loss of Scottish identity and its betrayal of the working class. Taylor was very much the product of West of Scotland Unionism. Like Michael Forsyth, he is a genuine populist. Taylor's parents, he told me in 1993, were Conservative because they thought it 'respectable'. His father had been a stockbroker's clerk who took over the business when his boss died. It failed; they had to sell up everything and his mother had to find work in a textile factory. She saved every penny she could. 'Put it this way,' said Teddy. 'We had a very tough time but a very happy home life.'

After university Taylor worked briefly on *The Glasgow Herald* and then handled industrial problems for about five years for the Clyde Shipbuilders Association. Again like Forsyth, who grew up in a council house in Arbroath, his Conservatism was a reaction against the results of Labour rule. He lived in Cathcart and was its councillor when he was chosen to stand for it at the 1964 election. He held the seat until 1979. He told me in 1993:

> I'm not convinced that the working-class Conservative votes were crumbling. You had a social change. People were moving out of the town. Respectable middle-class people, bank clerks and the like, were gradually moving into the new developments. The areas like Cathcart and Pollok were going down socially. But there's no point in hiding the fact that there was a working-class Tory vote based on religious divisions. That faded away.

Taylor offered a simple explanation for the failure of the Tory interest in Scotland. He said:

> We abandoned the working class. They did not abandon us. Unfortunately the impression was given that the Conservative Party in Scotland was a branch of the English Conservative Party.

He always accepted that Labour people in Glasgow were 'good people' who did things for the right reasons. The sincerity of the average Labour councillor in Glasgow was 'streets ahead' of what you would find in the average politician at Westminster.

> What convinced me more than anything that Labour policies did damage to the working class were things like council housing and comprehensive schooling. Look at the huge variation in educational performance in council schemes. Parental expectations are low. What they didn't realise was that Labour policies which were well intentioned and based on good philosophy sadly simply had the effect of imprisoning the working class by stopping social mobility.

While the Unionists had been flirting with the dubious delights of nationalism, the SNP had been drifting ever deeper into irrelevance. Dr Robert McIntyre, chairman from 1948 to 1956, had drawn up his Poujadiste policy declaration in 1948. In his belief in the economic discretion and freedom of the individual and the limited role of the state he was an odd precursor of Thatcherism. He accepted everything, wrote Hanham, except the modern bureaucratised state. McIntyre also insisted on stricter party discipline. This was the beginning of a period of drift and schism, a fallow period during which the SNP was overshadowed by the Covenant. Hanham also noted the policy statement's complete lack of interest in culture. Thus McIntyre not only broke with the idea that the SNP could be a broad front rather than a disciplined political party; he also severed the links with the poets and the intellectuals. People like Douglas Young and MacDiarmid were simply nuisances. Young went back to his teaching of classics, his poetry and his translations of Aristophanes, and in 1970 took up professorships in North America. He claimed not to be in exile, citing the frequency of his visits home. He died in 1973, much mourned. As for MacDiarmid, the obituary in *The Times* in 1978 barely mentioned his turbulent involvement in nationalism.

CHAPTER ELEVEN

Flower of Scotland

The next sequence of chapters deals with the failure of devolution, the central Scottish political event of my professional career. The story is convoluted, for it is told from several different points of view. There was the rise of nationalism and then its decline. There was the long process by which the Conservative Party disengaged from its devolutionary commitment. There were severe stresses within the Labour Party which led ultimately to the fall of the Callaghan Government in 1979. I have dealt with these as themes in parallel chronology and the reader may from time to time find it helpful to refer to the appendices – a summary of Scottish electoral behaviour since the war and a simplified chronology of devolution.

The cause and origin of all this political excitement was the rapid and, for the major parties, unnerving rise in support for the SNP from the early Sixties onwards. The devolution years really began for me in 1967. It was after midnight and on *The Scotsman* we were holding the Glasgow edition for the result of the Hamilton by-election. Seconds after the declaration – a stunning victory for Mrs Winifred Ewing over Labour – the late David Bradford, the political editor, came on the line and bawled out the intro which I took down in long hand and sent to the composing room. I can remember that it began with the phrase, 'The rising tide of Scottish nationalism . . .' and it expressed the mood of excitement. Mrs Ewing, though she lost the seat later (as a Euro MP she is now Madame Ecosse in the European Parliament), launched the SNP into the stratosphere of concentrated London media attention and from her victory is often traced the party's modern prominence. But Hamilton was not the beginning. It was a flowering.

Gordon Wilson is arguably the most important nationalist politician of modern times. He was perhaps the first, indeed, one of the few, to acquire genuine political maturity, and he made an enormous contribution to the party's modern development. He was a source of ideas; he was one of the parliamentarians not to crack up under the strains of Westminster; he learned how to play both sides of the party against the middle; in a memorable stramash in 1982, he confronted a crisis with courage, though there are many who today still question his judgment of that time, and purged the party of rival groups. In 1993 he remains, back in legal practice in Dundee, an influential figure in the background. In his mannerisms he is precise and lawyerish. He hates excessive displays of emotion. And yet there is passion there.

I first met both Wilson and Douglas Henderson, another of the 1974–79 parliamentary group, at university in the late 1950s. The nationalist club was in those days more of a social than a political organisation. We would hear a paper from a speaker and drink tea. Wilson, then, was hot on the economic case for independence, and to this day he remains much happier with logic than rabble-rousing rhetoric. Economic analysis is the channel for rational nationalists' more intense but rarely acknowledged feelings. These flow, essentially, from the inevitable tendency of a larger state to dominate, and attempt to absorb, a smaller brother. To call them anglophobic is, in Wilson's case, to over-simplify and mis-represent them though Henderson openly acknowledges that anglophobia, or a dislike of what he would call the English state's political, economic and cultural dominance, is a motor force of nationalism. Wendy Wood made an important distinction when she said:

> I've always kept it extremely clear in my mind that the English Establishment is separate from the English people. What I am against is the humbug of the English Parliament. The English people are victims in that they've had their nationality eliminated too.

Down the years I bumped into Wilson from time to time. Early in 1993 we dined together in Dundee. Downstairs, as we traced the events of his political career, a disco started up and my tape began to pick up its thumping rhythms. I felt remote from the kids enjoying themselves below. What did they know or care about the post-war growth of Scottish nationalism? Yet Dundee has a quirky and honourable place in Scottish history as a radical city. It was sacked five times by the English. In 1922 it preferred a prohibitionist candidate to Winston Churchill – the cruellest cut of all, as Wilson remarked. Dundee East was for 13 years Wilson's constituency. And in 1993 it saw, in the Timex dispute, a reassertion of union militancy in an age which had almost forgotten what it was like.

Like others Wilson locates the beginning of modern nationalism not in North Sea oil but in industrial decline, political disillusion and Scotland's resentment at being used as a range for weaponry and as a Nato 'aircraft carrier'. The rise of CND was a contemporary phenomenon. In 1955 the SNP was in a feeble condition. It had been weakened by the Covenant movement, which had siphoned off much energy. As noted earlier, the Tories had talked up the Covenant to embarrass the Labour Government which had a formal commitment to home rule. The price they paid was that this stratagem produced a generation of convinced Tory devolutionaries whose beliefs could not be absorbed by a fundamentally Unionist party.

The SNP's chronic tendency to schism was much in evidence. The nationalist movement is essentially fissile. Henderson believes the party needs fringe groups to allow a certain kind of activist to express a desire that politics should be lively and fun. Others would say it needs a vent for the continuous thread of batty nationalism. In 1955 there was a split, what Wilson called a 'very big fight'. The membership was probably no more than 1,000 and about a third left the party. The dissident group was largely Edinburgh-based and was led by an ex-major, James Glendinning, editor of *The Scots Independent*. It included Henderson, at that time still a student. In the vocabulary of the movement, the word nationalist, as opposed to national, has strong fundamentalist connotations. It aligns a group very much to the right. But, as Wilson remarked drily, it was 'too small to be authoritarian'. Henderson's recollection was that it was formed in protest at what was seen to be the feeble leadership of Dr McIntyre.

Between 1957 and 1959 it was difficult to choose between the small splinter groups. These included the Scottish National Congress founded by the octogenarian Roland Muirhead in 1950, and Wendy Wood's Scottish Patriots. James Halliday took over the chairmanship in 1956. He was a gifted teacher. Jane Scott, now married to my cousin Grahame Young, was his pupil at Dunfermline High School and he taught her history. He stimulated his students to work up to 'four hours solidly, twice a week'. Despite his known commitment to nationalism he taught with objectivity, humour, understanding and enthusiasm. In 1993 Jane wrote that he had inspired her to take history as her principal subject at Edinburgh University. Over the past 30 years she had retained a 'continuing memory and example of a teacher who inspired his pupils to acquire an independence of mind, while holding and acting positively on very clear personal views'. Wilson thought Halliday played a much bigger role than is usually acknowledged, though Henderson remembered the period as one of continued drift. Halliday assumed the office at a younger age even than Alex Salmond (who succeeded Wilson in 1990 at the age of 35).

Halliday was succeeded in the chair in 1960 by Arthur Donaldson, and under his leadership the party became dynamic. Donaldson had a first-class brain and was a good speaker. He specialised in the economic case for independence. He fought many seats for the party. He did not win but he fertilised the ground; it was in these constituencies that the party was later to prosper. Like many nationalists – for example William Wolfe and Wendy Wood – his nationalism had been influenced by overseas experience. He was a Dundonian who had worked for Chrysler in the US. Some gave him credit for the mechanisation of the American army; he was seconded to the public contract office in Washington. He kept in touch with home and joined the National Party of Scotland when it was founded in 1928. He married a girl from Forfar who, said Wilson, 'drew his attention when she biffed him for being sarcastic. He made some sarky comment and she hit him!' A case of love at first sight? 'At first blow.'

He returned to Scotland in 1936, took up chicken farming in Ayrshire and edited *The Scots Independent*. In the period before the war Germany was flirting with nationalist movements in Europe. Donaldson was approached by an emissary of the German consul but declined a meeting. However, in 1941 he was detained in Barlinnie under Regulation 18b (the regulation used to detain Oswald Mosley). He went ten days without food to test his resolve and then threatened a hunger strike. He was released after the intervention of James Maxton in the House of Commons. Donaldson was against industrial conscription of women, for two reasons. He thought it wrong in principle. But, like Tom Johnston from the very different perspective of the Scottish Office, he could see that all the modern industries were being established in the south where they would remain after the war was over.

The Donaldsons moved to Forfar and he became editor of the *Forfar Dispatch*. At one point he was banned from the press box at Forfar Athletic because of some cutting comments he had made about the team. In an honourable tradition of journalism, he went to the terraces and reported from there. He became a much loved citizen of the burgh. By the time he died in 1993 at the age of 91 he had served as provost and a street had been named after him. When Donaldson took over as chairman in 1960, the SNP had about 1,000 members and 20 branches. When he was succeeded by William Wolfe in 1969 it claimed 125,000 members and 470 branches.

In 1959 there were other stirrings. A group in Glasgow began to show concern about organisation. The industrialist David Rollo, who was party treasurer, used to finance the party office out of his own pocket though he was by no means a wealthy man. At the election of 1959 the SNP made a feeble showing, gaining less than one per cent of the vote, but there were 'glimmers of hope and activity'. Wilson said: 'Activity tends to lead somewhere; inactivity leads to inertia.' In the 1950s unemployment of one and a half per cent was regarded as worrying. And then it started doubling, from virtually full employment, year by year. It was also a time of very high migration. Many members of the large workforce were in industries approaching the end of their lives. He continued:

> This brought us back to a point raised by Arthur Donaldson. We had missed a lot of the light engineering industries, the development of radar, the motor industry, these were all the booming industries. Shipbuilding was beginning to tail off too. The end result was that there was a degree of disillusion.
>
> And there was the beginning of intellectual activity, people trying to think through the way Scotland should go. My wife came into the movement, for example, in 1961 or 1962, over the Beeching rail cuts. I came in for something quite bizarre – for somebody who has the reputation of being unemotional and so forth – the rocket engineers [in the Hebrides, the episode which inspired Compton Mackenzie's *Rockets Galore.*] It was something to do with the Gaelic language. I had never spoken it. I never got past [the primer] *Gaelic without Groans*. I started groaning very early on.

While working as a lawyer in Edinburgh, Wilson became active in Radio Free Scotland, a pirate station that would use the Radio Scotland wavelength after the programmes finished at about 11pm. Here he was motivated by a sense of injustice that the state should deny the SNP a fair slice of air time. The authorities were pretty relaxed about it. The Edinburgh police told him, with a 'sense of loathing', that their inquiries had been at the request of the Glasgow police. They asked him if he would attend an indentification parade; he politely declined and no more was heard of the matter.

At the begining of the Sixties William Wolfe began to make his considerable contribution to the rise of the nationalists. He was born in Bathgate in 1924, the second son of the eighth child of George Wolfe, a local magnate. George Wolfe had built up a successful business manufacturing shovels and also had a steel rolling mill. He was a pillar of the Evangelical Union, a schism from before the Disruption (now part of the Congregational Union). It stood out against the Calvinist doctrine of election lampooned by Burns in 'Holy Willie's Prayer':

> O Thou that in the Heavens does dwell,
> Wha, as it pleases best Thysel,
> Sends ane to heaven an ten to Hell,
>   A for thy glory,
> An no for onie guid or ill
>   They've done afore ye!

William Wolfe's nationalism may be traced from the death in 1924 of his brother at the age of seven. Wolfe was four at the time. His father, though loving, became withdrawn in his grief and Wolfe was thrown upon his own company. At the age of nine he found a copy of *Scouting for Boys* in his father's study and Baden-Powell became a kind of substitute father. After the war he became a keen scout leader and was county commissioner when he first contested West Lothian in 1962 – the first of eight attempts to defeat and then dislodge Tam Dalyell, all unsuccessful. (In

1973 he made one excursion from West Lothian when he unsuccessfully contested a by-election in North Edinburgh.)

In 1993 Wolfe was to be found living in a cosy terrace house in North Berwick, a douce town near the mouth of the Firth of the Forth, a place of pensioners and commuters. He had come through almost a decade in the political wilderness that had also seen stresses in his personal and professional life. He now realised, he told me, that as a teenager he had been carrying grief for his parents. 'I never wanted to upset them and behaved in an exemplary fashion towards my parents, which was a bit unbearable for other people, especially my surviving sister.' When the war broke out he was 15, a boarder at George Watson's in Edinburgh to which he had been sent after attending Bathgate Academy. He joined the army at the age of 18 and was commissioned before he was 20. He went to Europe on the day after D-Day. Then as an AOP pilot he went to India and Indonesia. There he had his first encounter with explicit political nationalism.

On the boat back from India in 1947 he found a sheet from the *Scottish Daily Express* blowing about the deck. In it he read of the Saltire Society. He joined its Edinburgh branch and became active in it while finishing the CA qualification he had begun before the war (he qualified in 1952). The branch chairman was the famous teacher from the Royal High celebrated by Karl Miller in *Memoirs of a Modern Scotland,* Hector McIver. He was put to work sorting out the bags of newspaper cuttings accumulated during the war. At the Saturday socials he met Douglas Young and other nationalists of the day. But their nationalism was too extreme for him and he found an outlet for his energies in the church and scouting. The Saltire Society, however, must have influenced his attitudes. He had returned from the war having mixed mostly with English people but without connecting his unequivocal sense of being Scottish rather than British to any set of political beliefs. Now he began to think differently. He noticed that his beloved Baden-Powell had very English attitudes which were expressed in the literature and periodicals of scouting. He began to become very concerned about emigration, the symptom of de-industrialisation:

> I started looking at the emigration figures – I had to write to the Ministry of Labour – but I knew from my own experience that Bathgate Academy, a marvellous school, was exporting most of its brains from Bathgate. Of the people who stayed on and did highers very few remained in Bathgate. I just thought of that happening all over Scotland, which it was. So I said, what are you going to do about it?
>
> In 1959 I wrote to all five parties and asked them what their policies were for Scotland. I can't remember if they all replied but the only one which seemed logical and right to me was the SNP which said that if we are a nation we should be self-governing and there's no half-way house. I had been studying emigration and I realised the economic implications of it all: we really would need to have complete control over our economy if we wanted to do anything about it. There was net emigration of over 50,000 at the time. It was more later but that was still very high. There were still shiploads leaving from the Clyde and of course a lot went to England.

Wolfe joined the SNP in 1959. He had gone into the family business but politics began to claim more and more of his time. He began to show a creative touch as a publicist and exploiter of issues. He questioned the reasons for the closure of the local shale oil industry and set up an organisation called the Social and Economic Inquiry Society of Scotland which straddled the political divide.

Now began a series of by-elections, starting with Glasgow Bridgeton in 1961. The SNP secured 18.7 per cent of the vote. Labour was down almost six points, and the Tory share fell by 16. The SNP candidate, Ian Macdonald, an Ayrshire farmer, was stimulated by his success to become the national organiser, the party's first full-time official. With others he energetically toured Scotland. Wilson said:

> Ian Macdonald had a very unusual style. I suppose it reflected his wisdom as a farmer. It wasn't intensive cultivation. Ian would go off and there would be a public meeting and he would form a branch. It was a case of throwing out the seed. If the seed fell on fertile ground the branch grew. If it was thin, and if it withered away, then Ian would come back next year and hold another meeting.

Wilson himself laboured in the vineyards on an honorary basis. He became national secretary in 1963 and lasted until 1971 when, in exhaustion after the anti-climactical but intense election campaign of 1970, he gave up. 'At that time I couldn't stand fools easily and I was making it too evident.' Wilson was the political co-ordinator. He reformed the party organisation in 1963. From about 1960 membership had doubled every year. Wolfe rattled the Labour and Unionist establishments with a brilliant campaign in the West Lothian by-election of 1962, taking 23.3 per cent of the vote. For the first time in 40 years, Wolfe later recalled, a Unionist candidate lost his deposit. Wolfe became deputy chairman in 1964, giving up his work for a time to contest the seat on a full-time basis. Labour used every trick in the book. On the door-step activists spread the rumour that the Wolfe companies used cheap labour, a lie which led to an action for defamation against a local councillor; in Linlithgow sheriff court Wolfe won the case but was awarded no damages by the sheriff. West Lothian is a constituency of burghs and villages and candidates have to attend meetings in about 20 venues; if they do not they risk gravely offending local opinion. A disruptive group of Labour supporters followed Wolfe around, heckling. The Labour vote held at 50 per cent.

Wilson recalled that 1963 and 1964 were years of disappointment. In 1963 there were three by-elections which were 'quite disastrous'. The first was in Perth and Kinross. Arthur Donaldson had done well there in 1959, with 15 per cent, and stood again. But this was no ordinary by-election. Sir Alec Douglas-Home had renounced his earldom so that he could become Prime Minister in succession to Harold Macmillan. He had supplanted George Younger as Tory candidate, an act of fidelity which was to stand Younger in good stead, for in the political life there is no greater virtue than loyalty.

Wilson was still working but took a week off. There was intense press interest. About 20 journalists, many of whom had never been to Scotland before, would attend the daily press conference. The young Nigel Lawson was one of Sir Alec's sidekicks. It was a largely rural constituency and he remembers the intense questioning at meetings on the esoteric subject of 'winter keep'. Donaldson came a poor third, with a mere 7.3 per cent of the vote. A few weeks later, at a by-election in Dundee West, Labour swept in with the SNP stuck at 7.4 per cent.

When yet another by-election came up at Dumfries a few weeks later, the party was punchdrunk and almost bankrupt. There was little support for the local team from the centre but a good candidate put the SNP vote up to 9.7 per cent. 'So starting from absolute disaster we moved to crisis and eventually felt things weren't so bad.'

By the end of the year exhaustion had set in. But at the general election of 1964 the party was back, fighting more seats than ever before and complaining again about broadcast coverage. It got only 2.4 per cent of the vote but it was changing. 'You could see it at every conference. And so even after a poorish election the party was still growing and in reasonably good heart.'

By 1967 the pace of growth was very rapid. That was the year of the by-election in Glasgow Pollok, won by Labour from the Tories at the general election in 1964 and retained by Labour in 1966. George Leslie, a popular Glasgow vet, stood for the SNP. By this time Wilson was a partner in a Paisley law firm, still convinced that his political future was as a backroom boy rather than as a candidate or an MP. In the by-election there was a tremendous swing of support to the party in working-class areas – in Pollok, Pollokshaws and the new housing schemes. But the Tory areas – the sandstone villas, the semis, – remained rock solid. The anti-Tory vote was split and Esmond Wright, who became an architect of the Scottish Conservatives' devolutionary policies, won the seat with 36.9 per cent of the vote (as recently as 1955 a Unionist had won with 61.3 per cent). In the Tory areas the SNP got only about five or six per cent but in the housing schemes its share of the vote soared in some places to 40 per cent.

For the SNP the impetus was building. When the Hamilton by-election came, on 2 November 1967, Winifred Ewing swept all before her. It was a truly sensational result, though the culmination of a process rather than its beginning. The SNP had become the conduit, north of the Border, for popular protest and dissatisfaction. The Government was in low water, with its economic policies in shreds (the Callaghan devaluation followed on 18 November). The by-election had been indirectly caused by the Cabinet reshuffle of August. Willie Ross was troubled by the demotion of Tom Fraser, the incumbent MP, supplanted as Minister of Transport by Barbara Castle. Fraser suffered for his lack of charisma and dreary presentational style. But Ross was worried because his friend was rather hard up. He solved the problem by appointing him chairman of the North of Scotland Hydro-Electric Board. Such use of patronage by Secretaries of State for Scotland, to console comrades for whom the fortunes of war have been unfavourable, continues to this day.

The impact of Hamilton was dramatic. For the first time the party received sustained attention from the London media. Mrs Ewing arrived in London in triumph. Scottish Office insiders remember that Dover House was besieged by her supporters most of whom had patriotically driven down in Hillman Imps built at Linwood. She herself had a lonely row to hoe. Scottish Labour members were rattled. Some subjected her to personal abuse of a kind that made her deeply unhappy. Walter Harrison, Labour's Deputy Chief Whip, recalled that she came to him in some distress. He put the word out and the attacks ceased. In 1993 Mrs Ewing's daughter-in-law, Margaret Ewing (formerly Margaret Bain) told me that some Labour MPs still maintained this dishonourable tradition at the Commons, where she was SNP parliamentary leader: some swore at her *en passant* and others kept up a *sotto voce* accompaniment of abuse as she or her colleagues, convener Alex Salmond and whip Andrew Welsh, tried to speak in the Chamber.

Back in Scotland, Hamilton produced a flood of new members. The fissile tendencies reasserted themselves. The old social creditists re-emerged and after Muirhead's death the 1320 Club was formed to carry on his work but became associated with extreme fundamentalism and infiltrated by would-be terrorists. It was proscribed by the SNP in 1971 and, a decade later, merged with Siol nan Gaidheal, the raggle-taggle army of activists from the housing schemes marching under the flag of caricatured celticism which was itself banned by the party in 1982. Wilson recalled:

> By the late Sixties the party had changed. It had become more sophisticated. New people came in with new ideas and people come into parties to change them. They usually find it changes them. But it takes time. The main problem was accommodating the growth. There were branches, followed by constituency associations . . . And we had a lot of inexperienced people who had never been members of a party for more than six weeks.

Wolfe became chairman in 1969 and by that time the tensions had grown. The party moved to the Left that year. 'Every ten years,' said Wilson, 'it moves to the Left with a big jolt and then it moves back gently to the Centre Left. Never Centre but Centre Left. Billy was Centre Left.' The shift reflected two things. First, the policy-making machinery attracted those of intellectual disposition and they tended to be to the Left. The national executive, set up in 1966, by now had 20 policy committees. The structure of national council, national assembly and national executive was a means of 'burning off' the party's intellectual and ideological volatility. (The fecundity with which it made policy and tried to control events created problems for the parliamentary group between 1974 and 1979.) Secondly, strong personalities were beginning to force their way through and were dominating the proceedings. Wilson said:

> There was a kind of flowering. There was a new movement open, as the SNP has always been open, in fact dangerously open, maybe dangerously naive, but it's been affected by a volatile turnover of membership – but you had all these people coming in.

The advent of intellectuals like Isobel Lindsay was accompanied by a growth in the Poujadiste element of small shopkeepers and businessmen. Year by year membership doubled. Wilson said: 'There was a tremendous flowering, a clash of ideas.' Nor was it easy to classify people on the spectrum. 'For example, Henderson was to the Right in some ways but not all. He came from one of the Edinburgh housing schemes though he went to the Royal High School.'

The 1970 General Election was regarded by the party as a disaster although it doubled its share of the vote, from 5 to 11.4 per cent. The SNP had got itself into another classic nationalist scenario, that of heightened expectations punctured by reality. Wilson continued:

> We're rather like the Scottish football team. It's a Scottish scenario. You've got to talk yourself up because in order to motivate people you've got to give them something to work for.

In 1970 Wilson was locked into the party headquarters as campaign director. He hardly saw sunlight for three weeks. It was a very sunny and hot campaign. The early weeks promised much. The party was bullish. Wilson said: 'In 1970 we had hopes not in the urban areas but in the rural areas. We hoped to keep Hamilton. That was Verdun, that had to be defended, *ils ne passeront pas*. In the event they did.'

The result was a disaster. On the Saturday morning after the election, Wilson recalled, they had gathered in an atmosphere of despair. 'As we waited for the Western Isles result, Henderson suggested that we might resort to prayer. Anway, Donald Stewart sneaked in and kept our parliamentary presence and credibility alive. He was the first nationalist to win a parliamentary seat at a general election, and he kept us in the game. That was crucial.'

By this time Wilson was exhausted. He gave up his work for the party in 1971. He felt he had become intolerant and authoritarian. He now spent more time on his legal career, became an expert on rating as chairman of the Paisley valuation appeals tribunal, and rediscovered pleasures like gardening. Such work can release the mind, and it was at this time that the idea came to him of campaigning on the issue of North Sea oil. This produced, from the graphic artist Julian Gibb, the slogan It's Scotland's Oil. This was a stroke of political imagination. In 1993 Henderson acknowledged Wilson's authorship of a 'brilliant' idea.

As we have seen, the roots of modern nationalism are to be found in industrial decline, relatively high unemployment, the softening of the Tory vote and what might be called a general sense of anomie or spiritual discomfort. If the Sixties had been a seeding and a flowering then the oil campaign was the sunshine that made for a vigorous bloom. It lent credibility to the SNP by removing many of the economic fears associated with secession or separation.

Wilson was the idea's author but others seized upon it and developed it, among them Wolfe, Isobel Lindsay and Julian Gibb. Donald Bain, then a young researcher, gave the campaign enormous impetus as his work began to show just how rich the North Sea gravy was. Macdonald was succeeded as organiser by John McAteer in 1968. He had been Mrs Ewing's agent in Hamilton and, in Wolfe's judgment, made an enormous contribution until his death in 1971. A series of leaflets on oil sold out.

The authorities played into the party's hands. They talked down the extent of the oil so that they found themselves wrong-footed by the SNP campaign. At a convention of riparian states they had also agreed a line of latitude that put most of the oil into Scottish jurisdiction. Wilson admitted that the party had distorted this convention which was designed to settle the question of which police force, English or Scottish, should be responsible for any offences in the oil field and to which legal jurisdiction any offender should answer. This point was much misunderstood, to the SNP's pleasure, but the jurisdictional line is a fixed part of its arguments about Scotland's entitlement to oil revenues.

The period of 1970–1974 saw the increasing agony of the Heath administration. The SNP capitalised on a growing loss of public confidence in the competence of government. Edward Heath retreated on UCS, was defeated by the miners, his industrial relations courts were discredited, and by 1974 Selsdon Man had become a coalitionist.

Stephen Maxwell joined the party organisation in 1973 as press officer. Cultural attitudes had brought him into the party. He had been raised in Yorkshire, the son of a Scottish family, his father a surgeon, his mother a nurse. In their house was an extensive collection of Scottish literature – Grassic Gibbon, Linklater, and the like. From Cambridge he went to the London School of Economics where he noticed that contemporaries jockeying for an entry into politics knew little and cared less about Scotland. At this point his attitudes were left-wing and to them he now added a commitment to Scottish politics.

He took up a fellowship at Edinburgh University, joined the local branch and became involved with *Scottish International,* the magazine edited by Bob Tait. In this milieu he met a number of Leftist intellectuals drawn to the nationalist movement. At a conference organised by *Scottish International,* Professor Donald MacKay, who had been commissioned by the Scottish Office to study the implications of North Sea oil, gave a paper which acknowledged its value and was criticial of Government policy. He was, Stephen believed, the first independent economist to do so. It was a time of genuine ferment. The 7:84 Company's satire on the economic exploitation of Scotland, *The Cheviot, The Stag and the Black, Black Oil,* was the theatrical expression of contemporary nationalism, and it struck a deep chord in the public mind.

Maxwell acted as Margo MacDonald's press officer in Govan where, in 1973, she surged to victory in the by-election with 42 per cent of the vote. She was sensational, a 'blonde bombshell' charming the nation on television. On the same night Wolfe failed to take North Edinburgh from the Conservatives. Here he found the first evidence that the Unionist parties were successfully countering the oil weapon. A pamphlet had attacked the 'greed' of Scotland using oil revenues to impoverish England and canvassers found it strongly echoed on the doorsteps.

Nevertheless, in the general election of February 1974 the SNP caused further consternation. It got 22 per cent of the vote and seven seats. In Parliament Donald Stewart was joined by Wilson who won Dundee East, together with Henderson, the broadcaster and journalist George Reid, Winifred Ewing, Hamish Watt, a farmer and dealer who came to be known affectionately in Parliament as 'Potato Watt', and Iain MacCormick, son of King John. Reid and Watt were converts – Reid from Labour and Watt from the Tories. Heath at first tried to form a coalition with the Liberal leader Jeremy Thorpe and Teddy Taylor was given the task of holding informal conversations with the nationalists. He stressed, when we talked in 1993, that he was no more than a carrier of messages and gossip. Discussions were taking place at a 'higher level', involving the whips, but the nationalists were asking more than he, an arch opponent of devolution, would have wanted to give.

Between the elections of February and October Henderson, the parliamentary whip, sustained the Labour Government almost single-handed. Wilson said: 'People forget that the only committee place we had at that time was on the committee on employment legislation.' Henderson himself recalled an anecdote of those days. It is to some degree second-hand but an anecdote is a fragile bloom and needs minimal validation.

> On the report stage of the Trade Union and Labour Relations Bill, repealing the Heath Industrial Relations Act, Bob Mellish, the Labour Chief Whip, came to him for help. Mellish told Henderson he was counting on nationalist votes. Tough luck, said Douglas. This is Thursday night and tonight we all go home. We have trains to Scotland to catch. Our whip comes off at nine. Mellish wheedled and cajoled. He was used to dealing with lobby fodder or, as Douglas put it, 'rubbish' – and if he kept the Scottish Labour MPs until five a.m. he did not care if they walked home. He realised, however, that Douglas was serious and gleaned from him the fact that there was a one am train to Edinburgh. It was the Newcastle service to which one sleeping car was added and taken on to Edinburgh.

Mellish returned to the office and discovered from his lists that Tom McMillan (Glasgow Central) was sponsored by the NUR. In the Kremlin Bar, as the Strangers' Bar was known because of the Scots Labour MPs' devotion to it, McMillan was on the drams, surrounded by his cronies. He rarely spoke but always did what the whips told him.

Suddenly a brash young junior whip burst in. Is Tom McMillan in the bar, he said in a peremptory voice. McMillan paled. I've done nothing wrong, comrade, he protested. The chief whip wants to see you, said the emissary. Now.

Shaken, McMillan immediately reported to Mellish. What can I do for you, comrade, he asked nervously. Mellish replied: The Prime Minister wants you to do a job for him. McMillan's mind reeled. Could this at last be preferment, the reward for all these years of loyal if silent service? He was quickly disillusioned. He was appalled to learn that Mellish wanted him to get 'these crazy fucking Scottish nationalists' on to the one a.m. sleeper. There's a phone, said Mellish. I suppose you know how to use it. Do so. Now. McMillan nervously picked it up and got through to a number at King's Cross. He said, This is Brother McMillan, MP. I want you to do a job for the union.

When the nationalists got to King's Cross, they found an angry crowd besieging the booking office. Their tickets were invalid. There had been an oversight. It was tough luck. They could get a refund if they wrote a letter applying for one. SNP members, clutching the tickets newly issued by the Commons travel office, walked through amid suspicious glares and catcalls and claimed their places. McMillan had forgotten to book a place for himself and travelled in the guard's van.

Walter Harrison, Labour's deputy chief whip, has a different recollection. He had been a corporal in the army and organised his whips on military lines. He had an army of 'squaddies' or secondary whips – his eyes, ears and legs. Tom McMillan was one of them. Harrison took the Scots Labour MPs' tickets off McMillan and gave them to the SNP.

The SNP was now ready for its greatest moment. On 7 September 1974, the first Labour White Paper on devolution (the second was published in 1976) proposed assemblies for Scotland and Wales. On 18 September an election was called for 10 October and two days later Parliament was dissolved. The SNP achieved 30 per cent of the vote and acquired four more MPs.

CHAPTER TWELVE

The Tory Young Turks

During the rise of the SNP, the major parties had not been at ease; indeed, they were badly rattled. Devolution in a sense was created by Westminster politics. It is a curiosity of the devolution years that the early responses made by both major parties were directed by London and caused severe stresses at home. They divided Tories searching for a modern Scottish identity from the party's largely anglicised Old Guard, the guardians of industrial Protestant Unionism like Teddy Taylor, and spokesmen for the mercantile class like Iain Sproat. Labour's divisions were as painful. The Wilson Government appointed a Royal Commission on the UK Constitution in 1969, and bought some time. Both major parties were to feel grateful to him. A year earlier Edward Heath came to Perth and delivered the Declaration of Perth. It arose from the report of a committee under the chairmanship of Sir William McEwen Younger. In 1967 it had advocated an indirectly elected assembly. Heath was misled about the true state of party opinion in Scotland. The divisions were to be revealed but were for the moment occluded by the imperatives of fealty to the leader.

Why should a Unionist Party have become converted to legislative devolution? The answer begins with the election defeat of 1964 and Willie Ross. In Scotland the party responded to defeat with a series of reforms. It wanted to drop the image of the grouse moor and modernise itself. The young radicals wanted to demonstrate the party's commitment to a Scottish personality and agenda. In 1965 it restored the name Conservative to its official title and although the word Unionist remained it was largely ignored. It broke up the anti-Labour coalition in local government which had successfully operated under the Progressive label. Lord Whitelaw, the last genuine Tory grandee and a pivotal figure in the early Thatcher Cabinets, was fond of an anecdote about James Stuart, the influential Tory Secretary of State for Scotland between 1951 and 1957. 'I never discuss politics with my constituents,' he said. 'They're all Liberals, really.'

The Young Turks were responding also to the boredom-inducing tactics of Willie Ross, now Secretary of State for Scotland in the Labour Government. For 13 years in opposition, between 1951 and 1964, this gruff, unimaginative, loyal and extraordinarily effective politician had preached the politics of grievance. In office in the Wilson administrations from 1964 to 1970 and from 1974 to 1976, he achieved a great deal for Scotland. In the late Seventies, after he had become Lord Ross of Marnock, I asked him to write, if not his memoirs, some retrospective pieces. He declined. Lord Carmichael told me in 1993 that Ross had a dislike for his chattering English colleagues who flooded the bookstands with their diaries or memoirs as soon as possible. Other contemporaries recall his unconcealed contempt for the diarists Richard Crossman and Barbara Castle, who made their activities, as 'chiels among you, taking notes,' all too obvious. The consequence is that Ross remains a seriously under-rated politician.

His personality was a combination of force, cunning and charm infused with patriotism both Scottish and British. He had been a schoolteacher, and retained a pedagogic air, dishing out or withdrawing approval. He had risen from the ranks to be a major in the HLI and, Lord Carmichael recollected, had as Mountbatten's signals officer accompanied him to receive the surrender of Japan. For this he got the MBE. He was schooled in military discipline. He gave loyalty and obedience and expected it from others. He found dissent very difficult to accept from younger Labour colleagues.

My brother David, from his days in political journalism, recalled that Ross was a man of simple habits. He would sometimes spend the night on a camp bed in his office at Westminster, eschewing more luxurious quarters, and so impervious was he to the London around him that on one occasion was unable to give directions to Paddington, of which he had barely heard. Harry (Lord) Ewing, who as a junior minister served under him in the Wilson administration from October 1974, recalled in 1993 that Ross, who had strong views about how drink seduced too many politicians, refused to let him have a cocktail cabinet in his ministerial office for the occasional entertainment of visitors. In 1993 John Smith, who had been Ross's first parliamentary private secretary in 1974, gave me this portrait of him:

> Willie Ross was strongly anti-European in an old-fashioned conservative way. He was quick-witted and strong-willed and he turned on the charm when he wanted to. He was very Ayrshire in his outlook. He was a military man and of course a man of the Kirk. He stood for a kind of image of Scotland.
>
> There was a legion of people he didn't like. But he had real bearing and style. He was a proper Secretary of State. He could charm the birds off the trees. I saw him at functions at Edinburgh Castle when he would absolutely charm foreign bankers. He was passionately Scottish too. He has some wonderful achievements to his credit. He could get things through. He was extremely good in Cabinet. He achieved enormous success in what he could get for Scotland in public expenditure terms. I think his technique was to secure Scotland somehow and then support the Chancellor in doing everybody else down. I said, Why don't you boast of your success? He said, You don't understand: the day you do that you can never do it again. He was willing to give up the taking of credit in order to secure the advance.
>
> When I was at the Department of Energy [in 1974–75] and Willie was Secretary of State, he expected Scots in other ministries really to be ambassadors for Scotland. He would say, You know what your duty is here. He felt I was on loan from him to the Department of Energy.

Evidence of Ross's essentially conservative nature came from his cross-bench friendship with the staunch opponent of devolution, Betty Harvie Anderson, the Conservative MP for Renfrewshire East from 1959 to 1979. There was a strong bond between them, and he showed his admiration for her by appointing her a member of the Wheatley Commission on local government. Indeed, Ross got into hot water at a Labour Conference around this time: when challenged about his tendency to give patronage on boards and quangos to non-Labour people, he said that he would appoint Labour nominees when he could find candidates of 'quality'. Harry Ewing remembered that Ross showed considerable deference to the Establishment until 1970. After the Heath general election victory, he was infuriated when some senior civil servants formed a welcoming party for the incoming Conservative Secretary of State, Gordon Campbell, and applauded him all the way up the stairs of St Andrews House as he arrived for his first day's work. Ross never forgot that and thereafter, when he re-entered Government in 1974, treated many of his civil servants with extreme suspicion.

Ross pursued the politics of grievance with such skill that, Harry Ewing recalled, Attlee remonstrated with him, warning him that he would fan the flames of nationalism. Harold Wilson too, according to Ewing, was uneasy about the consequences of his rhetoric and warned him about it. Margo MacDonald told me in an interview in 1993:

> Willie Ross was actually the biggest nationalist or chauvinist you could ever find. In a way this feeling was incorporated into the old idea of the British Empire: it could have all these nationalist groupings incorporated inside it. Willie was quite shameless about playing the Scottish card.

Others have argued that Willie Ross was one of the fathers of post-war nationalism. For years he banged on about Scottish grievances and disadvantage. When my brother David, working on a speech for him, asked what line to take, Ross would usually instruct him: 'Just say things are looking grim.' MacDonald said:

> Unfortunately he gave rise to a fashion which persists to this day, that of the girner. When he called the Scottish Nationalists the Scottish Narks Party it was a case of 'it takes one to know one'. It was something I always fought against. I just get angry at the girning, whining mentality.

Ross's line had two important boomerang effects. First it persuaded English politicians that Scottish discontents were of deadly seriousness and must be met. Secondly, it fuelled the discontent of the Scots themselves. George (Lord) Younger recalled in 1993 that Ross had been 'most massively boring' and continued:

> The Declaration of Perth was the combination of a number of factors. There were a lot of new Conservative members. I was new. There were all sorts of people like Alick Buchanan-Smith, Norman Wylie, Hector Monro and Jock Bruce-Gardyne. What hit us was the extreme tedium of the enormously lengthy deliberation on Scottish matters. This all arose from the great battle Willie Ross had against the Tory Government during 13 years. He and Tom Fraser and Margaret Herbison and various others got the technique very well of delay and delay and delay and were an awful nuisance to the Government on Scottish affairs. There was great tedium and boredom among all the Scottish MPs about Scottish business in the House. It was shared to some extent by the Labour MPs who all appreciated the political merit of what they were doing but they too were bored. I think we felt, as new members coming in, that it was all wrong that Scottish affairs should be boring. It should be among the most important and interesting things in the world.

In a way it was a bit of an echo of one of Willie Ross's great successes – it boomeranged in a number of ways and this was one of them. It also created Winnie Ewing. He was so successful in getting across the idea that absolutely everything was wrong that when he came into office and people suddenly discovered that everything wasn't all right, then Winnie was the answer to that . . . You got the Hamilton by-election and all that.

Also, we new Conservative members were a bit radical and reformist in those days. And we saw this situation and we felt, well, why not, let's address our minds to whether there's anything wrong with the system.

The series of organisational reforms were of dubious value and the commitment to parliamentary devolution caused acute internal stress. Younger described the enormous impact on the party of the loss of Pollok in the general election of 1964. This was one of the first intimations that the old Unionist religious vote was growing soft but it produced an over-reaction. For Robert Kernohan, at the time assistant editor of *The Glasgow Herald,* the loss of the Pollok seat had been a personal tragedy, because it cut off before it could begin a political career that promised distinction. He was unfairly blamed for what can now be seen to have been the result of an underlying social shift. Professor Esmond Wright regained the seat in the 1967 by-election. In fact, Wright was re-elected not because the Conservatives increased their share of the poll – they did not – but because the SNP split the anti-Tory vote and kept Labour out. Younger recollected:

We lost Pollok in 1964 which was quite shattering. To lose Pollok was unimaginable. The older hands saw very clearly that what was disappearing was the working-class Tory vote, the Unionist vote, and with supreme illogic of course, at that moment we chose to stop being Unionists and become Conservatives. That was part of the reorganisation Sir John Gilmour put through. [Sir John, Scottish Secretary from 1924 to 1929 and later Home Secretary, had before the war reorganised the Scottish Office.]

We had just had a defeat. We thought, there's something wrong here. We were looking for everything that could be wrong. One of the things that to many of us was daft was to be calling ourselves Unionists. I suppose we didn't have the length or maturity in politics to see why that was so. We just thought, Well, I'm not a Unionist actually, I'm a Conservative.

The decision to politicise the Conservatives at local government level also proved to be an unhelpful tactic because it broke up a successful alliance of disparate Progressives, Moderates and Ratepayers. Lord Macfarlane recalled in conversation the extreme resentment his father, Bailie Daniel Macfarlane, had felt at the time. As a Progressive he was councillor for Partick West from 1955 to 1964; depute river bailie from 1960 to 1961; and bailie of the burgh from 1961 to 1964. He stood down and the Conservatives subsequently lost the ward, though he later served as chairman of the Lower Clyde Water Board from 1970 to 1973. Many businessmen, including Sir Hugh (Lord) Fraser (of Allander), had served in local government under the Progressive title. Among them was a strong feeling that local government should not be politicised; although they were Conservative in sentiment, they had also a strong concept of public service. The change was one of the factors which sustained Labour's hegemony in local government in urban Scotland, though the reforms of local government, put through in the characteristically paradoxical pattern of Scottish affairs by the Conservative Government in 1973, had a more decisive influence by creating a powerful Labour local government establishment. Younger recalled: 'We were enormously frustrated at that time by the fact that Progressives wouldn't be Conservatives. It seemed to us that the Labour Party organised themselves jolly well in local government. We just weren't there.' In his *Herald* column in 1993 Brian Meek, a leading Conservative devolutionary who pursued his political career in local government, recalled the days when Edinburgh was more or less perpetually controlled by the Progressives. 'They were – nudge, nudge – non-political but right-wing and definitely anti-Labour.' When they became Conservatives, they had a 'rough ride'.

Teddy Taylor told me in 1993 that he thought the change in the party's name and the dropping of the Progressive label had been mistakes. He said:

> The change in name did great damage to us as did the change of name in our council elections in Glasgow. The Progressives were an independent Glasgow party. The abolition of the term Unionist – which conveyed that the Scottish Conservatives were something different from the English Conservatives – did us damage because people didn't regard us as a Scottish Conservative Party fighting for Scotland.

It has been implied that the Conservative commitment to devolution which began to crystallise at this time was a cynical series of palliative manoeuvres in the face of rising nationalist sentiment. This seems a touch unfair. There is no doubt that many younger Tories saw a need to assert the party's Scottish character and revitalise its internal debate. A Thistle Group of Scottish Conservatives had emerged, consisting of young Edinburgh graduates including Michael Ancram, Peter Fraser and Malcolm Rifkind. They met in a room in Rose Street, Edinburgh, held meetings and published pamphlets. Michael Ancram was its most active member. Rifkind himself, although he had been a founder, was in Rhodesia by the time it was set up. In 1993 Rifkind recalled that the Thistle Group had not been specifically devolutionary. He said: 'It had nothing to do with nationalism as such.' It had been a kind of Scottish Bow Group, composed of Young Turks who thought anybody over the age of 30 was an 'old fuddy-duddy'. It arose also from the perception that the Young Conservatives were not sufficiently political, a point which certainly chimes with my own memories. When I was at university the Young Conservatives were derided as something of a marriage market for the socially secure and politically naive. Rikfind said in 1993 that they were also conscious that the Conservative vote was declining and that the party had had insufficient political debate. He added:

> I was responsible for the name Thistle. We were trying to find something that would clearly be Scottish but would also imply that we had the tendency to make a nuisance of ourselves, to be uncomfortable. It was partly the impetuosity of youth.

As it happened, the leading members of the Thistle Group became individually pro-devolution. It gave evidence to the committee set up by Heath under the chairmanship of Sir Alec Douglas-Home to put flesh on his Declaration of Perth. Other committed supporters were shadow Secretary of State Michael Noble, Russell Fairgrieve and Alick Buchanan-Smith, the latter being regarded by political journalists of the time as among the brightest younger Scottish Tory talents of his generation.

111

Nevertheless Heath's declaration stunned the Old Guard. It committed the party to a constitutional review. Perth has a resonance in Scottish Conservative politics for most of the party conferences take place there. Its compactness and conviviality make it an ideal venue. It was here, in 1985, that George Younger, faced by a revolt by small shopkeepers, businessmen and domestic ratepayers outraged by the impact of revaluation, began moves towards the poll tax which were to contribute to Mrs Thatcher's exit from the leadership in 1990.

In his speech in 1968 Heath noted the trend towards standardisation and centralisation; and the fear that the Scottish identity would be submerged. In an interview in 1992 with William Russell of *The Herald* he could be found insisting still on the correctness of his Declaration of Perth – how often the word declaration occurs in the devolutionary cycle. It was influenced by his vision of European development: he was an early proponent of what today would be called subsidiarity. Indeed, after he had been deposed from the leadership in 1975 he came to support an assembly with strong economic and legislative powers but firmly within European union. There was not much to choose between this scheme and that proposed by Jim Sillars, from a very different perspective, when he formed his breakaway Scottish Labour Party in 1976. For the moment, however, the practical result of the Declaration of Perth was a constitutional committee under the chairmanship of Sir Alec Douglas-Home but many Unionists felt that devolution had been foisted on them quite against their traditions, instincts and judgment. According to Mitchell, the whips notified the leadership that about two-thirds of the Scottish MPs opposed Mr Heath's declaration, believing him to have been excessively frightened by the SNP. Among the dissident Old Guard, Betty Harvie Anderson was to have a great influence on Mrs Thatcher. She was one of those, contemporaries recalled, who convinced her that devolution would fatally injure the Union. Nigel (Lord) Lawson recollected in 1993 that Mrs Thatcher had also been greatly influenced by Teddy Taylor.

Younger in 1993 conceded that there had been an over-reaction. Heath, he said, had been aware of the fall in Scottish Tory representation, the rise of nationalism, the feeling that the Scots Conservatives 'weren't ringing the bell'. He continued:

> We persuaded Heath it was a good idea. He was very willing to be persuaded. But we were quite surprised by the strong reaction we got from the Old Guard after the declaration – Betty Harvie Anderson, Tam Galbraith [Cdr T.D. Galbraith, the father of the present Lord Strathclyde], Michael Clark Hutchison, all sorts of people, some of the grand old ladies and people like that. They were very virulently anti. We were surprised by the vehemence of their unhappiness about it.

In conversation in 1993 Brian Meek said he had been a 'bit surprised' when Heath went so far in the Declaration of Perth. He became leader of the Edinburgh Conservative group in 1971 and thought that an assembly would, if nothing else, be good for Edinburgh. He said of the opposition:

> It was the anglified Tory MPs who were against it. Betty Harvie Anderson was one of them. She was most vitriolic. She was pure tweeds-and-twin-sets. She was ahead of her time in that although she was married to a doctor she kept her own name. But she was a fearful old bat.

In 1970 Sir Alec's committee duly reported and recommended a devolutionary scheme which represented the most radical proposal ever produced by the Conservative leadership on this question. There was to be a Scottish convention of about 125 members meeting about 40 days a year. The 'essential principle' of the sovereignty of Parliament was preserved, and the convention would be able to take Bills, on second reading, committee and report stage, if they had been certified by the Speaker to apply only to Scotland. On return to Westminster they could be amended before submission to the Lords.

It was an ingenious attempt to turn the Grand Committee into a directly elected body, giving it legislative power, while reconciling it with the doctrine of parliamentary sovereignty. It would have had a reasonable chance of working had Conservative strength in Scotland remained roughly in equilibrium as a counter to Labour. The decline of the Tories in the Eighties created severe problems of balance for any schemes involving the Grand Committee. The Scottish Select Committee had to be abandoned after 1987 (it resumed work in 1992) because of the shortage or reluctance of Scottish Tory back-benchers to serve on it, and the Standing Committees considering Scottish Bills had to be supplemented by English Tory MPs. It remains a fascinating speculation: if the Douglas-Home proposals had been implemented would they have arrested the subsequent decline of the Conservatives in Scotland?

CHAPTER THIRTEEN

Lunch at the Garrick

On *The Scotsman*, from 1968, we had been pursuing devolution with increasing conviction and excitement. Alastair Dunnett in that year published a series of major editorials (written by Matthew Moulton, James Vassie, Willis Pickard and Andrew Hood) which revived the old Liberal federal programme. They caused much interest at the time and were even reprinted as a pamphlet. Eric Mackay carried on the policy with enthusiasm when he took over the editorship in 1972.

On the paper we discovered the joys of opinion polls, which throughout the history of home rule have usually shown majorities of about three-quarters for some form of constitutional change. These figures do not translate into electoral behaviour. This allowed Ian Lang in 1993 to say scornfully that devolutionary support was '75 per cent of nothing'. But falling upon ready ears, they had a catalytic effect, pushing the political and parliamentary system into a series of muddled judgments.

Our polls were done in London by Opinion Research Centre, and I would travel down to work with Nick Spencer on the results. We had great fun concocting yet more arresting stories based on information which, it must be admitted, did not vary much from month to month. Similar opinion polls by System Three were appearing in *The Glasgow Herald*, where the late Anthony Finlay was enjoying himself too. Between them they inculcated in the political firmament a pole star – representing the fixed idea that a large majority of Scots supported devolution.

The Heath declaration and the work of Sir Alec's committee was complicated by the Wilson Government's own concession to rising nationalism in general and Hamilton in particular. John Warden was at that time the political editor of *The Glasgow Herald*. In 1993 he let me have a note of his recollection of the immediate consequence of Hamilton:

> A lunch was held at the Garrick Club soon after Winnie Ewing took her seat in November 1967. By any standards Hamilton was a sensational result, but the home rule dimension threw Westminster politicians into a state of utter confusion and bewilderment as to what exactly the result meant or what needed to be done.
>
> The Cabinet, beset by economic woes (devaluation etc.), was equally at sea. Willie Ross, who referred contemptuously to the SNP as the Scottish Narks Party, was for playing down the significance of Hamilton. Harold Wilson applied the classic remedy of setting up a Cabinet sub-committee under Richard

Crossman, Lord President of the Council, to look into the significance of the SNP breakthrough and advise on the Government's response.

I doubt if this sub-committee had even met when Crossman hosted a Friday lunch for four or five Lobby correspondents in a private room at the Garrick. A fire blazed and the claret flowed round the table; other topical issues dominated but eventually Hamilton came up. Dick turned to me, as the only Scot, and asked what I would do.

Thinking more about what I expected the Government to do, I replied that a Royal Commission would seem to be the answer. This horrified Crossman who raised his hands to dismiss such an unimaginative solution and gave a scornful laugh. 'Here's a man who would set up a Royal Commission!' he mocked. (Royal Commissions were out of fashion since Wilson's famous quote that they 'take minutes but waste years'.)

Always an intellectual bully, Crossman felt challenged to give his own simple answer to a complex problem. His idea was to let Scotland have its own parliament, as in Northern Ireland. (The first cracks in the Stormont model had yet to show.) As the minister in charge of Scottish 'devolution', Crossman with his customary enthusiasm gave every indication that his mind was made up in favour of a Scottish Stormont and that it was only a matter of sorting out the detail.

Such was the finality of his tone and the lack of interest of others in the detail, that conversation moved on at once to other subjects. The lunch was on strict Lobby terms and could not be sourced. I intended to use it as background for my weekend column. Later in the evening the London *Times* man, George Clark, who had been at the Crossman lunch, phoned me to confess that he had written a news item about a Scottish Stormont. I felt obliged to file a story. But what was worth under half a column on an inside page of *The Times* merited the splash treatment it got in *The Glasgow Herald* next morning, a Saturday.

The next I knew was that on the Monday morning a delegation of senior Scottish Labour MPs, led by Willie Hannan (Maryhill), called on Harold Wilson at Downing Street brandishing *The Herald* story and demanding to know what was going on. Wilson managed to convince them that they had no need to worry. Crossman was furious about the 'leak' and wanted apologies. His Scottish Stormont plan was overwhelmed by Labour hostility, subsequent events in Ulster (the first vibrations of trouble emerged early in 1968) and Dick Crossman's move that year to social services.

Wilson took no further action. For the next 18 months Willie Ross and the Labour hierarchy allowed no concessions to the SNP, though I'm sure Willie used the nationalist threat to Scotland's advantage inside Cabinet. Ted Heath, in opposition, took up the running with his Declaration of Perth in May 1968 and the Douglas-Home report. At Westminster, a pro-devolution group of youngish MPs was formed by the late John P. Mackintosh and included Donald Dewar and Bob (Robert) Maclennan. They were ridiculed by Willie Ross who continued to stand against the tide.

At the Labour conference in Blackpool in autumn 1969, Jim Callaghan, then Home Secretary, found himself having to reply for the national executive committee to a devolution debate. It concentrated his mind on the subject. He began to think about a Royal Commission. Willie Ross agreed only if its terms of reference extended to England and Wales as well. Callaghan threw in the Channel Islands and the Isle of Man too, because the Home Office had some problems there. As a result the Crowther (Kilbrandon) Commission on the Constitution's remit covered 'the several countries, nations and regions of the United Kingdom'. And so it came about that I was right about forecasting a Royal Commission, but Crossman's solution of a Scottish parliament was borne out in its recommendations and subsequent Labour Party policy.

The Royal Commission did not report until 1973, by which time the Wilson Government had been supplanted by the Heath administration of 1970–1974. The commission recommended directly elected Scottish and Welsh assemblies with responsibility for transferred matters. The number of Scottish MPs would be reduced and the office of Secretary of State for Scotland would be abolished.

Labour's conversion to devolution was a painful process. The manifesto for the first election in February 1974 contained no commitment to it. As nationalism surged, Labour was committed to it by the time the second election was held in October but Scottish resistance to the idea proved a tough nut for the London leadership to crack. In June the executive committee of the Scottish Council held an extraordinary meeting one Saturday. There was a poor attendance because a Scottish World Cup game was being televised. By six votes to five it rejected all the devolutionary schemes proposed so far. Among the devolutionary five were Donald Dewar and George Robertson, both now Labour front-bench spokesmen. London was highly irritated by this tactless behaviour. The influential trade unionist Alex Kitson intervened on the devolutionary side. The national executive council's officers told their counterparts in Scotland to get the decision reversed, and in July the NEC formally endorsed devolution. Scotland duly fell into line and in September a special conference at the Glasgow Co-operative Hall in Dalintober Street called for a directly elected assembly. There was no doubting the sincerity of devolutionaries like Dewar but the party came to heel with unhappy reluctance. Andrew Marr wrote that it was a victory for 'fix and fear'. John Smith said in 1993 that the 'old guard had to be dragged round a bit'. He added:

> People like George Lawson, Willie Hannan and Willie Small were centralists. They thought it was a nationalist thing. They had this view, in common with many others, that during the war central planning had ended the chaos of before the war and that we could win the peace that way. There wasn't much opposition to nationalisation at the end of the war. Even *The Times* rebuked Mr Attlee for not nationalising enough. Then there was the Rosa Luxembourg question. Is nationalism antithetic to socialism? It's been argued back and forth. The idea that the Labour Party has to be centralist is a great error, in my opinion.

Willie Ross, Smith recalled, had to 'climb down a bit'. It was not that he supported the switch. He 'let it happen' but continued efforts behind the scenes to retard and dilute devolutionary schemes. Indeed, the evidence is that Wilson decided to override him. According to some accounts by Scottish Office insiders, Ross was not informed in advance when Wilson, in a parliamentary reply to Mrs Winifred Ewing, disclosed that proposals would be forthcoming. In 1993 the veteran Labour activist John Pollock gave this impression of how Ross had swallowed his resistance to making concessions to the Nationalists:

He was partly responsible for the change of policy in not vigorously denouncing it and stopping it. He sat in the [party] committee, allowing the discussions to take place, for once not saying fairly autocratically, Well, we're just not having that. He wasn't a prime mover but he was influential in that he was the one who would have blocked it previously.

Donald Dewar was a prime mover, very much so. He was on the Scottish executive. Donald had just lost Aberdeen South [to the Conservatives]. Previously Willie's answer to that kind of defeat would have been, We've got to hammer the Nats harder. Donald's was that the Labour Party needed to re-assess its position. I think Donald was probably the most influential person, along with Bruce Millan [Secretary of State for Scotland in succession to Ross]. There was a general change of mood.

The Labour executive also felt itself under pressure from the communists who were active and influential in the STUC. Since the war the Communist Party had strongly committed itself to Scottish independence and had given evidence to the Royal Commission to this effect. There were, of course, tensions in the STUC, because many of the British unions had no interest in devolution. Pollock recalled:

All through this period the STUC was pressing strongly. A problem for them was that the actual representatives on the executive from the trade union side were not strong proponents of devolution. Most unions are British unions. They were exactly in the same position as the Labour Party – they were taking instructions from their union head offices. It would be from the constituency representatives on the executive at that time that the pressure would be coming.

After the second election of 1974, in which the SNP gained 11 seats, the Labour Government retained office, owing its majority of four to its Scottish seats. No more evasion was possible.

CHAPTER FOURTEEN

An absolute show-stopper

Wendy Wood, of the Scottish Patriots, had been active since before the war, planting flags and staging demonstrations. Her group was small, personalised and eccentric. Wendy Wood commanded much affection and towards the end of her life found an enormous and appreciative audience as a story-teller on television. She was imprisoned on several occasions for refusing to pay fines. She had been born in England, spent much of her youth in South Africa, was good enough as an artist to be trained under Sickert in London, and then was brought by marriage to Scotland. A tour of the Highlands revealed conditions which moved her to anger and she espoused nationalism. In 1972 she staged a 'fast until death' in order to force the Heath Government to honour its promise that it would publish a Green Paper setting out its plans for an assembly. In a Commons written answer Gordon (Lord) Campbell, the Secretary of State for Scotland, repeated undertakings to publish it in due course after the Royal Commission had reported. Few people knew at the time that he himself was under enormous emotional stress. In 1993 he wrote to me as follows:

> What was not made public (but is no longer confidential) is that my daughter, Christina, was near death at that time from the fasting disease, anorexia, and was in hospital for weeks and months, aged 19. That is why I knew about weight loss and fasting in general! The Scottish Office and friends were good at keeping this quiet in the patient's interest, on advice of the doctors.

(The story of Christina had a happy ending. After some severe bouts of the illness and two unsuccessful starts at university, she made a recovery upon engagement at the age of 25. Married soon afterwards in 1980, she has been transformed. 'Having a husband and home to look after, and then children,' wrote Lord Campbell, 'has been largely responsible for her transformation.' She started again at the university and took a very good law degree. For four years she has been a magistrate and has worked in the Citizens Advice Bureau organisation. Her four children are aged from 11 to three and she efficiently runs her house and a cottage in Hampshire. In giving me permission to use these details, Lord Campbell concluded: 'Her story is good news for other parents of anorexics and my wife and I are in touch with several.')

Jim Sillars went on television to make an appeal to Wendy Wood, and to everyone's enormous relief she called it off. Everybody had a soft spot for Wendy Wood. My mother recalled how Wendy, towards the end of her life, heard the

118

doorbell ring at her house in Howard Place, next to the Botanics. A party of foreign visitors had found the tea room shut. Could she direct them to a café? She took pity on them, brought them in and gave them tea. Next day the doorbell rang again. Outside was an enormous crowd of foreigners, come for tea. Miss Wood had politely to turn them away. She died in 1981, aged 88.

Her protest dramatised what had become a general cynicism about the Conservative Government's commitment to devolution. In 1970 Heath had unexpectedly led his party to victory at the general election. Because of the Declaration of Perth and the report of Sir Alec's committee, the Government was committed to a scheme of devolution. Its failure to produce one reflected the party's growing unease. But the existence of the Royal Commission genuinely complicated matters and the death of Lord Crowther in 1972 genuinely delayed its report. Commentators of the conspiracist school were led to construct a theory that the decision, announced in the Queen's Speech in 1970, to give legislative priority to the reform of Scottish local government represented a delaying tactic. For the Conservatives it was by genuine coincidence that a long process of gestation on a new structure of local government had reached the legislative stage. It has been suggested that Willie Ross, who as Secretary of State in the outgoing administration had supervised the Bill's evolution, saw in the creation of Strathclyde a means of blocking a Scottish assembly, to which he often seemed bitterly opposed until 1974. Other, and more convincing, recollections are that he reluctantly acceded to it.

The impulse to reform local government came out of the bureaucratic process rather than from political calculation. The previous round of reform, in 1929, had spawned a proliferation of cities, burghs, towns and counties. Officials at the Scottish Office yearned for administrative efficiency and economies of scale. In a letter written in March 1993, Lord Campbell recalled:

> Another factor, little remembered over 20 years later, is that the four chief local authorities in the area [that became Strathclyde] had been at odds with each other. These were the councils of Renfrew, Lanark, Dumbarton and Glasgow. Not only did they not co-operate with each other but at times they seemed tempted deliberately to take a course contrary to that of a neighbouring authority.

The principles of reform were first set out in 1964 in a White Paper by George Pottinger, the gifted civil servant who had been secretary to the Balfour Commission but was to be disgraced in the Poulson scandal. His White Paper sank from sight when the 1964 general election supervened. The matter was remitted to the Wheatley Commission. Because of the uneven distribution of its population in a large land mass, it is extremely difficult to draw a coherent local government map for Scotland. Strathclyde emerged as a region containing about half the population of Scotland. Strathclyde and other regions became Labour fiefdoms. That it was a Conservative administration which created them is striking evidence of the consensual continuity in Scottish government at that time.

The regions arose from the estuarine principle adopted by Wheatley. According to this doctrine the naturally homogeneous areas of Scotland were delineated by the firths and river systems around which they clustered. Like all such generalisations it had limited validity. It outraged local pride in such places as Ayrshire and Fife. The reformers were also pursuing efficiency and co-ordinated management. Strathclyde certainly gave administrative convenience and economies of scale but the system grew increasingly less congenial to the Conservative administrations of the Eighties and Nineties.

After 1992 the Government proposed a return to a single-tier system. Strathclyde, this creation of Conservatives, was denounced in 1992 by John Major and Ian Lang. Major even called it a monster. By that time Conservatives had come to perceive the large Labour regions as sources of hostile propaganda which helped to explain the Tories' enduring unpopularity north of the Border. In correspondence in 1993, Ian Lang disputed my original use of the word 'uncongenial' to describe his attitude to Strathclyde in particular. He wrote:

> As far as Strathclyde Region is concerned, I have never denounced the administration of the region and I feel no animus towards the authority. Other local authorities have a much poorer reputation in my eyes than Strathclyde Region . . . The simple point is the misconception of Wheatley's estuarial principle and the sheer size of Strathclyde. It was that size which rendered so many parts of Strathclyde Region incompatible with each other and made the region as a whole incompatible with any structure of *local* government.

The reversion to a single tier was also a response to central government's persistent difficulties in controlling spending by local government, as Nigel Lawson's memoirs make clear. Lang wrote:

> We did use the means at our disposal to control local government spending, but these means were inadequate because we continued to believe that the choice of spending levels by local authorities must remain at local level. We have, however, while respecting that principle, tightened the capping regime because of the impact local government expenditure was having on overall public expenditure. One specific mistake that was made was failing to control spending levels at the time of the switch from the old rating sytem to the community charge – local authorities behaved irresponsibly then.

The evidence that Willie Ross acquiesced in the creation of Strathclyde as a stratagem is anecdotal. John Pollock was chairman of the Ayrshire Labour Federation for 25 years, a member of Labour's Scottish executive for 21 years, chairman of the party in Scotland in 1959–60 and chairman again in 1972. He left the ruling councils and his various offices in 1974 when he became general secretary of the Educational Institute of Scotland, the leading teachers' union, but chaired the STUC in 1982. He was a close political associate of Ross until they became estranged when Pollock led a teacher's strike which greatly embarrassed his old friend. Pollock told me in 1993:

> There was strong resistance in Ayrshire to being absorbed into Strathclyde. Fife got its independence but Ayrshire didn't because Willie Ross saw the creation of Strathclyde as the real block to a Scottish assembly. I chatted with him about that.
>
> One of the major factors with Willie was that it would be a clear nonsense to have a region with half of Scotland in it and an assembly as well. In being prepared to concede the arguments for Fife, and then failing to concede an identical argument for Ayrshire, one can see that the only difference was that factor. During the progress of the Bill, Fife was in with Lothian and then was

taken out. There was a bit of a cross-party agreement. The quid pro quo for that was that Ayrshire would also come out when it came to its turn. But that didn't happen. Willie Ross didn't want Strathclyde split up.

However, Harry Ewing and Scottish Office insiders to whom I spoke in 1993 disputed this interpretation. Their view was that Ross was sympathetic to the amendment splitting Strathclyde into four; indeed, he voted for it. They recollected that the reform was pushed through as it stood on insistent official advice: local elections were imminent and it was simply too late to change.

In the civil service, it was also widely believed that Gordon Campbell found the priority of local government reform a useful justification for delay on devolution. Insiders recall that in the internal deliberations of the Scottish Office after 1970 the Green Paper was barely mentioned. Campbell himself stoutly denied such an interpretation when we corresponded in 1993. He wrote about the interaction between local government and constitutional reform as follows (he began by correcting my faulty recollection):

> The Wheatley Commission unanimously recommended a region slightly larger than Strathclyde! They called it 'West' region . . . Far from there being any 'confusion' [a quote from AK's initial letter], what was happening was obvious – we had to wait for Kilbrandon. Geoffrey Crowther (chairman until his death in 1972) told me that he hoped to complete the report within two years. Everything changed after his death. When I inquired whether the Commission would mind if I published a Green Paper before they had finished . . . I was told that Kilbrandon and most of the members would resign! I would have been pre-empting their report. I wish you well with your book and in disposing of any false mythology.

In a separate note from his own papers Lord Campbell set out the timetable of events. In the interests of clarity it is worth reproducing:

> The Scottish Conservative manifesto of 1970 stated that the report of the constitutional committee under the chairmanship of Sir Alec Douglas-Home would form the basis of proposals which a Conservative Government would place before Parliament, taking account of the forthcoming reorganisation of local government.
>
> Sir Alec Douglas-Home's committee had reported at the beginning of that year (1970) suggesting a possible form of parliamentary devolution comprising a Scottish convention meeting in Scotland but directly related to the UK Parliament at Westminster. It stated that such a devolutionary plan would need to have regard to the new pattern of local government, following consideration of and action on the Wheatley Royal Commission's report on the reorganisation of local government in Scotland. Wheatley reported in September 1969.
>
> Another Royal Commission had been set up in 1969 under the chairmanship of Lord Crowther . . . Its task was to consider constitutional reform for all parts of the United Kingdom. It took four and a half years to produce its report which was published at the end of October 1973, only three months before an unexpectedly early general election.
>
> The reform of local government was effected in an Act which was passed

in October 1973. The important decision for the new structure, concerning the Strathclyde region, was not clearly decided until the late summer.

Had the Crowther/Kilbrandon Commission reported sooner (four and a half years is considerably longer than the time taken by most Royal Commissions), it would have been possible to have had Green Paper proposals ready for publication soon after the new structure of local government had been decided.

With the sequence of events as they in fact happened, Green Paper proposals were being prepared and would have been ready for placing before Parliament by the middle of 1974, had the early general election not taken place.

In correspondence Lord Campbell confirmed that the Green Paper would have been derived from the Douglas-Home proposals. He continued:

It would have been immediately criticised by some people as having no teeth and only tinkering with the existing Westminster system. On the other hand, Home did not raise the West Lothian problem because final decisions were to be taken by all UK MPs on the floor of the Commons, as with the Grand Committee procedure. [The Green Paper] would not have aroused any hostility of MPs from Northern England since it included no new executive likely to outbid the English regions.

The kind of proposals which would have been in the Green Paper could never satisfy those who want final decisions made separately from Westminster and also want Treasury and tax-raising powers. But with meetings being held in Scotland, easily accessible for the public, and with much more time for Scottish subjects to be discussed by a body unencumbered by Westminster duties, the Home formula could have been attractive to the majority of the public in Scotland who are not particularly concerned but who would have favoured decentralising measures.

George Younger took a less sanguine view. He said in 1993:

We got away with the Home committee with the Old Guard because Alec Home was on it, really. Sir William McEwen Younger was also very respected. It certainly is the case when we came in 1970 that the reason we couldn't go ahead was that we had to do the Wheatley Report. We certainly couldn't do both at once. And we felt more time was needed to thrash out the difficulties anyway. But if there hadn't been Wheatley we would have been committed to doing something on the lines of Home but we would have got into a fearful fankle trying to do it. Actually it's jolly imaginative but it's full of all sorts of difficulties . . .

I suppose one could argue that if we had done something like that there might have been a recovery. I don't know, really. It's a possibility. We would have had a very difficult time. The Betty Harvie Andersons of this world would not have taken kindly to it at all. It might have withered on the vine.

In a subsequent letter Lord Campbell conceded that there might have been opposition to his Green Paper from the Old Guard:

As regards the Old Guard, their reaction to the May 68 Declaration at Perth did not surprise me. In the Commons it consisted of about six Conservative MPs, with Tam Galbraith and Fitzroy Maclean the most prominent (I had known both of them for many years before I entered Parliament). What they feared most was the kind of ill-considered assembly which later appeared in the Scotland Act. Its instability would have created the 'slippery slope' towards breaking up the Union.

They would doubtless have disapproved of the stable and workable Home model as unnecessary – another tier with no responsibilities, etc. – and they could have aired their views on the Green (consultative) Paper. Whether a White Paper would have followed with the Conservative Government's views and, if it did, whether it would have dropped the assembly idea, is a matter of conjecture. I agree with George Younger that there was substantial opposition in Scotland in 1968–71 to any kind of assembly.

I was not involved in the decision to make the May 1968 Declaration. Michael Noble was Shadow, Scotland, and I was No 2 Shadow, Defence. Heath's initiative was evidently to meet an apparent clamour for an assembly, much emphasised in the media, and he called on Wilson, the PM, to set up a Commission to enquire. This he later did – for the whole of the UK.

The opposition in Scotland to such devolution was there, but virtually silent.*

PS. Perhaps not their fault. Most of the press concentrated on reporting the contrary view, so they were not heard.

Attention now turned to the Kilbrandon proposals. Their essential weakness was pointed out by their diehard Conservative opponent, Iain Sproat. As a price of the assembly they conceded the office of Secretary of State for Scotland (Scotland would be looked after in Cabinet by another senior minister, perhaps on a part-time basis) and a cut in the number of Scottish seats. Sproat remarked that there would be something phoney, ludicrous and disagreeable in 'somebody strutting about calling himself Prime Minister of Scotland' but with functions limited to roads and tourism. The CBI, in evidence to Kilbrandon, had identified what later was to become another standard text for opponents of the Scotland Act – the probability that an assembly would concentrate on social legislation, with the consequence of higher taxes.

The West Lothian question has proved enduringly difficult. Would Scottish MPs be allowed to vote on English matters in Westminster while the equivalent Scottish matters were devolved to a Scottish legislature? The question was forcefully put during the devolution debates by Tam Dalyell, and named after his constituency (West Lothian until 1979, now Linlithgow). In fact it had older origins. Mitchell traced it to A. V. Dicey's *England's Case Against Home Rule*, a book written in 1885 during the debates on Irish home rule. George Younger said of the West Lothian question in 1993: 'It's an absolute show-stopper.'

CHAPTER FIFTEEN

How best to lose?

The SNP's advance of October 1974 was almost a decisive breakthrough. With 30 per cent of the vote it won 11 seats but came second in 39. It was second to Labour in 33 constituencies, to the Conservatives in five and to the Liberals in one. Even so, it was a remarkable achievement. But in it lay the basis of the party's later difficulties. The electoral wheel of fortune determined the composition of the group that was summoned to the Parliament and the group that stayed behind. Into Parliament went 11 disparate personalities of uneven abilities. Behind stayed a remarkably talented and largely left-wing group. It was led by the chairman, William Wolfe, and contained thinkers and pro-active policy-makers like Isobel Lindsay, Tom McAlpine, Colin Bell and Stephen Maxwell. The economist David Simpson and the research officer Donald Bain kept up a supply of intellectual fodder. The prominent member of the extra-parliamentary party was Margo MacDonald, thought by Wolfe to be the most politically astute of all her contemporaries. Her narrow failure to retain Govan, which she had won in a by-election in 1973, was in his view something of a political tragedy. With his sponsorship and support, MacDonald used her position first as vice-chairman, policy, and then as senior vice-president, to dominate the media at home. She had exceptional media skills which aroused the jealousy of some members of the parliamentary group. Donald Stewart, the group leader, would complain bitterly about her activities. The MPs, because of the pressure of duties at Westminster during the week and in the constituencies at the weekend, found it hard to attend meetings of the national executive committee, held on Fridays.

Wolfe thought jealousy of MacDonald a much more important factor than ideological, strategic or tactical difficulties. Stephen Maxwell confirmed there was jealousy but felt the underlying conflict was as to who ran the show – the party in the country or the group. He said:

> My memory is of pretty fraught meetings of the national executive council, with Tom McAlpine, Isobel, Margo, Billy, all very ready to criticise the parliamentary party. There were long debates as to whether the parliamentary group should operate autonomously with freedom of movement. There was a real fear that it would be sucked into parliamentary politics.

By the time that Parliament limped to its end in 1979 very severe tensions had broken out between the parliamentarians and the thinkers and publicists back home. Douglas Henderson, the whip from February 1974 until 1977, made the point, in conversation in 1993, that nationalism is by its very nature apolitical, with a strong emotional content. Furthermore, the MPs had to behave pragmatically, taking the deals where they could find them. The group back home tried to dictate tactics to the MPs but could not possibly have a grasp of the inner workings of the parliamentary process. Where a Government has a small majority, deal-making is the name of the game. They also began to move the party to a strategic position which made Labour voters its first target. Since most of the MPs were not from the industrial belt but had been elected by voters from the Poujadiste or radical wing in largely east-coast rural constituencies, the result was that the party in Parliament and the party in the country moved along shear lines like rock strata under stress.

Henderson, an amusing and complex man unjustly lampooned by his enemies for being far out of sight on the Right, was a gifted parliamentary operator, earning the respect and in some cases the friendship of whips from other parties. A civil servant paid him what was intended to be a high compliment by saying that Henderson had the most convoluted mind he had ever encountered. He told me in 1993 that the parliamentary group got 'a bit fed up' with the thinkers back home telling it how to vote, often on relatively minor issues. Such behaviour gravely weakened his ability to operate effectively, for a whip gives nothing for nothing, especially when dealing with a tough and cynical operator like Bob Mellish, Labour's chief whip in the Wilson Government, and cannot afford to show his hand. Gordon Wilson, because of his shrewdness, steadiness, discretion and reliability, became the honest broker between the two groups. He sought, though with limited success, to enforce the distinction that the party in the country was responsible for strategy while the parliamentarians must be free to determine tactics day by day. Some members of the parliamentary group like Hamish Watt recalled that Wilson had a very strong personality and did not hesitate to use it to put pressure on them. In some ways, although Wilson was Stewart's deputy, he exercised more influence at critical times.

In the October election the SNP team was supplemented by the dependable and enduring Andrew Welsh, Margaret Bain, the journalist and publicist Douglas Crawford, and George Thompson, who later became a priest. Wilson considered Welsh a seriously under-rated politician. From time to time he had a decisive influence. Thompson was the man on the Clapham omnibus, the voice of common sense, and if there was a difficult decision Wilson tended to follow his lead. From a left-wing position Margaret Bain was and is on the fundamental wing of the party. She was inspired to enter nationalist politics by Mrs Winifred Ewing, who became her mother-in-law when she married Fergus Ewing. After her defeat by Alex Salmond in the leadership contest in 1990 she became seriously disillusioned with Westminster life but soldiered on with a facade of cheerfulness, disenchanted with Scotland's political inertia and extremely distressed by the suffering in Bosnia.

After October 1974 it seemed for a time certain that Scotland must secure some sort of Parliament. Stephen Maxwell said:

> I sometimes think it was the best chance Scotland had or will have to seize some political power for itself. It was a happy coincidence of the growing disillusionment with British politics, the discovery of the oil, and the availability of models of how small countries could prosper. The Scandinavian model was in full bloom and hadn't been discredited by later problems.
>
> The oil developments and what they told us about Scotland's status fitted in very conveniently with fashionable theories of under-development. You could

make a structural case that Scotland was an under-developed country, a third-world country with all the sources of control being outwith the country. These factors lent credibility to Billy Wolfe's attempts to build the social democratic alternative to the traditional nationalism of Dr McIntyre. The fact that Billy had been in the Campaign for Nuclear Disarmament helped. We felt it was helping to locate the SNP on the political spectrum far more clearly than it had been.

Apart from the standard spectrum of class politics, there were other scales of values against which nationalists measured themselves. Here again, unanimity was impossible. The question was whether devolution was a prize or a trap. There were those who believed in the 'big bang' theory and those who believed in the 'slippery slope', a progressive devolution. The party was ambivalent and the divisions in the party outside Parliament were mirrored in the parliamentary group. Henderson said in 1993 that it would have been easier if the group had been 20 or two. If the first, it could have dominated the national executive. If the second, then the balance of power would have gone the other way.

In an interview Isobel Lindsay told me that the devolutionaries had been in the majority on the national executive; they included herself, Stephen Maxwell, Colin Bell, and Margo MacDonald most of the time. But categorisation was not easy. Fundamentalists like Winifred Ewing were also 'gradualists' rather than supporters of the 'big bang'. Then there was the standard class spectrum of political sentiment. More of the fundamentalists were to the Right and more of the devolutionaries were to the Left. Lindsay said: 'It was a liberal-ish Right. You were never entirely sure how a debate would come out. Hamish Watt was on the Right – but he was a devolutionary.' Wilson told me: 'I have always been a pragmatic fundamentalist, but I'm always prepared to trim.'

Lindsay said the parliamentary group found itself under enormous stress. Its members were not prepared for Westminster, or for the rapidity with which they were socialised, or for the intensity of the scrutiny.

John Smith, when we talked, put it another way. He said:

> The SNP group was pretty hilarious. There was a constant party. They were well known on the Terrace. They affected disdain for this Parliament but when you have 11 people you become an important force. I don't think they understood the role they were playing, the importance of it, its crucial nature. They weren't unintelligent people but there was a festive mood about them.

Many gained the respect of other parliamentarians. Callaghan got on well with Donald Stewart – they were both Navy men – and Stewart is remembered with great warmth by politicians from all parties. Walter Harrison, Labour's deputy chief whip, had been in the habit of sharing a dram with him from the time of Stewart's arrival at Westminster in 1970. In 1993 he spoke of his complete integrity. Teddy Taylor also paid Stewart a glowing tribute when we talked in 1993. He said:

> Donald Stewart was one of the most respectable, honest, decent people I ever met. He was a man whose word you could trust an awful lot more than that of most politicians.

126

Harrison regarded Henderson as 'pretty smart', a high compliment in whips' lingo. Harrison was to be found living in retirement in a pretty house near Wakefield in Yorkshire. One May morning he gave me an intriguing account of some of the whips' black arts. The good whip needs cunning, integrity, an iron constitution and an ability to hold his drink. Harrison kept in constant touch with the SNP group, often addressing them collectively so that there could be no misunderstandings of his position. He said he fell out with them only once. They had agreed to support the Government on a division. On the strength of that Harrison let some of his exhausted front-bench men go home early. The SNP then told him they had changed their minds. Harrison was in trouble. As ten o'clock came the Nats waited eagerly for him to move that the question now be put. He studied his order paper. He half rose. Then he sat down again. He half rose again. Then the hour chimed and the amendment was thus 'talked out' under the timetable procedure. He was free to reintroduce the matter at his leisure. Had the SNP members been smarter, one of them could have moved it. They did not have that quality which a whip prizes in a parliamentarian – they were not 'cute'.

In Isobel Lindsay's view, the pressure of parliamentary and constituency work was intense. Because of the MPs' irregular attendance at the national executive, it had to appoint representatives to go to Westminster to liaise – Robert McIntyre (by then the president) and Tom McAlpine. Henderson believed the MPs lost touch with the Scottish press back home. The Scots journalists in London he found 'Westminsterised' and out of touch with sentiment in Scotland. In one incident Watt tore up telegrams sent by shop stewards protesting against the SNP's decision to oppose the Bill to nationalise shipbuilding and aircraft production, and on one or two occasions visiting members of the national executive were kept waiting by the parliamentary power in an irksome display of gamesmanship.

In 1976 Margo MacDonald instigated a hardline campaign for independence rather than devolution, a case, said Wilson, of the 'Scottish football team' scenario of being swept along by events – 1975 and 1976 being the years in which Jim Sillars led John Robertson and others out of the Labour Party into his Scottish Labour Party. MacDonald herself described to me in her progress towards a harder position. When she was elected in the Govan by-election of 1973 it was possible to go along the devolutionary line. 'We were nowhere on the horizon. Independence was understood by about three men and a dog.' MacDonald came very early to the conclusion that there would be a referendum and that no matter the question the answer would relate to how people felt about its subtext of independence. 'Very few people would be sophisticated enough to vote for a halfway house if they never wanted to progress beyond it or understand the implications of gradualism. Most folk would answer in relation to how they felt about separatism.' Her view was that tactically the party should say anything within limits, but 'understand that strategically the case you have to win is the independence case'.

The loss of hope was a creeping thing throughout that unhappy Parliament. As the tensions developed, Wilson reflected that there were some very powerful and able people who should have been elected but were not. They included Wolfe, who was not obstructive but, as a great admirer of MacDonald, endorsed her frequent appearances on the television and in the press. Wilson thought Lindsay would 'have made a superb MP. She was officer material, of ministerial calibre.' MacDonald, in his view, would have been much easier to handle inside the parliamentary group. Stephen Maxwell would also have made an excellent parliamentarian.

Wilson and MacDonald agreed about the moment when the party's star, having risen so fast, began slowly to sink. The SNP's decision to oppose the shipbuilding and aircraft nationalisation Bill, which was brought forward by the Government in 1976 and 1977, saw the start of the downward movement. (This was the Bill that provoked Michael Heseltine to pick up the Commons Mace and flourish it during a rammy over the Government's attempts to expedite the legislation.) The SNP's decision illustrated that the parliamentary group and the national executive were of different temper and aroused considerable criticism in Scotland. It also demonstrated the sometimes inconsistent influences which work on the minds of nationalists. The decision did not arise only from a dislike of nationalisation as such. It came from the party's traditional fears about industrial control passing out of Scotland. Centralisation in general and the removal of the marketing function to Newcastle in particular were reasons enough for opposition in Wilson's mind. MacDonald said there was a perfectly valid reason for opposing it. 'But there were guys on the Clyde who knew that the only way they could hold on to their jobs was through nationalisation. The SNP was compromised by this vote.'

The opinion polls, having ridden so serenely high, turned down. It was also damaging that the Bill made Wilson an 'on-the-job absentee'. He was deputy leader of the group throughout the Parliament but disappeared into the committee giving detailed legislative consideration to the Bill. Like a mole he had gone underground and in all practical terms he was out of SNP politics for about 15 months. He became an absentee member of the parliamentary group and came off the national executive. 'That was a bumpy passage,' he said.

A second setback for the SNP came when Jim Sillars formed the Scottish Labour Party. It was not that he seduced anybody from the SNP, though it was one of his followers, John McAllion, who was to cost Wilson his seat in 1987, McAllion having by that time rejoined the Labour Party. It was Sillars's failure to cross the line or resign his seat, drawing Labour dissidents into the SNP, which Wilson identified as being a lost opportunity. Two prizes went begging – the capture of a significant Labour politician and a by-election campaign driven by the excitement of the Sillars defection.

Henderson, Lindsay and Wolfe did not attach as much importance to the nationalisation question. They felt that the decisive setback for the SNP was the Lib-Lab Pact, and Wilson agreed that this was the true watershed. This pact was made when Labour's first devolution Bill failed in 1977. It died for lack of parliamentary time when the Liberals refused to support the Government's time-table motion. David Steel, Henderson believed, delayed home rule for at least a generation by accepting the pact which saved Callaghan from an election. It moved the leverage from the nationalists to the Liberals. It took the SNP out of the limelight. The longer the Parliament continued, the weaker the SNP grew. Hamish Watt believed, when we talked in 1993, that there could have been, instead of the Lib-Lab Pact, an SNP-Lab Pact. Donald Stewart and he were due to discuss this with Callaghan but Gordon Wilson's powerful opposition to the idea, he recalled, put a stop to it. Wilson and Henderson reckoned that had an election been called at that point the SNP would have won between 25 and 30 seats, thus guaranteeing the creation of a strong Scottish parliament.

The Government hung on, brought in the second round of legislation with separate Bills for Scotland and Wales, and conceded the referendum to placate the rebels. Devolution as an issue had become tedious. The public's attention began to turn elsewhere, and for the SNP MPs it was the beginning of a decline that led to the electoral disaster of 1979. Lindsay has rueful memories, too. 'The Lib-Lab Pact got a very negative press in Scotland; the *Scottish Daily Express* denounced Liberals as traitors. The SNP supported the Bill but not without difficulty.'

Tensions were renewed when the amendment introducing the 40 per cent rule came up again at the report stage and third reading of the second Bill. This rule, introduced by Labour rebels led by George Cunningham, caused the Government much grief. It said that if less than 40 per cent of the electorate voted Yes in the referendum which the Government had now conceded then an order to repeal the Scotland Act should be laid before Parliament. Michael Foot and John Smith, piloting the leglislation through (see Chapter 17), were not the only ones to be caused embarrassment. For the SNP it caused a serious split. Isobel Lindsay recalled that the majority in the parliamentary group gave signals they were going to vote against it. The national executive made a decision, by a substantial majority, that they should vote for it. She continued:

> Because there was little time between the national executive decision and the vote there was great stress. I leaked this to the media to try to ensure the parliamentary group abided by it – I wanted to put it into the public domain – because the majority mood, with Gordon Wilson dissenting, was to vote against it. Had the referendum taken place in the autumn, rather than the spring, things might have been different. By the time of the referendum, in the event, there had been the winter of discontent, the popularity of the Government had slumped, there had been bad weather, bad politics, bad industrial relations, an atmosphere that all changes were for the worst.
>
> If we had voted against the amendment and the Bill had not gone to the referendum stage, then we would have been permanently blamed. The Labour Party would have said that we had washed our hands.

In the event, the parliamentary group, having opposed the 40 per cent rule when it was introduced in committee, abstained when it came for consideration at report stage. Henderson and others argued strongly at this period that the Bill should be opposed root and branch. Its failure to transfer real power made it in their view fraudulent. The party had lost its touch. This was confirmed at the Glasgow Garscadden by-election in 1978 when, in a constituency dependent on naval shipbuilding on the Clyde, the SNP fielded a well-known unilateralist, Keith Bovey. He got 33 per cent of the vote but Donald Dewar triumphantly returned to Parliament with 45 per cent, increasing it to 61 per cent at the general election in 1979.

The party fought the referendum campaign of March 1979 without enthusiasm. Maxwell was the party's referendum director. They sent out 'mountains of leaflets'. Many of the MPs – including Henderson and Stewart – hardly campaigned at all. But even before the campaign started the party made what Wilson believed to be a major error in strategy. In the executive he and Maxwell argued that the next general election should be fought on economic issues. Wolfe and MacDonald asserted that the chosen ground should be the constitutional issue. At a meeting in January 1979, Wilson and Maxwell lost the vote. 'In the end that had a nasty twist because we fought the constitutional issue at a time when it had burnt out.'

Around this time Wolfe and McIntyre were summoned to a meeting with the parliamentary group. Henderson did not, when we spoke, have any recollection of it; but Wolfe recalled that the MPs kicked him around over the activities of Mac-Donald of which Douglas Crawford and other MPs had been critical. Wolfe told me that McIntyre was at this meeting and afterwards he and Wolfe became estranged.

By this time what Maxwell called the mismatch between the parliamentary group and the party in the country could no longer be concealed. Back in Scotland the thinkers and intellectuals had decided, after analysing the referendum results, that those most susceptible to the SNP were Labour voters. People like Henderson knew that this was an analysis of limited application and that it was potentially damaging, for his constituency of Aberdeenshire East was quite different to any-thing in the industrial belt. Wilson said:

> This is one of the abiding paradoxes of the SNP. It's an anti-Tory ethos in East Aberdeenshire, a radical tradition. It's not left-wing and he (Douglas Hender-son) was taking a risk in supporting trade unions because though they were anti-Tory there they were also anti-union – fishermen, independent contractors, small farmers, small shopkeepers or workers in the fish factories who had never been fully organised. Douglas was one of those people who had properly but wrongly been categorised as on the Right. In nationalist terms he went towards the fundamentalist side of the party but was essentially pragmatic.

After the indecisive referendum, a new parliamentary game began. Callaghan was at first well disposed to moving the repeal order with a view to its rejection. Michael Foot was pressing for it. During that period, day by day, the SNP expected an election to take place. The refusal of the Callaghan Government to move the repeal order led the SNP to table a vote of no confidence. 'This was not done with the intention of bringing down the Government,' Wilson said. It was done in the hope that the prospect of a hanging would concentrate the mind.

When the Callaghan Government fell in 1979, it did so on the Conservative motion of no confidence which had, in Henderson's phrase, hi-jacked the resolution tabled by the SNP. Wilson was keen to dispose of the 'myth' that the parliamentary group acted contrary to the views of the party. In fact it was obedient, in some cases reluctantly, to a unanimous vote in the national council. He had wanted to bring down the Government nine months before because the SNP would have saved more seats; its position was eroding the longer the Parliament lasted. Wolfe told me in 1993 that he had not wanted to bring the Government down but that at the national council meeting there was an irresistible 'mob' sentiment. Hamish Watt, whose personal agony is discussed more fully in Chapter 17, remained, in 1993, convinced that a tragic error of judgment had been made. Before the SNP forced the issue there was, according to Wilson, a meeting between Donald Stewart and Callaghan. Callaghan was at that point willing to move the repeal order, Foot was pressing for it. Wilson said:

> The SNP motion was signed by every MP. They knew there was a high risk. Many of them knew their days were numbered. In retrospect, if time had been allowed, we might have come out of it with four MPs rather than two. We hoped that had we got guarantees we would have changed our mind. If they had moved the repeal order and put on a three-line whip, and even if they had been defeated, we might have supported them in the subsequent confidence vote. That would have been different. If the Government had made the effort, they would have shown their honourable intentions. Even so, it was a matter of assessable

loss. We couldn't really win, because an election had to be held anyway. The Government was simply hoping to buy time so it could have a give-away Budget.

In Lindsay's account of events the parliamentary group had been influenced by the national executive and the national council to the point where the MPs were more or less driven to bring the Government down.

> Left to its own devices the group would not have voted to bring the Government down. I was strongly in favour of them doing so – I thought the Labour Government would make a major concession. They made no concessions, like implementing the Scotland Act. They thought a lot of their own backbenchers wouldn't support them but I think they also thought the SNP would not vote against them. There was a lot of misinterpretation. Right up to the last minute I thought something of substance was going to appear. It was a failure of management on the Labour side.
>
> The vote in national council had been unanimous. The fundamentalists and the devolutionists were united – the fundamentalists because they didn't want any cosy relationships with the Labour Government and the devolutionists to see what they could get out of it.

In 1979 Wolfe approached Wilson to ask if he would agree to become chairman. Wolfe was being squeezed this way and that. He had been deeply saddened by the meeting at which he had been rebuked. His shovel-making business – making mostly forestry equipment – was in crisis. He had learned that in business the salesman is king and had driven thousands of miles a year selling the products of Chieftain Forge. They had a disaster with a potato tilling machine developed at the request of the Potato Marketing Board. There were stresses in his personal life. Throughout the Parliament he had found Wilson absolutely reliable in his dealings. More than anyone else he (Wilson) had tried to reconcile the two wings of the party. Wilson, in his attempts to maintain a separation between strategy, a party matter, and tactics, an issue for the MPs, had gone so far at one point as to resign for a brief period in 1978 from the parliamentary group deputy leadership as a signal to it that it could not act in isolation from the party in the country. The general view in the group was that things were falling apart.

Wilson, Lindsay, MacDonald, Wolfe and Maxwell had wanted the SNP members to pull the plug on the Government. Maxwell said:

> We'd lost the game and we should try to keep a party that had some sort of self-respect. We'd fought the battle and lost; we should have gone down with all flags flying and lived to fight again. If we continued to support the Government which was quite obviously not going to concede anything very significant we'd simply split the party and we'd lose the election anyway. When Jim Sillars came into the party in 1980 that was his constant theme – the folly of bringing down a Labour Government.

Maxwell's predictions were right on both counts. Maxwell said: 'We were all pretty exhausted. It had been a period of intense and frequent campaigns and crises.' Electoral disaster followed. John Smith said in 1993: 'To go from 11 to two MPs because of your own actions – it's pretty astonishing, isn't it?'

131

The SNP now began a period of intense infighting. Those who came up with the analysis that Labour voters were most open to the nationalist argument might have had second thoughts had they been privy to a conversation between Teddy Taylor and Mrs Thatcher soon after he became shadow Secretary of State for Scotland in 1976. He told me in 1993 that it had gone something like this:

> Mrs Thatcher said to me, Teddy, I want you to help me destroy the Nats. I said, I can do that, Margaret, but in so doing you'll lose Teddy Taylor. She said, You will always be in Cathcart, Teddy. She said, You're not serious, are you? I said, Yes I am.

Mrs Thatcher feared that the SNP might replace the Tories as the alternative to Labour in Scotland. In such circumstances the move in the other direction by the SNP was for the Conservatives a distinct relief. Though he says it himself, Taylor ran a good campaign. He went on the stump in the SNP seats outside the central belt. His prediction came true. He lost Cathcart, one of only two Tory losses, because the collapse of the SNP vote let Labour in. 'In decimating the SNP,' he said, in a typical Teddy quote, 'I decimated myself.' In 1980 he was found the seat of Southend East, from where he continues to take an interest in Scottish politics when not too occupied with his anti-European campaigns. In a way he was also a victim of the devolution years. When we talked in 1993, I had the impression of an exile.

CHAPTER SIXTEEN

A graceful disengagement

Peter Fraser, now Lord Fraser of Carmyllie, was a young prospective Conservative candidate in 1975. He first became aware that something was seriously amiss with the party's commitment to devolution in 1975 at the Dundee conference. He was about to go on to the platform and make a speech about the need for an assembly when Alick Buchanan-Smith drew him aside. 'Don't commit me to too much, for I won't be able to deliver.' To those at the centre of events it was obvious that serious and sustained opposition had developed within the party north and south of the border.

Once Mr Heath had, in 1975, been removed from the leadership after the electoral failures of 1974, Whitelaw was replaced as shadow devolution spokesman by Francis (later Lord) Pym, with Leon Brittan as his junior. Pym was sympathetic to devolution but encountered increasing if tacit resistance from Mrs Thatcher, other members of the shadow Cabinet and English Tory MPs. The stalemate produced a prolonged charade of obfuscation and equivocation. Pym and Brittan did not say yes to Labour's White Paper, *Our Changing Democracy*, when it came out in 1975; and they did not say no. They engaged in an elaborate series of consultations. Peter Fraser remembered feeling highly flattered that Brittan, on a visit to Edinburgh, asked him for his opinion. The leading devolutionary, Brian Meek, together with a sympathetic colleague in the local party, took Brittan to the Caledonian Club in Edinburgh and filled him up with the club whisky and their opinions. 'He went off into the night promising to tell Mrs Thatcher of our views. We also saw Francis Pym.'

Four identifiable groupings had now emerged. A group of diehard Unionists gathered round Teddy Taylor, Iain Sproat and Betty Harvie Anderson. There were the Rifkind moderates who wanted a directly elected assembly with legislative and deliberative but not executive powers. Buchanan-Smith, Michael Ancram and Brian Meek were in this group; it would be reasonable to add Sir Alec Douglas-Home. Russell Fairgrieve, party chairman from 1975–80, led the 'maximalist' position favouring a more powerful assembly. Finally, there was an even more radical group committed to a quasi-federal and autonomous assembly. James Mitchell, in *Conservatives and the Union*, put Heath in this group.

By 1976 it was clear that the anti-devolutionaries were getting on top. Sproat lobbied and campaigned tirelessly. In May, Keep Britain United was launched in Glasgow. He had hoped it would be all-party but Tam Dalyell refused to become part of it and it was pretty exclusively Conservative. Teddy Taylor was involved and a 15–strong parliamentary committee was formed, including five Scottish MPs.

Its members from the party outside Parliament included James Goold, at that time deputy treasurer of the party in Scotland. Sproat hinted that Mrs Thatcher was sympathetic. The party conference later that month endorsed devolution but by a majority of only 2–1 which, Sproat alleged, did not fully reflect the real feeling in the hall. Mrs Thatcher then pledged herself to a directly elected assembly with an evident lack of enthusiasm.

When the first devolution Bill, the Scotland and Wales Bill, was published by the Callaghan Government in November 1976, the Tory devolutionaries found themselves undermined. No one could like the Bill. On that point at least there was unanimity. In correspondence in 1993 Lord Campbell, who lost his seat to Mrs Winifred Ewing in February 1974, said the Labour Bills had two grave defects. First, they did not solve the West Lothian question and so contained a 'source of immense trouble later from objecting English and Welsh MPs whose case would have been unanswerable'. Secondly, they would have set up two rival executives, the assembly's executive and the Secretary of State. Under the distribution of powers, the Secretary of State and the Scottish Office retained the major share. 'This would have been a formula for misunderstanding and conflict.' He added:

> The main worry about such proposals, both for Labour and Conservative, was that an unstable or unworkable form of assembly would create a situation where there was pressure for separation from the UK (the hope of the SNP) or for central government in London to step in and take over before the new system disintegrated, reached deadlock, or collapsed.

Two days after its publication the shadow Cabinet decided to oppose it at second reading with a three-line whip. The next day Buchanan-Smith, Rifkind, Younger, Hamish Gray, Hector Monro and John Corrie met Mrs Thatcher and the Tory chief whip Humphrey Atkins. They asked that Buchanan-Smith be released from the obligations of collective responsibility. A week later Buchanan-Smith resigned from the front bench. As junior spokesman with responsibility for devolution, Rifkind felt honour-bound also to resign. Monro, Corrie and Fairgrieve all offered their resignations but these were refused by Mrs Thatcher. Whitelaw advised that the doctrine of collective responsibility had to stand even in opposition. George Younger wrote to me in 1993 in the following terms:

> Alick and I and Hector Monro and Malcolm Rifkind were all very unhappy at the decision of the shadow Cabinet to vote against a second reading. As a result of that Alick resigned his post as shadow Secretary of State for Scotland and Mrs Thatcher called me in to ask me to take his place. I refused to do so because I held the same views and could not therefore go along with the vote. I should explain that at that time I was not on the front bench as I had ceased to be shadow Secretary of State for Defence early in 1976 when Ian Gilmour was moved from the Home Office to Defence. I had no further resignation to offer apart from refusing to take the post of shadow Secretary of State.
>
> I should add that we were all clear that we could not support the Scotland Bill as it stood should it go through Parliament without amendment, but we felt that at the second reading the party should have abstained and reserved its fire for a third reading when the exact nature of the Bill would have been clear and we would have had an opportunity to make amendments.

Malcolm Rifkind gave me a similar account of this episode:

We had a policy which committed the Conservative Party, including Mrs Thatcher, to support the principle of devolution and the principle of a Scottish assembly of some kind. At that time we envisaged that assembly as having legislative powers. The Conservative Party was never a supporter of it having executive powers, in other words a Scottish government as well as a Scottish parliament. The support and the enthusiasm was for some sort of legislative supervision over the work of the Scottish Office. The Labour Party published its Scotland and Wales Bill which provided for not only legislative devolution but also executive devolution. We were all opposed to this, including Alick. We thought it was the wrong structure. It went too far and created a real risk of separatism.

Having said that, we were very concerned at the clear desire of the shadow Cabinet to vote on second reading against the Bill. We argued that as the party was committed to the principle of devolution and some kind of assembly then if our disagreement was not with the principle but with the kind of devolution being proposed by the Labour Government, then we didn't argue that the party should vote for that Bill. That would have been foolish. We argued that the proper course of action was for an abstention on second reading. We would try to change it in committee. If we failed, we then could in proper conscience vote against it on third reading.

Alick reported to us that the shadow Cabinet had decided not to accept his advice and that given the feeling in the parliamentary party as a whole had decided that it would be proper to vote against on second reading on a three-line whip. No voting for, no abstentions. We discussed it and Alick decided that he could not in conscience support that view. He had a majority of his Scottish colleagues with him. I supported him as did Russell Fairgrieve and John Corrie. There were various discussions, with Mrs Thatcher and the Chief Whip; Willie Whitelaw was very much involved. The conclusion was that there had to be a vote against on a three-line whip. A number of us took the view that this was unwise and the proper course was to offer our resignations. The initial reaction was that if I and one or two other junior spokesmen were prepared to abstain then we wouldn't be required to resign. I took the view that if Alick resigned the proper course of action was for those who agreed with him to do the same. I had been the junior spokesman assisting him on devolution and so I was in a particularly difficult position.

In public Mrs Thatcher did not disown devolution until the Eighties, and even then with some caution. But she seems to have been moving towards rejection more or less from the time she dislodged Heath from the leadership in 1975. Teddy Taylor told me that when he joined the shadow Cabinet in 1975 he had the impression she had not yet made up her mind. He said:

It was pretty clear that she had doubts about devolution. I think she would probably have gone along with it if she had been convinced of the arguments. Quite a number of the shadow Cabinet were pro-devolution. I was quite a loner in the beginning.

He had in the first instance been appointed shadow Trade Secretary. He said:

I often wondered why. I felt very excited by it. It was a huge job. I got the impression that Mrs Thatcher wanted someone in the shadow Cabinet who was Scottish and did not support devolution. We had a delightful and honourable chap called Alick Buchanan-Smith [as shadow Secretary of State for Scotland]. I got the impression that the reason she wanted me to do this huge job . . . was perhaps some kind of threat [to Buchanan-Smith].

What retarded Mrs Thatcher's rejection of devolution was the support for it in significant quarters in Scotland, from what Taylor called 'the Scottish Conservative establishment'. Taylor continued:

She had contacts in Scotland, I think with the office-bearers of the party, who consistently sent down messages saying: You mustn't abandon devolution. There was also a chap called Francis Pym who was in the shadow Cabinet and was a conveyor of messages from the Scottish Tory establishment. The messages were consistently in favour of devolution.

Right to the end, Taylor recalled, he had a terrible battle. Buchanan-Smith he respected as 'an honourable, decent chap.' He added:

The real battle I had was with Francis Pym. He was pushing it with all sincerity and with the support of the Scottish Tory establishment. Sadly for me, although I was shadow Secretary of State for Scotland [the job to which he was moved when Buchanan-Smith resigned], they used Pym as their vehicle. I wasn't on the same wavelength. They said that if you support devolution you'll get votes in Scotland. I remember on one occasion Pym grabbed my hand and smacked it, rather like a schoolteacher, as if to tell me I was going too far.

The decisive reverse for the devolutionaries came with the shadow Cabinet's decision to oppose the Bill. Taylor said:

I think in 1977–79 we succeeded [in reversing the policy on devolution]. It was about 1981 before Mrs Thatcher starting saying it. On the other hand, she knew I was saying it on her behalf.

The evidence that Mrs Thatcher had decided against devolution from an early point is thus overwhelming. She brought a leading 'anti' into the shadow Cabinet, in a job for which he acknowledged he was not yet qualified. She encouraged him to speak up against Pym. Now he began the work of conversion in Scotland, again with what must have been her approval though it remained tacit. Brian Meek had an anecdote about Teddy Taylor at that time:

Teddy Taylor arrived at Lothian Regional Council to talk to the Tory group there, accompanied by George Younger. Teddy was at his best, smoking fags and eating Rollos as only Teddy could. He gave us this stridently anti-European speech. How many people here support devolution, he asked. About 12 people put their hands up. And he turned to me and said, You've got a lot of pinkos here.

Taylor himself said his technique was to give the party line but with clear contrary signals:

At first, speaking in my capacity as shadow Secretary of State for Scotland, I put forward the party's official line – that we still had some thoughts of doing something on the lines of the Alec Douglas-Home model. But I said it in such a way as would indicate total lack of enthusiasm.

On second reading, 70 MPs of both parties defied the whips. Five Tories voted with the Government.

For the Tory devolutionaries this was the decisive reverse. In 1993 Lord Lawson told me that a change of policy had become inevitable because the Heath line was so difficult to sustain. It was not even a question of a simple division between English and Scottish members; the divisions among the Scottish members themselves were acute. The party was therefore much more comfortable with the diluted policy that began to emerge. In Scotland devolution began to be a dirty word. When Betty Harvie Anderson had made clear her intention to stand down at the next election as MP for West Renfrewshire, Meek was on the parliamentary list at the time and decided to apply. He recalled:

> We went to be interviewed in the hotel in Glasgow Airport. The second question was, Are you in favour of devolution? I had to say yes. There were only about two other questions. The chairman shrugged and said, Well, what can I say? That was it. After that I came to the conclusion there was no point going for any parliamentary seat. Anybody after that who was in favour of devolution had to be an established figure such as Buchanan-Smith otherwise there was no chance of being selected. Allan Stewart was against devolution, he was for hanging, he had all the correct attitudes – and he was chosen.

Michael Foot introduced the devolution bill, giving assemblies to Scotland and Wales, in November 1976. He indicated that the Government would be willing to consider a referendum. Scottish devolutionaries on both sides found the going increasingly tough. The Tory anti-devolutionary caucus, calling itself the Union Flag Group, led by Taylor, Sproat, Betty Harvie Anderson and George Gardiner, formed a tacit alliance with the Labour dissidents and sceptics, among whom Robin Cook, Neil Kinnock, Tam Dalyell and George Cunningham were prominent.

The first Bill died in March 1977 when 22 Labour rebels voted down a timetable (or guillotine) motion to curtail debate and secure the Bill's progress. This was a victory for the prolonged guerrilla warfare conducted in committee by the Union Flag Group. According to Mitchell, it was responsible for 338 of the 1062 amendments tabled in total. Mrs Thatcher made no attempt to restrain the diehards. In response to the resignations of Buchanan-Smith and Rifkind she had let it be known that discipline would be slackened. Mitchell pointed out that it was the diehards rather than the devolutionaries who benefited. Progress on the Bill was slow and the Government was forced into the guillotine motion. Heath was abroad and Buchanan-Smith, who abstained, may have been slightly placated by a speech by Francis Pym over the previous weekend which had proposed that a constitutional convention should meet to investigate whether broad agreement could be reached on a scheme in three years.

Heath grew increasingly bitter. Defiantly he went to Glasgow in April of 1977 to demand that the assembly be given powers to raise revenue. But devolution was moribund. It look a long time dying. Labour pressed on because its Government stood on the rotten plank of the Lib-Lab pact. But devolution acquired its terminal illness from the failure of bipartisan support for it and the deep fractures it made in both major parties. For this the backing of the Liberals and the nationalists was insufficient compensation.

CHAPTER SEVENTEEN

The loss of illusion

After the second election of 1974, the Wilson Government pressed ahead with devolution despite serious misgivings at the highest level of both Government and civil service. The Cabinet Office began to work on the details, and devolution spread like a blight, pervading all branches of government. The Scottish Office found itself in a position of some ambivalence. Ross remained the reluctant convert, diluting and delaying wherever he could. Ted (Lord) Short was put in charge as Lord President of the Council and Leader of the House. During the election campaign Short had visited Harry Ewing as he defended his seat of Stirling, Falkirk, and Grangemouth against bitter SNP assault. By dint of a vigorous campaign he hung on, with 43 per cent against the SNP's 40 per cent. On Short's recommendation, and without consulting Ross, Wilson appointed Harry (Lord) Ewing as the Scottish voice in the devolution deliberations with the rank of parliamentary under-secretary at the Scottish Office. Ewing had a very difficult time. Ross made clear his displeasure at the appointment and insisted on attending every ministerial meeting to keep an eye on what went on. He made an alliance wherever he could with the Whitehall departments who were showing increasing resistance to yielding powers and functions to an assembly. He was instrumental in making sure that the proposed Scottish assembly would have no economic teeth and that the Scottish Development Agency would not be devolved to it. The SDA was his creature and he was not prepared to dilute his control or patronage. Ewing recalled that at one meeting, when the transfer of the SDA to the assembly was discussed, Ross growled: 'This is devolution, not separation.'

Old Scottish Office hands will tell you that in the tortuous gestation of the devolution bills, a subtle shift began to take place. Others say there was nothing subtle about it; that as far as Whitehall was concerned the devolutionary spring was followed by winter without any summer at all. At first, the Scottish Office approach had been to specify what functions and responsibilities should remain at Westminster and Whitehall. The assembly would take the rest. The approach was quickly reversed. The assembly's functions were now specified with increasing niggardliness. The Scottish universities, recently much expanded and many of them suddenly anglicised, fought a successful campaign to evade the assembly's clutches.

Ewing's difficulties were compounded by the curious behaviour of Short's deputy in the Privy Council office (with the rank of Minister of State). This was the MP for The Wrekin, Professor Gerald Fowler, an old chum of Wilson. As the deliberations advanced towards completion of the promised White Paper, a ministerial meeting was held at which a confidential draft was circulated. The civil servants registered the names of those who received a copy. By a curious chance there was one copy too few. Ewing, believing himself a master of the subject, generously said that he could do without, and did not receive a copy. The next day the document, in full, appeared in *The Scotsman*.

So porous had the Government become that a procedure had been instituted to investigate serious leaks. This was clearly one of them, and Ewing was visited by the civil servant responsible for making inquiries. He was told that he was a prime suspect, and that he had so been identified by Willie Ross who was deeply suspicious of his friendship with fellow devolutionaries Alex Eadie and Jim Sillars, with whom he shared digs in London. Ewing was incensed, and was able to demonstrate his innocence by referring the investigator to the register of those who had received copies. He confronted Ross, who could offer no convincing explanation for the injustice. He then found out that Gerry Fowler had subsequently been identified as the culprit. He had handed the document over to Tom James in the bar on the evening of the meeting. With a manifest lack of even-handedness, Wilson did not sack him. He moved him and replaced him with Lord (Norman) Crowther-Hunt, a member of the Royal Commission who was often confused with its first chairman, Lord Crowther. By now thoroughly incensed, Ewing went to see Wilson. He demanded that a note be circulated clearing him of any complicity in the leak. He said he would resign if this were not done, and make public the reasons for his resignation. Wilson complied with ill grace.

The Government eventually produced the White Paper, *Our Changing Democracy*, committing itself to devolutionary legislation. Its perceived inadequacy, in particular its omission of economic powers from the assembly's responsibilities, propelled Sillars out of the party along with John Robertson. They led the breakaway Scottish Labour Party that caused an enormous but ephemeral excitement and imploded in confusion and bitterness. The SLP was infiltrated by various Marxist factions and collapsed at a spectacularly chaotic conference.

Wilson abruptly resigned in March 1976 for reasons which have never been satisfactorily explained. Callaghan became Prime Minister and Bruce Millan Secretary of State for Scotland. Callaghan had wanted to appoint the engaging but politically wayward Dr Dickson Mabon to the Scottish job. Now there was just the sort of individualist Ross could not accommodate. Harry Ewing told me that Ross went to Callaghan and said that if Mabon were appointed he (Ross) would 'raise the roof'. Ewing, too, strongly supported Millan's appointment. He thought he was an under-rated politician capable of holding the highest offices of state. To have passed over him, he judged, would have been a disastrous and unacceptable error. Millan in 1993 was serving a second term as one of Britain's two EC Commissioners.

The removal of the baleful and hostile figure of Ross, and his replacement by the much more sympathetic Millan, at once created a significantly more constructive atmosphere. Michael Foot, as Leader of the House and Lord President of the Council, took charge of the devolution legislation and John Smith, as Minister of State for the Privy Council, went in to do the hard work of detail both in the Chamber and in the Cabinet Office Constitution Unit. A more positive and committed team of civil servants was put in place. John (Lord) McCluskey took charge of legislative progress in the Lords, as Solicitor-General for Scotland. Some of the most thoughtful debates were to take place in the Lords as the peers struggled to reconcile the contradictions which the enemies of devolution exploited.

It has been said that Callaghan was never keen on devolution and he was taunted throughout his premiership with the charge of expediency. When we talked in 1993 Michael Foot clearly felt there was substance to the suspicion that Callaghan had a certain lack of enthusiasm and he confirmed this in the note he sent me after our lunch in his favourite restaurant, The Gay Hussar in Soho. He wrote:

> The Prime Minister had never been enthusiastic about devolution in Wales, and was never over-enthusiastic about the proposition for Scotland. However, he went with the party decisions on the matter and did his best to assist them.

Donald Dewar said that in his view Callaghan had a limited if genuine belief in decentralisation. It has also often been said that John Smith was never emotionally committed to devolution but a master of its complexities and an able parliamentary advocate of it. This is an interpretation which Smith rejects. He told me in 1993:

> That's not true. Just because I happen to express myself in a guarded way – I thought there was a logical and clear argument which could be made and should be made. But I'm very committed to it, very committed indeed.

Smith recalled that when winding up the debate in March 1977 which killed the first Bill on the guillotine motion, he was handed a note from the Chief Whip saying the Government had lost. He continued:

> I had to pretend we were going to win. We were defeated and that was it. Enoch Powell said, There's a terrible stench in the chamber. Will someone please take this dead Bill away? The Lib-Lab pact revived it. Callaghan had me in and said, Right, get the Liberals to suppport it.

The following month the Lib-Lab pact was announced, promising the Liberals regular consultations on policy, and the Government survived a no-confidence motion by 24 votes. Smith went back to see (Sir) Michael Quinlan, one of the senior civil servants at the Cabinet Office Constitutional Unit.

> I told him that the Prime Minister had said there was to be no nonsense with departments. If there was any difficulty about anything it was to go back to No 10. I said, that's quite important. Michael Quinlan said, It's more than important, it's pure gold.

Having learned at the feet of Willie Ross, Smith did not hesitate to use the Scottish Labour mafia. He said:

> I found that every time we proposed something Whitehall objected to it. If we wanted to give something more on the economic front to the Scottish Assembly you'd get DTI objections. Fortunately I had Gregor MacKenzie [the MP for Rutherglen and Minister of State, who died in 1992] at the DTI and he would send over the briefing they had done. So I had the brief that was to be given against me.

Smith had to fight on three fronts. He had to overcome Whitehall's resistance to change. He had to deal with the Labour rebels. And he had to keep the Liberals happy. He recalled:

The Liberals . . . that had its complications. The first meeting I had with David Steel wasn't a great hit. He said they wanted a federal solution. What does that mean, I asked, parliaments for other English regions? No, said Steel, I can see you don't have time to do that. But devolution with a federal philosophy? I told him, You can't have that, David.

He tended not to come after that and [Sir] Russell Johnston came instead. I didn't think they had very much to contribute, quite honestly. They were not a great fund of new ideas. It was quite amicable. I had late-night sessions with Russell over a glass of whisky and he'd phone me in the morning and say, What was it we agreed? And he'd say, Wee Steelie won't like that! It was good fun.

The pact was sustained with some difficulty. Smith continued:

At this time Denis Healey was kicking John Pardoe down the steps of the Treasury, causing immense strains to the pact. There was a liaison committee which Michael chaired which was to supervise the pact. There was a constant series of complaints about Healey, to which Michael would say, Well, he just treats you the way he treats us! So what's the complaint? I said to Michael: Would you tell him to behave himself because every time he insults them they come along and cause trouble for me.

One of Smith's first actions was to persuade Foot that it had been a serious error to lump Scotland and Wales together. This had maximised the Labour opposition. Neil Kinnock had hinted to him that doing Scotland only would be an acceptable way forward. The Government ploughed on with separate Bills for Scotland and Wales.

The crucial parliamentary session was that of 1978–79. Comparisons with the Maastricht debates of the Nineties are inescapable. For the Callaghan Government, as for the Major administration later, endless constitutional debates and cross-party manoeuvring preoccupied the whips and enfeebled the Government's capacity to pursue its legislative programme. Michael Cocks, who had succeeded Bob Mellish as the Labour Chief Whip, complained at one point to Cunningham: 'You realise you're bringing Michael Foot's shingles back!'

Smith adopted two strategems to deal with Whitehall resistance and Labour rebellions. First he made sure that everything he did was authorised by Foot. He said in 1993:

Michael Foot was a powerful figure in the Government. A troika ran it – Jim Callaghan, Michael Foot and Denis Healey. Michael was powerful with Jim because Jim was very grateful for Michael bringing the Left in behind the Government. In fact I think Michael put me into the Cabinet.

Secondly, Smith tried to contain the Labour rebellion by making sure that the devolution proposals were at all points endorsed by the party conference. He recalled:

The Labour rebels had not been able to do anything openly because after we got the first trouble from them I made certain that we got everything through every conference. The Eric Heffers of this world would spend their time giving you wee lectures about conference decisions. I thought, Well, I'll give them conference decisions.

But the rebels found a way through. On 25 January 1978, Cunningham, an expatriate Scot who sat as Labour MP for Islington South-West, successfully introduced an amendment inserting the 40 per cent rule. This stipulated that if less than 40 per cent of the registered electorate endorsed the Scotland Act an order would be laid before Parliament to repeal it. On this topic conference was silent and Smith, though strongly opposed to it, could not contain the revolt this time. The amendments incorporating the rule were carried against Government wishes. Gardiner (now Sir George and a Maastricht rebel) crossed the floor of the House to shake Cunningham's hand; but their alliance was informal rather than explicit, as Teddy Taylor insisted when we spoke in 1993. The closest it got to formality was when a number of Tories, including Betty Harvie Anderson and Norman Lamont, joined Cunningham and other Labour MPs on a trip to Shetland. They sought to exploit the fact that if Orkney and Shetland stayed out of the devolutionary scheme most of North Sea oil would, beyond argument, remain within the ownership of the UK since it was in Shetland waters according to the standard conventions. The island councils in fact persuaded Jo Grimond to propose an amendment to this effect, which was carried but subsequently removed.

Cunningham's rule was to have a major impact, both in providing a focal point for opposition to devolution itself in Parliament and during the referendum campaign. Cunningham gave a full account of it in an article published in *The Spectator* in January 1989, on the anniversary of his sensational success. He wrote that, in the middle of the second reading debate in 1976, the Cabinet reluctantly agreed to referenda in both countries. 'On the ground of that fatal concession,' wrote Cunningham, 'we planted the delayed-action bomb that later blew up devolution.' He continued:

> Beside those of us in the Labour Party who were prepared to vote directly against the Bill there were others who would only inflict wounds. We were a mixed bunch – future members of the SDP like Bruce Douglas Mann, Colin Phipps and myself, but also left-wingers like Eric Heffer, Dennis Skinner, Joan Lestor and, of course, the present leader of the Labour Party [Neil Kinnock].

They met regularly to plan strategy. At their first meeting after the summer recess in 1977 Robin Cook, then member for Edinburgh Central, said that during the recess he had found only one constituent remotely interested in devolution, and he turned out to be a member of the SNP. Cook opposed devolution but felt bound by the Labour manifesto commitment to it. He found the idea of a minimum test therefore very attractive but thought it should specify that a third of those eligible to vote should approve the proposition. The amendment was first proposed in this form by Bruce Douglas Mann. Cunningham's amendment to the amendment increased the minimum to 40 per cent. In two divisions the measure was included in the Bill on Burns Night of 1978.

Cook believed, when we conversed in 1993, that Foot had made a tactical error. Foot wanted to kill the percentage stipulation altogether and believed that if it were increased to 40 per cent its manifest absurdity would seal its fate. Cook advised Foot that in his judgment the calculation was misguided, and so it proved. Cunningham wrote:

On the day before the crucial vote was due, I overheard John Smith, Minister in charge of the Bill, say in an unguarded moment that the order of business was to be changed so that my amendment might not come to a vote at all. I rushed into the chamber, denounced the Government for skulduggery, and sent briefing to all members. The embarrassment forced Michael Foot to withdraw the idea. So it was that the 40 per cent test was voted into the Bill at one minute to eleven on January 25, 1978 – by 15 votes. The whips were surprised that my lists had been more accurate than theirs and sought revenge by another procedural abuse, hanging about in the division lobby to prevent Jo Grimond's Shetland amendment being called before the guillotine fell. But they reckoned without Myer Galpern, the ex-Lord Provost of Glasgow, who was in the chair that night. Myer despatched the Sergeant at Arms into the division lobby, sword in hand, to sort out the whips. As Big Ben started to strike eleven Jo moved his amendment and the Government went down to another heavy defeat. As one member of the press lobby said, it was a Burns Night massacre.

In 1993 Walter Harrison, the Labour deputy chief whip, gave me an explanation of what happened. There were three divisions in rapid succession – the Cunningham amendment changing the Douglas-Mann amendment from 33 to 40 per cent, the original amendment as altered and the Grimond amendment. The whips had been trying to prolong the divisions in the hope that the Grimond amendment would not be taken. Had they succeeded, it would have fallen victim to the guillotine. He recalled he 'had been pinned against the wall' in the lobby. The Cabinet's embarrassment, when it met the next day, is recorded in Tony Benn's *Diaries*.

The Government's second mistake came when it sought to remove the Cunningham amendment on report stage. It chose not to do so itself but left the task to a back-bencher, the maverick, loveable and infuriating Dennis Canavan. It came as a surprise to no one that he failed. Cunningham wrote:

> I could not have asked for a better man – Dennis Canavan was as unlikely a
> person to win over waverers then as he is today. Michael Foot made the mistake
> of speaking too early, leaving me with almost the last word in a highly charged
> House. We won by 45 votes.

Cook failed to secure approval for his amendment to bring the threshold down to 33 per cent. Perhaps Callaghan came close to blaming Cook and Cunningham for his Government's defeat in the 1979 election. But the industrial troubles of the 'winter of discontent' more gravely damaged confidence in its competence. Strikes by lorry drivers and 1.5 million workers in the public sector coincided with a winter of exceptional severity. The nation's television screens were full of apocalyptic images of anarchy and incompetence.

The failure of the Yes vote to achieve 40 per cent in the referendum meant that under the terms of the Cunningham amendment the Government was obliged to move an order repealing the Scotland Act. Cunningham estimated that 100 Labour back-benchers would not follow the party line of opposing repeal. The 11 SNP MPs made their demand that Callaghan proceed with the motion and put on a three-line whip to secure its defeat.

It was a pivotal moment in British politics. Michael Foot takes up the story. He revealed that a compromise was available to Callaghan that might have bought time, allowing the Government to run to its term in the autumn and might even have prevented the election of the Thatcher administration.

On 4 March, the Sunday after the referendum, Foot rang Callaghan and told him there was a possible solution to the dilemma. His suggestion was that the orders repealing the Scotland Act should be laid. The House should be invited to vote against the repeal of the whole Act. But, 'as an encouragement to our anti-devolutionists not to sabotage the proposition', an assurance would be given that the Act would not be put into operation until the next Parliament. The matter could thus be considered afresh by the electorate. This seemed to him a 'fair way round' for anti-devolutionaries, while retaining respect for the majority verdict in the referendum itself. This was known as the 'Frankenstein' solution. It commanded much support in the party although the anti-devolutionaries did not care for it. Foot continued:

> However, it was evident from the start, even from that Sunday morning conversation with him, that he was going to be hostile, that he would consider the idea, but his enthusiasm was obviously muted, even on the telephone.

During the next few days, and at Cabinet meetings on 8 March and 15 March, it was evident that Callaghan had a different approach of his own. It was 'primarily' his idea that the Government should propose talks to the Opposition parties:

> He did not claim it was a solution, but I think believed that it might offer a way out . . . I think he believed it would sow some dissension in their ranks and at any rate would not involve any adverse decision against us.

Foot and the rest of the Cabinet went along with it because it did not entirely rule out the other solution:

> At the first Cabinet on the 8th, while not opposing him in any sense, I underlined that I would certainly wish, as would some others, to consider the matter very carefully before we were ever put in the position of recommending the House of Commons to reject the whole Scotland Act because of the vote on the referendum. That in my view would have played into the Scottish Nationalists' hands over a much longer period. And all of us who took this view had reserved our position.

The idea of talks held the field for the week or two that followed. Over the weekend of 16–18 March, it became apparent that the different parties, particularly the SNP, were taking up harder positions. There was much talk of the Tories putting down a motion of no confidence now that they had seen that the SNP was prepared to do the same.

On the evening of 21 March, the night before Callaghan was to make a statement on the Act, Foot went to him and proposed that a motion should be put down calling on all parties to respond to his invitation to talks, and that the repeal orders (for the Scotland and Wales Acts) should be debated in the week beginning 7 May. Foot recognised that there was a danger of this motion splitting the Labour Party afresh but it did offer the chance of taking the initiative out of the hands of the Tories or the Nationalists. The Tories might still put down their motion of no confidence but it would look weaker and the other opposing forces might by that time have been dissipated.

Callaghan appeared to give this idea a considerable welcome and in his own hand made an amendment to the proposed wording. He and Foot met at 8 p.m. At 11.20 p.m. – 'a late hour for him' – he rang and indicated that he did not think it would be right for him to proceed in this way:

> He did not give any very powerful reason but said it was clearer to proceed in the manner of merely proposing the talks themselves. I did not try to argue the matter that evening but suggested we might discuss the matter further the next morning before the Cabinet, and he agreed. However, nothing happened and it was only on my pressure that I got to see him for a minute or two before the Cabinet started. Normally my meetings before the Cabinet took place with him in his room upstairs and we would have ten or 15 minutes . . . But on this occasion he did not come down until the last moment and when I met him on the passage on the landing upstairs, he said he didn't think that we should discuss it any further.

Callaghan proposed to go ahead with the statement on laying the repeal orders without reference to Foot's proposed motion and had his way in Cabinet. An attempt by the Chief Whip to revive the matter at the end of the meeting failed. Foot continued:

> It seemed to me then, as it did on a number of other days afterwards, that his patience had suddenly snapped. He wanted to invite the election and the decision that would lead to it. It was, in my opinion, a very considerable error.

In our conversation, Foot also said:

> I'm not blaming or criticising him for it because he was fed up by all the attacks being made on him for manoeuvring to try to keep the party and the Government in office. He was fed up with attacks generally, the invective of the Tory newspapers. He'd been responsible for a similar motion about the Boundaries Commission when in the Labour Government in 1969. People thought he still felt the wounds of the attacks in 1969. He hadn't done anything wrong at all. He'd introduced an order delaying boundary changes.
>
> I felt devolution was the right thing for Scotland. I don't want Scotland to leave the UK because if it did we would never get a decent UK Government ever again.
>
> Of course our objective was beyond that: I wanted to keep the Government going until the autumn when we thought we had a better chance of winning. We'd made something of a new agreement with the trade unions after the winter of discontent which also would have kept us going over these two or three months.
>
> When Callaghan turned that down, we didn't have a strategy. We knew that the others would vote against us. I think Donald Stewart [the SNP group leader] would have much preferred the agreement to carry on though others in the SNP wanted the opposite course. When they voted they voted for their own demise.
>
> The Government had made a really big effort to carry through a decent

devolution, some of us because we were strongly in favour of that kind of government anyhow, real devolution. Some of them went along with it just for party or tactical reasons, including maybe Callaghan himself.

Callaghan made his statement, that the repeal of the Scotland Act would be laid before Parliament without delay, on 22 March. On Monday, 26 March, a meeting was held in Callaghan's room attended by Denis Healey, the Chief Whip, Merlyn Rees and Foot. Callaghan 'almost urged' that they should have no further talks with the smaller parties whatsoever. He seemed to think there was something 'discreditable' about their discussions with the Welsh Nationalists. Foot strongly contested this view. Healey and the others were strongly in favour of 'trying to do everything we legitimately could' to win the vote on the Wednesday night. Foot's note continued:

> As the discussion moved that Monday morning, I think his spirit revived some-what, although there were still signs that he believed we should even court the possibility of defeat.

The talks went ahead. The Pneumonoconiosis bill was brought forward to secure the support of the Welsh Nationalists. That same Tuesday discussions had been arranged between Roy Mason (Northern Ireland Secretary) and the Ulster Unionists Enoch Powell and James Molyneux, on an entirely private basis. (The Queen's Speech on 1 November 1978 had promised five more seats for Northern Ireland reflecting Callaghan's desire to secure the support of Northern Ireland MPs.) Foot continued:

> Here again there was nothing whatsoever for anybody to be ashamed of. These discussions derived from the approach which Enoch Powell had made to me three or four weeks before. But I told him the previous weekend that I doubted very much whether they could proceed further . . . Therefore that . . . had to be taken into account too . . . The paradox of Roy Mason's conduct of the affair was that he alienated the Unionists and the Social Democratic Labour Party in almost the same degree.

In his memoirs, Lord Donoughue, then head of the 'kitchen cabinet', confirmed Foot's impression of Callaghan's fatigue. He wrote that by then the Labour Government had more or less given up. The Liberals had indicated they wanted an early election before the EEC elections in June because they knew they would do disastrously in these. They also believed the Thorpe case would come to court in July and damage them even further. (Jeremy Thorpe had resigned as Liberal leader in 1976 after allegations made against him by the male model Norman Scott. In April 1979 he and others were found not guilty of conspiracy to murder Scott.)

Thus the loose coalition on which Labour depended was falling apart. The Government was just drifting to disaster. 'It was a curious experience to be in a Government that knows it will inevitably be defeated before long. It was like being on the sinking *Titanic*, although without the music. Neither ministers nor civil servants did anything.'

When the vote of confidence took place on 28 March Callaghan instructed that there was to be no wheeler-dealing to win lobby votes, and he specifically ordered Roy Mason not to try to buy off the Ulster Unionists (though this did not prevent the Labour whips from soliciting their votes and in the end securing two).

Before this, Donoughue described the mood in Downing Street during the Winter of Discontent, which broke Callaghan. 'There was a deathly calm in No. 10, a sort of quiet despair ... The Prime Minister was clearly very tired, both physically and mentally. It was equally clear that he was very unhappy at having to confront the trade unions. His whole career had been built alongside the trade union movement and he seemed to find it quite impossible to fight against it.'

Cunningham wrote in his article in *The Spectator* that 'mercifully the SNP had never been good on parliamentary procedure. They thought that only the Government could bring the repeal order to a vote, but they were wrong. They could have done it themselves and, if they had, there just might have been enough Labour rebels fearful to repeat their anti-government votes when the nationalists were poised to bring the Government down.'

This is an interpretation that Douglas Henderson completely rejected when we met in 1993. When Callaghan spoke contemptuously of the SNP being the first turkeys in history to have voted for Christmas, he was not, in Henderson's view, deliberately driving its MPs to vote against the Government. Hamish Watt, who had succeeded Henderson as whip, was appalled by the prospect of his electoral destruction at his own hand; for him Callaghan was talking no less than the truth, for he (Watt) was being asked to behave 'like a fool'. One theory was that Callaghan, sensitive to taunts of being in the power of the SNP, thought he could finesse it and sneak through to survival. Foot recollected that his spirits had rallied to the point 'he thought there was every reason to do everything we could to win'.

According to Henderson, Callaghan had been advised he would win the vote or at least tie. The whips calculated that two SNP doubters might abstain – Watt and George Reid. Both Watt and Reid had come to the SNP from other parties, Watt from the Tories whom he had come to hate, and Reid from Labour. In 1993 Watt told me that he was not a nationalist, for he disliked nationalism; but he wanted a Scottish parliament.

Harry Ewing recalled that he had taken a much less sanguine view than some of the whips. He told Callaghan, who had consulted him, that only Reid was a possible waverer. (I recalled Reid coming to my house in Edinburgh in the early Seventies and over a drink telling me of his decision, after an agonising internal debate, to switch to the SNP. In Parliament he made Henderson's life a bit of a misery by the frequency of his intended resignations. At regular intervals Henderson would receive a letter from Reid informing him of his imminent resignation which would be followed by a major series of speeches on social democracy. After the 1979 election Reid went to Geneva to work for the Red Cross and Watt later fell out with the SNP group in Grampian Region.)

In the circumstances every vote was vital but Harrison decided that the Labour MP Dr Alfred Broughton, who had heroically offered to be present, was too ill to travel from Yorkshire; he died the following Saturday. Harrison recalled that, because of the intense scrutiny of the press, Broughton had stopped answering the phone and it had been necessary to use an elaborately coded procedure to maintain communication. Foot believed that Dr Broughton's absence, and the failure of the SDLP member Gerry Fitt and the Irish Republican MP, the late Frank Maguire, to support the Government, was the 'double blow' that brought it down.

Henderson believed the Government's major miscalculation was to have underestimated the hatred that Maguire had for British policy in Northern Ireland. Maguire and Fitt had sustained the Government in 1976 after defeat had driven it into the Lib-Lab Pact. Fitt had become increasingly disillusioned with the Callaghan Government. He had been incensed by the deals it was prepared to make with the Ulster Unionists and felt deeply patronised when Callaghan, in a clumsy attempt to woo his vote, invited him to his room and, though habitually grippy with drink, offered him a gin. The price of his support, Fitt indicated, was the dismissal or resignation of Roy Mason.

Maguire made a rare excursion from Fermanagh to London. According to the account of Henderson and others, the whips locked him up in their office with liberal quantities of whisky. They escorted him into the chamber in time for the division. He was smiling broadly and all seemed well. But when the time came he stood behind the Speaker's chair, with his arms folded, and refused to move. Henderson recalled that the whips tried to pull him into the lobby but he stood firm. Through his bluff, according to this account, he had the satisfaction of bringing down the Government. Later he told Henderson: 'I came to abstain in person!' Watt's memory was that he was simply too intoxicated to vote.

Something more serious may have been in question. Ewing believed that Maguire was dissuaded from supporting the Government by Fitt, who had become completely estranged from Mason. Fitt confirmed that this was the case when we spoke in 1993. According to some accounts, the real explanation for Maguire's failure to support the Government was that he was intimidated by terrorists. Robin Cook in 1993 recalled that on the day of the crucial vote he was followed to Westminster from Ireland by his wife and 'two men in raincoats'. They never left his side.

Harry Ewing had no recollection of this but found it perfectly credible. In those days security in Parliament was still relaxed. Fitt himself dismissed the idea of IRA intimidation. He did say that Maguire was close to the IRA. The men in raincoats, I infer, could have been IRA 'minders'. Cook's view that their presence was minatory was corroborated by Walter Harrison. On the night the Government fell, Harrison had hidden away somewhere in the Palace of Westminster – even 14 years on he would not tell me where – two Ulster Unionist MPs. He did not name them but scrutiny of the division list on 28 March indicates that they were John Carson and Harold McCusker. They voted with the Government. He had been given the promise of their votes and was trying to prevent the operation of what whips call the 'revolving door'. A whip may secure the vote of one MP but his support may repel another: one comes in but another goes out, hence the metaphor. Harrison feared that if Maguire or Fitt found out about the Ulster Unionists, there was no chance of their supporting the Government. There was little chance anyway, as Harrison recognised early in the day. He never tried to wheedle Maguire or Fitt. He took no for an answer from Fitt without further argument and, conscious of the men in raincoats, marked Maguire down as pretty doubtful. Foot had an enormous regard for Fitt's courage but thought, when we talked in 1993, that it would have also been more than his life was worth to have supported the Government. Later, as Leader of the Opposition, Foot recommended Fitt for a peerage. A reflection of the universal respect in which he was held came when Mrs Thatcher endorsed this on a bipartisan basis by putting him on the Government's list rather on that of the Opposition.

Harrison advised the Chief Whip that he thought the Government was about three short. But he took his two Unionist birds away to a secret nest while his colleagues worked on Maguire and Fitt. Sufficient ambiguity may have then entered the calculation to encourage Callaghan to take the gamble but his dismissive references to the SNP also suggest that he was pretty fed up anyway and did not much care if it worked. Smith said:

> I think it was true Callaghan was fed up. He thought we might win the vote. Maguire was supposed to come. It was close enough to gamble . . .

Smith confirmed Foot's view that Callaghan was influenced by the attacks launched on him when he delayed boundary changes in 1969. Smith continued:

> That was heavy on his mind . . . He had got such a terrible attack over that. He thought there was a price you did not pay, a kind of unseemly hanging on to office with all sorts of curious deals . . . That sort of thing, trying to be a Smart Alec, did not appeal to him.

The motion of no confidence was carried by 311 votes to 310. Harrison, who had hoped for the votes at least of Watt and Reid, and perhaps of another, recalled that there had been much whispering among the SNP members throughout the night. He had addressed them as a group three times in the course of the evening. Watt told me he spent an absolutely miserable evening. His constituency party had mandated him to vote with the Government. He had been elected in Banff by Labour voters and knew they would reject him, as indeed they did, should he help to bring Mrs Thatcher to office. He recalled that Gordon Wilson, in particular, had placed him under the most extreme pressure. This tended to confirm my own subjective conclusion – that Donald Stewart, Watt and Reid were all deeply unhappy about voting against the Government. Watt had the impression that Walter Harrison, by the time the divison was called, thought the Government had sneaked through and did not care so much about what the SNP would do. This came as something of a relief to Reid and himself. After the division, some SNP and Labour members thought the Government had just won. A teller, Jimmy Hamilton (Motherwell North), gave a misleading thumbs-up. When Watt realised the truth, it is said that he tried to 'cancel' his vote – permissible if you can get to the other lobby in time. He made a dash for it but it was locked just as he reached it. According to the folklore, he beat despairingly at it, demanding entry in vain. In conversation he told me that this was not true; he did discuss reversing his vote with the Labour whips but the lobby door closed before any conclusion could be reached. John Stradling Thomas, Number Three in the Tory whips' office, apparently dined out on an anecdote from that night. Using a pre-arranged code, he indicated to Mrs Thatcher that they had won by one vote by raising one finger. He used to remark that he was forever grateful that they had not won by two. Murdo Maclean, the Glaswegian civil servant who carries out the delicate negotiations between Government and Opposition at Westminster (he is private secretary to the Chief Whip but known as 'Usual Channels'), then visited Mrs Thatcher to negotiate the terms on which parliamentary business might proceed until the election.

In this atmosphere of tragi-comedy did Labour lose office. Had he played his cards right, Callaghan might have soldiered on. But his big mistake had been late in the previous summer when he decided, at the last minute, against an October election. Cook was at the printer's getting his election literature run off when the stunning news of the postponement came through. Cook recalled that very little attention had been given to proposals on public-sector pay on the assumption that an election would supervene. Out of such carelessness was the winter of discontent born. Perhaps Callaghan 'bottled out'. Perhaps he liked being an elder statesman a little too much.

His miscalculations ushered in the Thatcher years. The Conservatives were elected and the SNP crashed to two seats. A squeeze forced many older industries to shut up shop. Labour entered a prolonged nightmare as the Bennites assaulted the party machine. And civil war broke out in the SNP.

Cunningham was one of the Labour MPs who left to join the SDP. He later became chief executive of the Library Association and retired in 1992. He told me in a conversation in 1993 that the significance of the rule was that it made opposition to devolution more credible. Until then the 'juggernaut had been bowling along with no thought that it could be stopped'. He was bitterly attacked at the time for introducing what was described as a new principle but could point to many international examples of constitutional change requiring to pass a minimum test of public endorsement. Afterwards he discovered that Denmark had a constitutional test almost exactly similar to his own famous rule. The West Lothian question, he felt, was insoluble within the existing Westminster framework but thought that more people were coming round to the only answer, a federation of England, Scotland and Wales.

At home in Edinburgh the devolutionary dream dissolved. It had become clear that it was going to be much closer than all those early opinion polls had suggested. For Eric Mackay and those of his colleagues who had devoted so much energy to the campaign, it was a bitter disappointment. Neal Ascherson, one of the journalists who had come north to be in on the excitement, packed his bags and went back to London. Like the rest of us he had over-estimated the strength of devolutionary feeling. As John Maclean had come to hope towards the end of his life in 1923, Tom Nairn had predicted that nationalism would overcome class divisions. Its cohorts would smash the failing post-imperial state. The residuum of Scottish journalism was not enough for Ascherson, and he resumed his career as a commentator of international standing. The loss of a proper Scottish political agenda was felt keenly enough by those who stayed behind.

Eric himself had believed passionately in the rightness of the cause. Perhaps subsconsciously the reasons were partly professional. He saw that a parliament in Edinburgh would enhance *The Scotsman*'s importance and its claim to be Scotland's national newspaper. The circulation had risen throughout the Seventies to an all-time record, for one month, of just over 100,000 (it stood at the time of writing in 1993 at about 86,000). Much later, when I was editor of *The Herald*, our circulation controller John Wallace said he thought at the time *The Scotsman*'s claim of 100,000 represented an over-estimate of one month's figures and on the historic table of circulation figures the maximum for any six months is given as 98,000. But Eric was pretty pleased at the time. The Eighties dissolved into disappointment and industrial troubles, and for this generation life at *The Scotsman* was not the same again.

We overcooked devolution but we weren't the only ones. In the real world among the ordinary folk away from the taverns of the chattering classes, and especially outside the central belt, there was much scepticism. Of the rural regions only the Highlands (and the Western Isles) voted Yes and the positive vote was largely concentrated in Labour's industrial heartland. Labour campaigned for a Yes but eschewed an alliance with nationalists or Sillarsites. There were significant dissident voices, like Tam Dalyell, Brian Wilson, and Norman and Janey Buchan. Yet, for all its hesitations, Labour had got out the vote; the lukewarm and splintered SNP had not. Some of its MPs, like Henderson, detested the Act as a fake and an insult. The Conservative Party officially campaigned for a No. The dissident devolutionaries fought, some actively like Buchanan-Smith, some passively. Splintered, incohesive, the Yes campaign was a disaster. John P. Mackintosh was sorely missed.

By contrast Teddy Taylor masterminded a pungent and brilliant No campaign. While the Yes side struggled with hardly any finance, Taylor was well funded. Nationalist conspiracists have suggested (in the book *Britain's Secret War*) that the state intelligence services put money into the No campaign. The book's low level of accuracy must undermine its conclusions but it is an enjoyable bar-room speculation. We shall never know the truth of that. The No side had all the best tunes and played them well. The mercantile classes thundered of the danger of exclusion. Insurance companies made apocalyptic threats to decamp. One even more or less ordered its staff to vote No.

I think I realised the game was a bogey when Sir Alec Douglas-Home appeared on the television to advise a No vote because the Act as it stood was unsatisfactory; we should wait for something better to come along. It was a magnificent if somewhat hammy performance. This quavering old aristo, this loyal servant of the British state, had done his bit for the Union once again. He had spelled out his doubts about the Bill during the debate in the House of Lords, and his anxieties were principled (despite the taunts he had to suffer). He had sought to address the West Lothian question by including a provision that Bills referred to the assembly should be certified by the Speaker to apply only to Scotland. But it was a sad moment. Sir Alec, having flirted with devolution, now banished the old girl because she hadn't passed the medical. It was he, too, who had helped Churchill evade the expectations he had raised with his quasi-nationalist rhetoric in 1950. Contemporaries believed, when we talked in 1993, that this was a weight on his conscience. It explained his endorsement of the Declaration of Perth, his committee's devolution scheme of 1970 and his constructive attempts, during the Lords debates on the Scotland Bill, to find solutions to the West Lothian question.

The referendum remains the best evidence we have yet had of how Scottish opinion is likely to respond when faced with hard rather than theoretical ideas. It should not be forgotten that a majority of 51.6 per cent of those who voted did so in the affirmative. Nor is it fanciful to assert that had there been a clear political consensus in favour of devolution Scotland would have endorsed it convincingly. In fact the result was not so surprising. It was Labour's measure and the rest of Unionist, Conservative or Liberal Scotland viewed it with suspicion as a formula for Labour dominance. The assembly, its diet of powers steadily reduced by a centralist civil service and Parliament, was an emaciated figure by the time the Scotland Act staggered through the final stages. It raised problems so severe that constitutional tensions between England and Scotland must have flowed from it as Thatcherism rose in England and fell into disrepute in Scotland. The abstention rate of 36.4 per cent of the official electorate testified to a nation's confusion. The part that the two parties had played in creating this confusion raises questions. Was it the calculated response of the British state, absorbing, placating, wearing out and defeating threats to its coherence and integrity? Or was it all just an enormous muddle by a Government which had failed to deal with its central challenge – the need to confront the labour movement and remove the rigidities from the labour market which independent economists, and Conservatives, had identified as being a key cause of industrial decline?

The referendum demonstrated to Unionist politicians in the Eighties that home rulers could not muster a workable alliance capable of producing change. That remains as true today as it was then. Yet a more sensitive reading of the referendum result must show that for all the uncertainties and doubts Scotland expressed very considerable unhappiness about the way the Union was working. The discontent grew through the Thatcher Eighties but the SNP was unable to exploit it. The reason why the Union survives is that, despite what the opinion polls imply, there is a rock-like alliance between Conservatives and Labour in favour of it. So far the Nationalists have only knocked a few chips off it. The devolution years made it wobble but it stayed on its plinth firmly enough in the end. The opinion polls continue to give the same message but the constitutional issue is invariably given a relatively low rating in tables of political urgency. When these lines converge on the graph the desire for home rule will become much more difficult to resist.

CHAPTER EIGHTEEN

Pushing water uphill

Of all the Scottish politicians of the post-war period none has had more obvious political gifts than Jim Sillars. He has everything: he is a brilliant debater and skilful parliamentarian, a pungent writer, a trenchant propagandist; he has passion and sincerity. His deficiencies are equally obvious. He lacks patience, he is impulsive, he can take the huff and his judgment can suffer as a result. The political wilderness is familiar territory for him, and his career shows that personal relationships are a more important aspect of politics than most historians acknowledge.

In 1993 I met Sillars for lunch in the Caledonian Club in London, just round the corner from the office in Belgrave Square where he was working for the Arab Chamber of Commerce. He told me a story about himself which, he said, explained his character. When he was 15 he was apprenticed to a plasterer and was one of a team working on a job. Although he was the junior apprentice he found he was expected to do the labouring. On further inquiry he discovered from the boss that the job had been priced to allow for three labourers, a junior apprentice, a senior apprentice and a journeyman. The boss had not employed any labourers; he was skimming more profit by making the junior apprentice do the donkey work. Sillars walked off the job. There was an enormous row. His father was called to a meeting. But it was to no avail and that day the plastering trade lost a recruit. This story reveals Sillars's impulsiveness and a refusal to accept dishonourable compromise. Few politicians reach senior office without swallowing at least some principles in the larger cause. Sillars has always found this exceptionally hard to do. His is a restless political spirit. He is principled to a fault, and once or twice has nearly bankrupted himself in the pursuit of ideological honesty.

He has written, in his book *Scotland: The Case for Optimism*, of the agonies he felt when, with his friend the Paisley MP John Robertson, he left the Labour Party to form the Scottish Labour Party. Turncoat and traitor were among the milder terms of abuse (though he used his own mastery of invective to give as good as he got). As Willie Ross remarked, there is for such people a special kind of hell.

Sillars had been raised in the Labour culture. He began as a railwayman like his father, served in the Navy, joined the fire brigade and was active in its union. When an injury made it impossible for him to continue as a fireman, he became a party hack in the Ayrshire Labour Federation and later joined the staff of the Scottish Trades Union Congress before being chosen, by one vote, as the Labour candidate for the South Ayrshire by-election of 1970. Unlike the Labour movement in Glasgow, which had strong roots in the Irish Catholic working class, the Ayrshire Federation was both nationalist and presbyterian in its culture. In 1993,

Michael Foot remarked in conversation that Willie Ross, the most effective politician that the Ayrshire Labour tradition ever produced, was 'a bit of an Orange-
man'. In fact, as John Smith reminded me in 1993, the Ayrshire tradition was not
Orange but covenanting. He recalled that when Sillars had been fighting the by-
election in South Ayrshire:

> There were some people who said Tam Dalyell would not be welcome in certain
> villages because of the recollection of his ancestor who had put their ancestors to
> death – Bloody Tam Dalyell, the founder of the Royal Scots Greys. He attacked
> the covenanting conventicles and put them to the sword. Some of the villages
> might have given Tam a warm welcome.

The STUC was also strongly nationalist in the sense that it resisted amalgamation
by or absorption into the TUC, which was consistently hostile to its autonomy and
hoped it would wither on the vine. The point to remember is that Sillars grew up in
a tradition that was both socialist and intensely Scottish.

Margo MacDonald first encountered Sillars during her victorious by-election
campaign in Govan in 1973. Sillars, appalled by the inadequacy of the Glasgow
Labour establishment and the poverty-ridden constituency, worked against her
with increasing despair about Labour's relevance and prospects. They became
friends but their friendship did not become romance until the referendum
campaign of 1979 when they conjoined against the indifference of the major
parties. (Sillars joined the SNP in 1980 and married MacDonald in 1981, a date I
remember easily because it was a front-page story not long after I had become
editor of *The Herald*).

Sillars's career cannot be understood without reference to Ross. Eventually
they did not rub along. This was a painful matter for Sillars, because in his
formative years in the Labour movement he had been Ross's protégé. When Sillars
won the Ayrshire South by-election in 1970, taking 54 per cent of the vote and
containing a strong SNP challenge from his old sparring partner, the Labour
apostate Sam Purdie, Ross said of him: Here is a future Secretary of State. Harry
Ewing believed he regretted this remark and spent much time trying to live it down,
not because of anything Sillars had done but because it had greatly annoyed many
senior Scottish Labour politicians who thought they had a superior claim to preferment. Ross was to say sourly that while everybody thought of Sillars as a future
Secretary of State, Sillars thought of himself as the next Secretary of State. Ross was
fond of saying such things, John Smith recalled, but did not really mean them.

To observers it became clear in the early Seventies that Ross had turned
against Sillars. I had lunch with Ross in Rule's, London, in about 1972 and he
spoke of his dislike of those who thought they could run before they had learned to
walk. I am pretty sure he was referring to Sillars. Ross said he wanted loyal helpers
prepared to earn their spurs in committee but, as John Smith remarked in 1993,
there were 'a lot of people that Willie didn't like'.

When the death of Emrys Hughes created a by-election in South Ayrshire,
John Pollock could have had the nomination for the taking. He was Hughes's heir
by right and service. He declined, having no taste for a Westminster career, the
constant travelling and the 'basic removal from everything in Scotland'.

John Pollock told me in 1993 that he believed that had Willie Ross been a
more imaginative man he could have kept Sillars in the Labour Party. Reading
between the lines of Sillars's book *Scotland: The Case for Optimism*, one can sense

that Sillars desired Ross's approval. His contempt is for the 'careerist' time-servers and cronies on whom Ross relied. The book contains a revealing episode. Sillars and Ross were travelling back to Ayrshire on the same train. Deeply troubled by the SNP threat, Sillars had written a long memorandum on how Labour should respond. It included a recommendation for devolution. He had shown it to his friends, flatmates and fellow Labour MPs, Harry Ewing and Alex Eadie. Before they settled down for the night on the sleeper, Sillars gave it to Ross, who read it overnight and handed it back in the morning with a dismissive comment. The subtext, perhaps, was that Sillars as a novice MP had got above himself. As they walked down the hill from the station at Kilmarnock, Sillars tried to explain that his concern was not for the SNP but for the condition of the Scottish people. 'Ross is a most difficult man to engage in a dialogue unless he is telling you something. I got nowhere with him.'

Their relationship deteriorated. MacDonald said: 'Willie didn't really like him. He wouldn't even give Sillars a lift to the station.' Sillars's friendship with John Robertson, a Ross discard who had taken to the Commons watering holes with perhaps excessive dedication, could not have pleased Ross. On Sillars's questing and troubled political consciousness Robertson was to have a considerable influence. MacDonald got on better with Ross than did Sillars. He showed her a significant act of kindness when she arrived at Westminster for her brief stint as SNP member for Hamilton in 1973; in the tea room he gruffly but kindly showed her the way to read a Bill, the preamble and the schedules. She said: 'Willie was a very unimaginative man. He preferred people who knew their place. So it wasn't just Jim.'

John Pollock observed when we talked at his house in Longniddry in 1993 that Sillars found being at Westminster 'terribly frustrating'. He added:

> This is what happens to people when they get into the structure of government. Things get hyped in the Scottish press and television but when you go south you find these things are terribly small. And then there is an inability to get things done. For Jim it was the frustration of a socialist. Jim has always been pretty impulsive. He's so full of energy, so full of ideas. There was no way he could just accept the normal plodding pace that other MPs were running at.

Pollock thought that Willie's biggest failing was that he did not like criticism:

> Willie gave absolute loyalty to the party and Harold Wilson and he expected the same from everybody else. He was quite savage in his criticism of individuals who were in fact very good supporters of his but who argued against his view on any issue. Jim was just too independent of mind to agree with everything that was said.

Sillars's first response to nationalism had been to oppose it head-on. After her victory at Hamilton in 1969 Mrs Winnie Ewing came to a public meeting at Ayr and made an 'offensive and venomous onslaught' on the Labour Party. Sillars saw red as she boasted of her virtues and 'poured scorn on the kind of people I knew and respected'. Some idea of the pain that Sillars was to cause himself by leaving Labour can be sensed from the following passage from his book as he describes his feelings on hearing Mrs Ewing:

The Labour Party is the most important institution in the history of the working people and that part of the intelligentsia which gives itself to progressive causes. Labour was not born in a vacuum but emerged from a movement of struggle for justice which had its roots buried in the formative years of the industrial revolution. The heartbreak, the sense of solidarity, and the stepping-stone victories of that struggle are in its genes.

The result of Sillars's anger was a pamphlet, signed also by Alex Eadie, called *Don't Butcher Scotland's Future*. This was followed by *Exposed: The Truth about the SNP*. Both sold out. But when he retained his seat in South Ayrshire in the general election of 1970, his beaten SNP opponent Sam Purdie made a speech which was to haunt Sillars: 'I don't know what Mr Sillars is so happy about. His party has just swept the board in Scotland again but now we have a Tory Government we didn't vote for.' His doubts grew during the years of the UCS work-in and the STUC-sponsored assemblies to protest against rising unemployment. Quite early in his parliamentary life, he ceased to be a Unionist. His fear that the Scottish interest would be swamped in a larger political and economic system carried through to the European question and explained his decision to oppose membership of the EC. He campaigned against it in the 1975 referendum (a position which aligned him with the SNP).

However, his opposition both to the SNP and to EC membership had a quixotic impact on him. This is quite clear from a speech he made in the Commons on 3 May 1972. Here we find Sillars's political attitudes in transition. His work in gathering material with which to bash the Nats had stimulated an interest in the history of Scottish nationalism, and he spoke of it with authority and insight. And he showed his perception that European membership would change many of the calculations that had for so long locked Labour into the Union. Sillars was to enunciate this formally as policy after the referendum endorsed European membership in 1975 when he led the breakaway Scottish Labour Party, but the perception was dawning on others too in 1972. John Pollock recalled:

> I gave evidence to the Royal Commission that Scotland's future was as an integral part of the UK. In 1972 I wrote to Willie Marshall [Labour's Scottish Secretary] that all our evidence to Kilbrandon would be invalidated by our EC membership. That was because the minute you accept that in the long run the major dominant economy to which Scotland belongs is the European economy then that removes the restrictions that you must have relating to the specific relationships with England within the UK.

Sillars said when we met in 1993 that he came to hate Westminster. But as a new boy he spent much time in the chamber listening to the great parliamentarians of the day – Wilson, Heath, Jenkins, Crosland, Macleod, Powell. In the corridors, smoke rooms and tea rooms he found himself associating with Robertson, Ewing and Eadie. Robertson had entered Parliament after winning the Paisley by-election in 1961 but had made little mark. Sillars wrote:

> John was sunk in political gloom, going through the motions of being an MP. He was openly despised by Willie Ross; his opinion was rarely sought and no-one listened to his speeches. The snobbish clan who ran the Scottish group in the early and late Sixties, Peggie Herbison, Willie Ross, Tom Fraser, and supporting

players like George Lawson of Motherwell, successfully shouldered John out into the cold.

Sillars believed the reason was the second speech made by Robertson in the Commons, in 1961, in which he had described the conviction to which he had moved – that the only answer was a Scottish government. Robertson was on the Right, Sillars on the Left, and they were an unlikely pairing. But they became close friends, sharing their thoughts on economics, self-government, and the 'Scottish cringe' – by which they meant their country's habits of deference and lack of self-confidence. Margo MacDonald said: 'John Robertson was important. He influenced Jim a lot. He was an intellectual. He liked a good drink but there was much more to him than that.'

Early in 1974 the four published a pamphlet, *Scottish Labour and Devolution*. In the February election the SNP's advance, to seven MPs, was too menacing to be ignored. At the Ayr conference in March, the party's uneasiness was obvious. A devolution motion was greeted with boos and shouts of derision. At a reception Willie Ross was 'woundingly insulting' to John Robertson. But the national executive's decision against devolution in June was reversed at the Dalintober Street conference in September, and by now it was a stampede towards devolution. The party went into the October election with a commitment to a Scottish parliament. The Scottish manifesto (but not the British manifesto) said it should have substantial executive powers in the fields of trade and industry. As the threat from the SNP grew, Sillars recalled that even Tam Dalyell became a convert to a parliament 'with teeth' which, he said, could be working by the autumn of 1976.

When Parliament resumed Sillars was suspicious of the leadership on two counts. First, he thought they would try to silence him by giving him a junior job in a UK Department. He declined Wilson's offer of an under-secretaryship in the DHSS. He broke the code further by revealing to the Scottish press the fact that he had turned Wilson down; this indiscretion earned more disapproval from Willie Ross. In Harry Ewing's judgment, this was a decisive and even tragic moment in Sillars's career. Barbara Castle had positively wanted Sillars to serve under her. By now, Sillars recalled in his book, his admiration for Wilson had turned to 'contempt and distrust'. Once this decision had been taken, Ewing believed, Sillars's exit from the party was ordained, for now all doors were closed to him within it.

Sillars also became increasingly anxious about the strength of the party's commitment to the promises forced out of it under electoral duress. Eadie had already accepted a job at Energy and Ewing was the Scottish Office's devolution Minister with the rank of parliamentary under-secretary. He continued to share digs with them. Despite Ross's suspicion, Ewing and he were punctilious in respecting ministerial confidentiality. Ewing told me that Sillars, out of genuine delicacy, never asked him to breach it. But from other sources Sillars did learn of the resistance Ministers were meeting, as they tried to draw up the devolution legislation, from Whitehall departments and from Cabinet Ministers with contacts among North of England Labour MPs.

His conviction that Labour's commitment was reluctant and skin-deep was confirmed with the publication in 1975 of the White Paper, *Our Changing Democracy*. He was appalled by it. It was a scheme for a constitutional skeleton, with 'no flesh, no muscle, no power and completely pinned down by Westminster'. Above all, the assembly would have no economic power. The rest of the Scottish Group disagreed, holding that the White Paper met the manifesto commitment. That weekend Sillars had a meeting with two close associates outside Parliament – his old friend and aide from Ayr, Alex Neil, and the journalist Bob Brown. Neil has been a Sillars loyalist from their early days. He went with him into the SNP in 1980. Brown, former *Herald* news editor and Scottish correspondent of *The Guardian*, was a committed socialist, sufficiently trusted by the Labour Party in Scotland to be allowed to sit in on executive meetings as an observer and adviser. Sillars wrote: 'We decided the best thing was to quit and flush Labour's betrayal into the open'. On 10 December, he resigned from the Scottish executive and the Scottish Labour Group.

In his book, and in conversation, Sillars insists that the decision to form the SLP was spontaneous. He was undoubtedly egged on by journalists and others outside Parliament. Brown had planted the idea of a Scottish Labour Party in articles in *The Herald* under the pseudonym James Alexander. Other journalists active in an advisory role were Chris Baur, later editor of *The Scotsman,* and Neal Ascherson who had even, in a *Scotsman* article, gone so far as to say that a 'new Scotland' was emerging and that Sillars was its future Prime Minister. Today such claims seem ludicrously extravagant but in the nationalist euphoria of the time they did not seem unreasonable. *The Scotsman,* in particular, seized upon the possibility of the SLP and ran it on the front-page day after day. Our motive, as I recall, was journalistic as much as political. This was a good Scottish story; we were eager to develop the new Scottish agenda; and we wanted to show the paces of our star, Neal Ascherson. Opinion polls too showed an apparent degree of public support for the SLP, though in answer to a hypothetical question.

Sillars's disillusion, sense of rejection and impatience all combined to drive him towards a step that, given the political promise with which his gifts endowed him, must surely now be regarded as a major misjudgment in career terms. He wrote: 'It was a typical Scottish rush down hill, with blood flooding to the head'. John Robertson joined the charge, with some reluctance. Bob Mellish, then the Labour chief whip, told Sillars he was wasting a great career over nothing. There would not be an assembly. The English MPs would not permit it. Sillars's account, later disputed by Mellish, was that he offered to resign on the promise of a prompt by-election. Some weight is lent to Sillars's version because he repeated the offer publicly in February 1976. In the event he and Robertson carried on as MPs until the end of the Callaghan Government in 1979.

Labour turned on them with bitter denunciations and personal insults, but they found few new friends. The SNP was not welcoming. MacDonald recalled:

> Jim and John Robertson never wanted to found a party. They wanted to operate as a group. I suggested they should be offered the SNP whip. Douglas Henderson said, Never. At one point he said of them, They're finished, washed up.

In fact Sillars and Robertson operated to all intents and purposes as if they were still taking the Labour whip. John Smith said in 1993:

> I went to Jim and persuaded him we could deliver the second Bill. I explained that we would take the Scotland Bill on the Monday, the Wales Bill on the Tuesday and guillotine them both on the Wednesday. Taking them on a roll like that was the first smack of a firm approach there had been. He thought that was quite good. He thought about it and came back and said, Yes, I think you can do it. I went to the chief whip and said, There's another two.

Walter Harrison, Labour's deputy chief whip, amplified this account:

> I had the same relationship with Jim as when he was in the Labour Party. I could trust him. We had a good working relationship. When he left the Labour Party of course, he didn't get the same service of communication about parliamentary business, and so on. So I became their unofficial whip. I did this without any official instruction, just as part of the job I was doing in the communications game. We would get warning in good time of what the future business was going to be. And I used to let Jim know.
>
> Because I gave something to Jim, he naturally communicated back. I would tell him when it was critical, whether it was a soft whip or a hard whip. This allowed Jim and John to arrange their business in Scotland. A lot of them [in the parliamentary Labour Party] didn't like me doing it.

But, as Harrison explained, he was there to sustain a Government. He took his decisions and he took the consequences. His relationship with Sillars remained very close, as this anecdote illustrates:

> On this occasion I rang Jim. He'd leave a message on his answering phone. On this Sunday morning we were on a critical vote on the Tuesday. The answering machine, in Jim's voice, said, I'm away on constituency business and with the bad weather prevailing will be away for some time. Leave your name etc. During the day I rang back on the hour. The same message was there, every time. I began to get worried. If I missed Jim on the Sunday, I would lose him once he got down to Westminster. At eight p.m. I rang once more. The same message came down the line. But this time there was an addendum. And if it's Walter Harrison, Yes, tell him I'm coming on Tuesday, said Jim's recorded voice.

The SLP had its inaugural meeting in January 1976. It very quickly fell apart in chaos, destroyed by activists from the International Marxist Group who had entered it. Sillars wrote of the trauma of leaving the Labour Party. He was tormented by the feeling of being a traitor. His soul was crushed by the emotional agony of viewing as worthless all that a few months before had been regarded as good. His burden of sadness was 'permanent and heavy'. But the recriminations were not all one-way. John Pollock recalled:

> For the bitterness that grew up Jim has a responsibility, because of the savage way he criticised his former colleagues after the breakaway, for example his criticism of the STUC where he had actually been employed and his criticism of individual members of Parliament who had been doing at that time what he himself had been doing recently. It created tremendous bitterness. And of course Labour have never tolerated people who've changed parties, or at least they've tolerated them going in but not going out. They've always regarded them as traitors to the working class and so on. So that bitterness that grew up made it difficult for those who were on the gradual path of trying to get devolutionary policies within the Labour Party and stopped the evolutionary process.

The remaining years of that Parliament were for Sillars a long goodbye. It was then, I suspect, that he came to hate Parliament. He had a contempt for most of the SNP parliamentary group. Some say Willie Ross, too, thought they were a rabble, a

Síol nan Gaidheal: procession in Lochgilphead (1982)

The Thatchers at Perth (1982)

Ernest Saunders (1985)

Malcolm Rifkind's post-election news conference. With him is Lord Goold, chairman of the Tory Party in Scotland (1987)

First meeting of the Conservative Scottish Business Group in Edinburgh. From left: Sir Ian MacGregor, Lord Goold and James Gulliver (1988)

Professor Ross Harper (1989)

Tories at the RSAC Club. From left: Neil Thomson, Brian Meek, Michael Forsyth and Malcolm Rifkind (1990)

Bill Walker (1992)

Malcolm Rifkind and Michael Forsyth (1990)

The SNP's Gordon Wilson (1992)

George Younger on Prestwick Airport's runway (1992)

John MacCormick (right), with Gilbert McAllister

SNP convener William Wolfe, at the Bannockburn rally, with the parliamentary leader from 1970–79, Donald Stewart

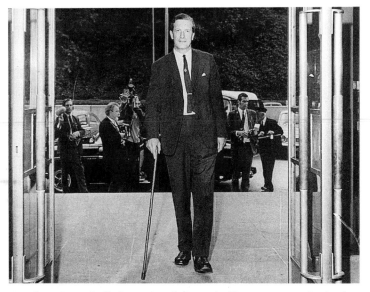

Gordon Campbell (later Lord Campbell) arriving at St Andrews House in 1970 to take up his duties as Secretary of State for Scotland in the Heath administration. The applause given him by some senior civil servants as he mounted the staircase made Willie Ross suspicious of them thereafter

discredit to Scotland because of the fondness some had for the more convivial side of Westminster life. MacDonald said in 1993:

> Jim never wanted to join the SNP. Winnie had shown a total insensitivity to work done in the community by Labour people. He was disgusted by the parliamentary group. He calls himself an atheist but he's really a Calvinist. Willie Ross found them disgusting too. He thought they gave Scotland a bad name.

The referendum campaign was a personal and political disaster. Sillars was in poor health, with an ulcer, and wrecked his personal finances by underwriting pamphlets and other activities. Labour's feeble campaign, its ability to ride two horses at once, convinced him that it was nothing but a 'self-serving, power-grabbing machine'. They were no match for the well-oiled, well-financed No campaign so brilliantly led by Teddy Taylor.

In the dying weeks of the Parliament Sillars lobbied hard to persuade the SNP not to bring the Government down, working particularly on the reluctance of Hamish Watt to do so. When that failed, he put up a good fight at the general election. He took 31.4 per cent of the vote. Labour's winner, George Foulkes, had 35.2 per cent.

Now Sillars began his journey to the SNP. The journey had for some time been inevitable. He had dragged his feet because of his distaste for the parliamentary group and for the anglophobia of its traditional wing. MacDonald said: 'Alex Neil took him into the SNP. He told him that if they were really serious there was nowhere else for them to go.'

When the 1979 Group was created, some commentators believed that its true purpose was to make it possible for Sillars to join the SNP. This MacDonald emphatically denied when she talked to me in 1993:

> We didn't form it to get Jim into the SNP. That had nothing to do with that. Stephen [Maxwell] and others of us had been trying for years to get the SNP to accept our basic strategy. It was now so clear. The people who voted Yes in the referendum were the people who had voted Labour in the general election and were likely to identify themselves as being working class. We now had the incontrovertible proof. It was recognising the group of people most likely to be converted to the idea of independence.

The SNP was about to enter a period of civil war that was to end in MacDonald's own resignation in 1983. Sillars's involvement in the campaign of civil disobedience in 1981 is discussed in the next chapter. But he rode out the crisis, was not expelled during the purge of internal groups, and survived to become the hero of the Govan by-election in 1988, the constituency where he had first fought as a party hack against MacDonald and had been appalled by the poverty and neglect endured by those who lived there.

In the SNP, his victory at Govan meant that he was, in MacDonald's words, 'walking on water'. He could have run for the leadership, when Gordon Wilson decided in 1989 to give it up, and might have won despite the traditionalists' dislike for him. He decided not to do so but his expectations that the party would unite behind Margaret Ewing were shattered by Alex Salmond's decision to run for the convenership. As a result of this episode Sillars and Salmond became estranged. The rift's beginning may be traced to the SNP's decision not to participate in the Convention for the Constitution summoned in 1988 by the Campaign for a Scottish Assembly.

It had become clear to Wilson that it had been used by Donald Dewar as an 'elephant trap' for the Nationalists, in that it would have committed the SNP in advance to a devolutionary conclusion. Salmond took a different tactical view though there was no strategic disagreement. He felt the SNP should go along with the convention to the point that it could be shown that it would not discuss independence as a serious issue or allow it to be presented to the people of Scotland. He also thought the SNP should argue within the convention for a multi-choice referendum (independence, devolution, the *status quo*).

On these tactics Salmond thought he had the agreement of Sillars. What happened next remains unclear except that there was a failure to consult Salmond about the decision to withdraw. Isobel Lindsay told me:

> Alex and Jim used to be so close. The split took place earlier than Jim's decision to support Margaret Ewing against him. Alex was the only office-bearer who was not consulted on the decision to withdraw from the Convention for the Constitution. In January 1988 the SNP had taken part in discussions. And then a week later they held a press conference to withdraw from the convention. It was taken by Jim, Gordon and Margaret. They said afterwards they had consulted all the office-bearers by phone except Alex who they said was unavailable. Now he wasn't unavailable. They assumed Alex, at the time a senior vice-president, would want to participate. That was the first time I had seen hostility openly expressed between Alex and Jim. Before that Alex would never criticise Jim. I was suprised that Gordon allowed this to happen.

Isobel Lindsay was one of those who dissented from the decision not to participate and allowed her membership of the SNP to lapse. The loss of so considerable an intellectual was a high price for the party to pay. Friends of Salmond did not blame Wilson for the failure to reach him. Though they acknowledged that their relationship had not been cordial ever since the 1979 Group expulsions, they dismissed as 'absurd' the idea that the two men had not spoken to each other for more than two years. Their belief was that Wilson had delegated the task of reaching Salmond. What puzzled Salmond was the fact that Sillars did reach him over that weekend – but did not mention the impending announcement even though some newspaper-men knew of it by then.

Their estrangement was compounded by Salmond's decision to contest the convenership in 1990. Again, what happened is not clear. Wilson had by now 'hit a wall of fatigue' and decided to give up. Sympathisers of Sillars told me that at a meeting in Dundee Wilson had indicated his preference for Margaret Ewing, believing Sillars to be the only other credible candidate. Wilson has acknowledged that such a meeting took place though he would say only that he made no secret of the fact that Ewing was his preferred candidate. In any event Sillars decided not to run because he wanted to unite the party and not stir up the old fundamentalist animosity. He believed that Salmond was not ready for leadership. He had come into Parliament only in 1987. He was inexperienced. He had not yet learned to handle people. Sillars, Alex Neil and others then held a series of meetings to persuade the party that Ewing should not be opposed. MacDonald said:

Jim was adamant that Alex Salmond wasn't ready. Margaret on the Monday said she would do it. Jim said we'll support you on the basis that it's a collegiate leadership. If Jim had run he would have won, he was walking on water, but he thought the SNP was on a roll and the last thing it needed was splits.

Friends of Salmond saw the matter differently. They believed that Salmond might not have stood against Sillars had he run. One said:

> The reason they wanted Margaret to be leader was to pull the strings behind her. Their support damaged her campaign very considerably. She lost control of her own campaign. Funnily enough, if Jim had decided to run himself, Alex might well have accepted that, in the sense that he felt there was a case for that. It would have been a seismic shock for the SNP, certainly. But at least it would have been an honest thing to do. What wasn't acceptable to Alex was the idea that you could run a party without being the convener of it. The whole idea was ridiculous and dishonest. But if Jim had gone upfront and accepted power and responsibility, such as it is in the SNP, then Alex might have had a different view of things.

Sillars endorsed Margaret Ewing's campaign but Salmond won overwhelmingly. Though he subsequently encountered difficulties on the national executive, his power rested on his support in the party at large.

By the time he lost Govan at the 1992 general election, Sillars told me that he had spent £44,000 of his own resources on nursing the constituency. His office there had become a kind of welfare service. Here he showed all his gifts as a demotic politician, for he knew that if he were to retain the seat he could only do it on the streets. He had a column in *The Sun,* by now an unlikely supporter of independence (as part of a Tory strategy to split the anti-Conservative vote by talking up nationalism), the fee for which he ploughed back into the constituency. This had the effect of making him *persona non grata* with some of the other media. He formed an alliance with the Roman Catholic archdiocese, at that time deeply incensed by the attitude of Strathclyde Region's Labour establishment to its denominational schools, many of which were facing closure. Sillars endorsed the Catholic position and the archdiocesan magazine, *Flourish,* returned the compliment (it was angered at one point by Neil Kinnock's failure to provide it with a response to an invitation to give his view of the educational issue and drew attention to it by running white space where Kinnock's reply should have been).

The Catholics' flirtation with nationalism was entirely tactical. It was a warning to the Labour establishment that Catholic support could not be taken for granted. In the 1992 general election Sillars was duly defeated by Ian Davidson, the Strathclyde councillor most closely associated with the programme of school reorganisation. After his defeat, Sillars went into a typical huff. On television he denounced Scots as '90-minute patriots' and departed once more into the wilderness. When we met in 1993 he told me, rather disgustedly, that Scottish politics had become trivial, a matter of 'roads and sewage'.

I do not think we have heard the last of Jim Sillars. For all the controversies that have followed him, you do not hear many people speak ill of him. George Younger said he was the best constituency neighbour MP that he ever had. When Sillars said he would do something, it was done. John Smith said in 1993:

> I get on very well with Jim. I never had a cross word with him, actually.

Others spoke with admiration of his parliamentary skills. Like all politicians of class, he has a coterie of devoted loyalists though he has a tendency to expect them to be acolytes. Just as much as Mrs Thatcher, Sillars needs clear-eyed friends rather than uncritical fans.

John Pollock believed that Sillars's major contribution was, by adopting the policy of Scotland in Europe, to have put Labour and the SNP on convergent lines. Ironically the policy was not adopted by the SNP until the Salmond leadership. Gordon Wilson could not have accepted it and there remains a significant anti-EC rump in the SNP. John Pollock said:

> In the long term you eventually get a situation in which more and more decisions are taken in Brussels and not in London. The potential is there for gradual constitutional change, with Scotland and England in a partnership with neither able to dominate the other but in which they are not separate either. By going for Scotland in Europe, the SNP has moved away from independence. The question for them now is: Which outside forum does Scotland participate in? It makes the SNP policy much more sensible but also pushes it towards what was always the basic Labour policy – that the first priority for Scotland in economic terms is that it must always be part of a bigger economic unit. The Nationalist route of doing everything at one fell swoop would cause short-term and there-fore possibly long-term chaos for the economy. But I am not so frightened now as I was at one time by the idea of the separate-path route for the English. If you have a gradual build-up of partnership then you do it without the revolutionary disruption, by evolutionary stages.

Pollock believed that Sillars had tried to shape the SNP in the image of his own Scottish Labour Party and that had Margaret Ewing won the leadership election he would have been king-pin of the party. To the young Alex Salmond has now fallen the difficult task of balancing off the factions but despite their estrangement he remains very much a Sillarsite: his nationalism is not cultural in its inspiration but founded on economic analysis. Ever since the pre-war days of John MacCormick the mainline nationalists have shown a distaste for the cultural fringe since it is a classic route for entryism by bampots and tartan terrorists. Salmond is a socialist. Above he all he owes to Sillars the policy of Scotland in Europe.

In Pollock's view, Sillars had not given up the hope of the leadership; he believed it was his destiny to change Scotland. Isobel Lindsay said:

> With Jim it's chemistry. He's a classic personality type. They're marvellous in certain situations. They're great in wars, at the high point of battles, a lot of energy, a manic force. But it goes hand in hand with enormous egotism and then things go into reverse in a dramatic way. It happened with the 90-minute patriot speech and it happened again in 1983. When Margo was expelled he went off in a huff to Saudi Arabia.

The thing to remember about Sillars, I conclude, is that he is a socialist first and a nationalist second – a proposition with which John Smith agreed in conversation – and that he is in painful exile from the movement in which he was raised and nurtured. I believe John Pollock is right in his assessment that he has tried to turn the SNP into a socialist party of the kind for which he strived in 1975 and 1976, and that the resistance he arouses in the SNP from the traditionalist wing flows inescapably from the party's heterogeneous nature. Sillars is not a cultural nationalist.

But I give the last word to Margo MacDonald, who loves him: 'Sometimes I say, Were we just wrong, Jim? He says, No, we weren't necessarily wrong. We were just trying to push water uphill.'

CHAPTER NINETEEN

Civil war

After the election of 1979 the barely suppressed animosities festering in the SNP broke out into open wounds. Gordon Wilson became chairman in September. The conference had been postponed from June because of the election. He was opposed but as one of the two remaining MPs had, as he said, 'something of an advantage'. He got about 60 per cent of the vote and began a period that was to test his political skills to the utmost. Many people to whom I spoke in 1993 felt that he mishandled matters, that he over-reacted to the crisis. I am not so sure. At some cost his decisive but instinctive action eventually made peace possible.

The party was exhausted and demoralised. There was disillusion with democratic processes. The quarrels that had gone between the parliamentary group and the intellectuals outside it were now crystallised. Wilson said: 'People did not know which way to go. And then they went in two directions. One group went towards fundamentalism and the other towards socialism.' Jacobites reappeared. There was, said Wilson, a curious mixture of 'Jacobinism and Jacobitism'. You have to remember, said Wilson, the political desert in which the party now found itself. The group was destroyed, there were only two MPs (Wilson and Donald Stewart), everything was 'swirling around and inchoate'. The same thing was happening inside the Labour Party. 'They had Militant. We had Siol nan Gaidheal (Seed of the Gael).'

The 79 Group, with its triple principles of independence, socialism and republicanism, was essentially the creation of a younger generation of party intellectuals and activists led by the full-time officials like Roseanna Cunningham, a research officer, and Duncan Maclaren, the press officer. Most of the histories attribute the group's emergence to Margo MacDonald or Stephen Maxwell but, according to Roseanna Cunningham, neither was present in the formative discussions. Gavin Kennedy, one of the moving spirits, was an authority on political entryism from his days in the Trotskyist Socialist Labour League. The leadership reflected the values of the older generation of nationalists. They felt uneasy with the radical left-wing attitudes of the 79 Group. Even the 79 Group was torn between two tendencies. People like Gavin Kennedy and Andrew Currie came from various points on the theoretical or hard Left. Alex Salmond was concerned about how the SNP should respond to the rapid de-industrialisation going on in the central belt, particularly in his home patch of West Lothian. Here members of the labour movement, identified by the 79 Group analysis as the ripest of political plums, were putting up significant if ultimately hopeless resistance in the form of worker occupations. Isobel Lindsay, who did not join the group, found its labourism old-fashioned and inappropriate when the old economy was dying. Stephen Maxwell hoped that the group would

166

not adopt old-fashioned labourism and instead espouse radical democratic politics. He lost. He recalled in 1993:

> I remember a meeting in [what is now] the Copthorne Hotel in Glasgow. We were getting big attendances at the time and there were about two or three hundred people, and we had a big debate about this. People who had been in the Labour Party came down like a ton of bricks on any idea of radical democracy, which put the stress on democratic institutions, rather than on traditional Labour Party policies like nationalisation.

In 1993 Salmond told me that he thought that the big mistake had been the group's espousal of republicanism, and Margo MacDonald confirmed that this had alarmed some otherwise sympathetic nationalists.

Siol nan Gaidheal was set up the same year; its favourite protest was to burn the Union Jack. It was called proto-fascist; and while it was infiltrated by extremists that was unduly to enlarge its importance. It recruited lads from the housing schemes and they marched about with their dirks and regalia. Wolfe became involved in it marginally, on the principle of keeping an eye on it (he had won the presidency in 1980 in a contest against Donald Stewart). Its Gaelic credentials were largely spurious. It fed off the boredom and dissatisfactions of the housing schemes, as Tommy Sheridan's Militant group was to do in the Nineties. Isobel Lindsay believed it was essentially harmless:

> It was opposed to my vision. But these were poor people from the schemes – Drumchapel, Easterhouse and so on – they had their flags, their bands, their regalia. To call them proto-fascists was ludicrous.

In 1981 Sillars made an emotional speech at the Aberdeen conference. He told the nationalists to put their money where their mouth was and spoke of cell doors clanging shut. Stephen Maxwell felt he was rather taken by surprise when his eloquence persuaded the conference, against the advice of the chair, to commit the party to civil disobedience. Shrewdly Wilson responded by giving Sillars the responsibility for carrying out the policy. It was his bed; let him lie in it.

The decision, however, produced a creative initiative from Alex Salmond, giving a sign that here was emerging a powerful political intelligence. The only thing you can't keep down, Wilson told me, is talent and Salmond has talent. He had been a member of the party since the age of 19. He joined the Government economic service from 1978 and the Royal Bank of Scotland as an economist in 1980. His proposals to put the conference resolution into practice showed a subtle mind at work. The campaign was within the law and it was aimed at the Labour grass-roots, bypassing the leadership. The soil was fertile, for in Scotland as in the UK generally, it was a turbulent period. There had been riots in Brixton and Toxteth. At the end of 1980 inflation stood at 15 per cent, unemployment at 8.8 per cent and manufacturing output had fallen by nine per cent; it was pronounced the worst recession for 50 years. In Scotland there was a spate of industrial closures to which workers responded with a series of sit-ins and occupations, notably at Plessey in Bathgate. In early 1982 Salmond produced a pamphlet called *The Scottish Resistance*. Apart from the foreword it was a compendium of workforce occupations, of which almost a dozen were taking place. At Plessey an SNP legal team, including the brilliant young advocate Jonathan Mitchell, went in to help the workforce. In a famous victory it secured the reversal by the courts of an interim interdict granted to the company to end the occupation. The propaganda value was enormous and it was legal. Once they got past the full-time union officials, Salmond recalled, they got an excellent response from the shop stewards. The Government as a result amended the law to make such occupations illegal beyond argument.

By contrast Sillars, the putative leader of the campaign, showed a much less certain touch. He and some supporters entered the Royal High School building in Edinburgh by breaking a window and scrambling through. Their intention was to hold a debate on Scottish unemployment in the chamber that had been prepared for the assembly. The leadership, including Wilson, was conspicously absent. The response of the authorities was low-key. Sillars was fined £100. This was no O'Connell Street, no Easter Rising. This was Scotland.

Wilson's desire to confront what he perceived as a parasitic growth of dissidence had to be postponed for 18 months. It had become clear to him by the 1981 conference, that there was a 'poison gathering in the party like a boil'. An attempt to confront the splinter groups in the national council failed. Both could combine to defeat the centre. 'At this point,' said Wilson, 'I had to fall back on patience.' Though he was often outvoted on the executive during this struggle for power, nobody could take him on and hope to win. Sillars was beginning to push his way through and the 79 Group was clearly split. 'It was rather like a civil war. There were lots of friends on opposite sides.' Isobel Lindsay, despite her left-wing credentials, was not in the 79 Group.

As the 1982 conference at Ayr approached, the turbulence in the party had produced a third force – that of fundamentalists reacting against the 79 Group. 'It was a very grim time,' said Wilson. The emergence of the new splinter was alarming. It was called the Campaign for Nationalism in Scotland. Set up by James Halliday and Winifred Ewing, it included Dr Robert McIntyre. Isobel Lindsay recalled: 'McIntyre was an evolutionist but with a strong dislike of socialism. He would say, Never use the word collective.'

On the eve of the conference Wilson had lunch with William Clark of The Herald and told him he thought a split could be avoided. Margo MacDonald recalled that he had even circulated to senior colleagues the text of a speech in which he said that the SNP was big enough to encompass different strands. What appeared to change his mind was a fringe meeting held on the eve of his speech by the Campaign for Nationalism. Members of the 79 Group went to the meeting and were subjected to considerable abuse. Clark had it all over the front page of The Herald the next day. Roseanna Cunningham told me in 1993 that she believed that the 79 Group people had been set up and lured into a stramash (which remained verbal). Wilson reacted badly to the headlines. He undoubtedly was also extremely concerned about the negative image being projected by Siol nan Gaidheal. That year their activities had brought disrepute on anyone associated with the SNP. Bill Clark remembered 1982 as the year in which the old easy attitudes to security at Scottish Conservative conferences ended, and the activites of Siol nan Gaidheal took some of the blame. In a note to me in 1993 he gave me this account of the Scottish Tory conference in May of that year:

> Inside the Perth City Hall the strains of the great organ soared to reach the highest notes of Elgar's Land of Hope and Glory. Emotions ran high as the 1500 Tory faithful prepared to welcome Prime Minister Margaret Thatcher.
>
> Outside the hall emotions were also running high, but in a different fashion. Siol nan Gaidheal, the nationalists' extremist wing, had earlier marched

to the city hall behind flags and Roman-style standards.

Their motley appearance had caused some amusement among the dozens of ordinary onlookers. Some wore leather jerkins, wild Tammies, kilts to the ankles, were bare-armed and bare-chested and chanted slogans of hate against Thatcher.

The police were wary of them but not alert enough. As the Prime Minister's car arrived alongside the side entrance to the hall a roar went up and more than a dozen of the Siol protesters charged down the street.

The Prime Minister in a kingfisher blue suit was looking relaxed in the evening sunshine but her smiles vanished as she saw the onrushing men. As police officers moved forward the party's Scottish director, Mr (now Sir) Graham MacMillan guided the Thatchers towards the door.

He pushed the Prime Minister through and in an instant the Siol members were at his heels. One swung back his foot and kicked him on the backside.

'I remember it all right,' said Sir Graham, who now lives in Bury St Edmunds. 'I had a damn sore leg for a spell. Mrs Thatcher was most surprised and not best pleased at what happened.

'She was very grateful to me for getting her in out of the squabble. But it was exactly the job I had done for other Tory Ministers.

'I saw it developing and realised things could turn ugly. That was the last time the police took a fairly relaxed attitude at conference. I was determined there would be no more of that.'

Mrs Thatcher's departure from the hall after her keynote speech was almost as undignified. The Siol supporters again made to charge and Mrs Thatcher, who had been waving to the crowd from the steps of the hall, was hustled into the rear seat by senior police officers.

This time it was Denis who suffered. He was heaved bodily into the front seat of the Jaguar and the car drove off at speed with his leg flapping from the open door.

The following year the Tayside Police threw what the press labelled 'a ring of steel' round the City Halls and sealed off all streets leading towards it. They even closed shops in the area bringing protests from the local Chamber of Commerce.

Isobel Lindsay made a perceptive comment about Wilson's habitual air of calm rationality. 'He was always very anxious to avoid the tinge of extremism. Under the surface Wilson was quite an emotional man, although the emotion was firmly repressed. He strongly disliked it when they sang *Flower of Scotland* at the conference, and this dislike flowed from strongly repressed emotions of his own.'

The SNP conference was held at Ayr, in what Wilson called a 'Zeppelin' hanger. The temperature rose to about 90 degrees, producing 'environmental politics' in the sense of hot tempers. Andrew Welsh moved a resolution reversing the policy on civil disobedience after the abysmal failure of the assembly break-in. Hostility to the policy was abated when the conference heard of Salmond's successful campaign aimed directly at the workforce, and this reduced the size of the majority by which the policy was abandoned. But the splits were now deep, wide and evident. Wilson had decided 'almost instinctively that it wouldn't disappear'. He reached the decisions the previous evening. 'I said that the following day I would propose a motion, which I had got through the agenda committee by one vote, that all groups, that is Siol nan Gaidheal and the 79 Group, should be disbanded.' He also said that the price of defeat would be his resignation. Lindsay said:

> I created a lot of enemies around that time partly because I supported banning the factions. In retrospect I think it may have been a mistake. I was in the chair and supported it. I thought the 79 Group was soft at the edges and that people would re-merge with the mainstream. That would have happened. Siol nan Gaidheal was minor. We should have tried to do something for the young people in the schemes. But when I saw the fundamentalists also organising themselves into a group, I knew they had clout. They were preparing to bring out a newsletter. I thought if they got going that would harden attitudes in the 79 Group and we'd never have an end to squabbling. There were quite a lot in the 79 Group who thought that this was all part of a plot, that Gordon Wilson was collaborating with the fundamentalists. They thought he knew that this group was going to be formed in order to give him the excuse to be even-handed. Now I'm almost certain that this was not the case because Wilson had very bad relations with Winifred Ewing and not particularly good ones with Robert McIntyre and some of the others involved. He did regard them as being in their own way troublesome. But I think there was enough strength of feeling in the party for the traditionalists to have done this off their own bat.

Andrew Currie was on the platform when Wilson issued his ultimatum. He rose and walked out. About 100 people followed him. Roseanna Cunningham recalled that as they filed out into the sunshine they were subjected to abuse from those who remained in the hall. Oaths flew. Get out and don't come back was the message delivered in pretty free French. Outside, they stood about on the grass without much idea of what to do or say.

About six months after the motion had been passed, the national council (the delegate body representing branches and constituencies and meeting four times a year) named the groups. Wilson said: 'That was my mistake. I should have named them in the conference resolution. On the other hand if I had done the motion might not have been carried.' The national council then named six people, including Margo MacDonald, Kenny MacAskill and Alex Salmond. Sillars was not among them but argued their case on the executive whose job it was to expel them. It was a 'horrendous year because people were really split, the conflicts were bitter'. But matters were brought to a head, forced to a decision, and eventually a healing process took place. Six members of the 79 Group were expelled. A special appeal hearing was held, at which the dissidents were represented by counsel. Salmond, though expelled, was allowed to address it and made a powerful speech. Wilson approved a healing compromise – that those expelled could return if they admitted they were in error and accepted the conference decision. Most did so; Margo MacDonald did not. She had resigned and now turned to a career first with Shelter, the housing pressure group, and then in the media. She rejoined the party in 1992. Roseanna Cunningham believed that many people left and never came back, her brother Chrisopher being one of them. A Scottish Socialist Society was formed under Stephen Maxwell's chairmanship. It was intended as a broad-based group on the Left and designed to attract members of the Labour Party. One or two did join, it published some pamphlets but it fizzled away as the onset of the 1983 general election brought some back into the SNP fold and others drifted out of active politics altogether.

Wilson believed that the party could hardly have avoided a period of confusion and regeneration, and that it lasted about five years. The Social Democratic
Party had been formed in 1981, and until its poor showing at the 1983 general
election was siphoning off third-party support necessary for any SNP revival. In
1983 Wilson retained his seat. He lost it in 1987, re-apprenticed himself to the law,
and began his final period as chairman, resigning in 1989. The creative spirit re-
emerged. He enjoyed leading from the front. There was a period of renewed
growth, culminating in Jim Sillars's victory, somewhat to his own surprise, at the
Govan by-election of 1988. After Salmond succeeded him in 1990 the party
committed itself to campaigning for independence in Europe. This would not have
been acceptable to Wilson while chairman and some in the party remained, in
1992, full of doubts about it. In conversation in 1993 Maxwell expressed the
feeling that the policy, posited on the idea of continued progress to European
political and economic union, was out of date. There was clearly a danger, in his
view, that the SNP, by identifying itself with what was essentially the Establishment
position – pro-EC, pro-Maastricht – was in danger of cutting itself off from its
traditional source of electoral support in disaffected elements in the population.
Anti-European sentiment was growing, especially in the farms and fishing fleets that
used to be fertile SNP territory.

In my judgment, for what it is worth, the analysis of the referendum voting
which led to the foundation of the 79 Group was faulty. It was true that it was the
Labour voters who turned out to say Yes. But that was not because they were ripe
for independence. It was because they were loyal to Labour. And the rest of
Scotland voted No, partly because it did not like the Scotland Act and the confusion which surrounded it and partly because it was reacting against Labour. A
Scottish assembly, like Strathclyde, would have been a Labour fiefdom. Teddy
Taylor said to me in 1993 of the referendum, where his undoubted genius as a
campaigner swelled the No vote:

> You have to remember that the Tory Party was not very enthusiastic [in voting
> No]. We got together a great campaign. It's one of the few contributions I've
> made to society, though it may have been a negative one. Most Scottish Tories
> would have said, We want something. But we don't want that nasty Labour
> plan.

Since then the Labour vote has held fairly firm at general elections although it is on
a gently declining curve. It was the Tory vote which was soft. And the Liberal
Democrats have ousted the SNP as the party of protest in some rural seats and in
parts of old industrial Scotland where left-wing politics make little appeal to the
remnants of the old Unionist vote. Mrs Thatcher's perception, in the middle
Seventies, that the SNP might more or less wipe the Conservatives out in Scotland
as the alternative to Labour was a factor the left-wing SNP theorists completely
missed. I am forced to the conclusion that their aim was to bend the SNP to their
own ideological mould.

By 1993 Wilson was still pulling some strings from his position of accumulated authority (he was too young still to be thought of as a grand old man). At the
root of his nationalism, in my judgment, is a strong feeling of the disequilibrium
inevitable in a Union of nations of unequal size. His sense of Scotland being
swamped and submerged has been expressed not in emotional terms, or in the
unlikeable language of anglophobia, but in the rhetoric of economic analysis, a

171

tradition now continued by Alex Salmond though from a more left-wing perspective.

For William Wolfe the 1982 conference was a nadir. He was treated like a leper and though he was president disbarred from chairing key debates. He was at the time under considerable personal and professional pressure, but what had alarmed his colleagues was the outspoken attack he had made on the Pope's visit to Scotland in 1982. Ten years later he was to exorcise the guilt he felt over his outburst when in an article in *The Herald* he explained his feelings at the time but apologised for having offended people. After describing his upbringing in the Evangelical Union Church, he wrote: 'An egalitarian philosophy was nurtured in me, and I abhorred the separate school system whereby the Scots community is divided against itself from the age of five upwards.' He explained his dislike, as one brought up under a presbyterian church government, of patriarchal and hierarchical systems. Isobel Lindsay recalled Wolfe as he struck his colleagues at the time:

> He always had a fey side. He was always quite rational but he had romanticism tempered by realism. His attack on the Pope's visit in 1982 came out of the blue. I had known him for 15 years and had never identified any anti-Catholic feeling. I didn't know whether he joined the masons or whether he had been a member all along. He had certainly never mentioned them. At a Burns Supper we were at together he went through the entire masonic ritual when it came to singing *The Star o Rabbie Burns* – the last verse is sung standing on the table. It was all of a pattern – paranoia about the papal visit and back to a kind of fundamental presbyterianism. He denounced the Catholic church as undemocratic; it had subverted all that was truly Scottish. I was quite taken aback. He identified most of the world's dictators as being Catholic. When I mentioned Hitler as disproving the rule he told me Hitler too had been a Catholic. He had got himself into the appalling logic of a fundamentalist. He developed an interest in Jung.

In April 1993 I visited Wolfe in his house in North Berwick. From the back window we could see the Firth of Forth lapping gently on a golden beach. We sat in front of an open fire and he talked of a political life of failed endeavour. But he was reconciled to it. He did not regret that he had never gone to Westminster. And in the party he was out of the wilderness now. He had a sense of reconciliation, having apologised for his attacks on Catholicism. Eighteen months before he had been re-elected to the national council and was taking a keen interest in current SNP events again. At the time there was a classic SNP split on parliamentary tactics. The three MPs had decided to vote with the Government in return for undertakings about how many places Scotland would have on the Committee of the Regions, due to be put in place by the Maastricht Treaty, and the stipulation that all the major parties would have a nominee and an alternate. The deal quickly dissolved amid mutual rancour but Wolfe's relish in the politics of it all was engaging. He was by now divorced and in May he married Kate McAteer, widow of John McAteer the SNP organiser who died in 1971 and a Roman Catholic. And on that happy and uncharacteristically harmonious note we leave the SNP to its uncertain future. The only thing that can be said with certainty is that it will not be dull; perhaps, as Teddy Taylor predicted, nationalism will zoom, sometime soon. After writing this paragraph, I happened to receive a note from Wolfe. He said, in a reference to some current issue: 'I see stour on the horizon!' His political antennae were twitching and he was happy again.

PART IV
THE BACKLASH

CHAPTER TWENTY

The last consensualist

Since taking up the editorship of *The Herald* in 1981 I have had the opportunity of observing at reasonably close quarters three Secretaries of State for Scotland. On the whole I have had friendly if occasionally strained relations with them. All three – George (now Lord) Younger, Malcolm Rifkind and Ian Lang – had to survive periods of severe political stress that would have tested the equanimity of a saint, and those of us who work in the press do not really comprehend how the criticisms we cheerfully and often superficially throw out hurt those who must tackle real questions of power, patronage and resources. On the whole politicians pay excessive attention to the newspapers, or at least some of them do, and after a setback they usually come bouncing back.

Donald Regan, chief of staff in the Reagan administration, gave a sardonic account in his memoirs of how his enemies, led by Nancy Reagan, undermined him. The President read his own home-town paper, the *Los Angeles Times*, and tended to believe what was in it. And so Donald Regan's enemies planted stories there, by the judicious use of leaks, to the effect that the President had lost confidence in Regan. The President came to believe it was true. Similarly, Nigel Lawson in his own memoirs gives an enjoyably bitchy account of how Mrs Thatcher's press secretary, Bernard Ingham, would filter that morning's press before presenting a summary to the boss. His close links with *The Sun,* and its complicity with his leaks, tended to delude Mrs Thatcher about her mastery of the popular mood.

By the time George Younger became Secretary of State for Scotland in 1979, he was seasoned in the affairs of the Scottish Office. He enjoyed the patronage of the powerful figure of William (Lord) Whitelaw who had not forgotten his sacrifice of Perth & Kinross in 1963. Younger, philosophical and pragmatic, accepted the changing climate and served under Thatcher loyally if at no time with enthusiasm for the doctrines of the New Right. Like Whitelaw himself, he remained a consensualist but did not make it too obvious. He got 'over the wall' into the Ministry of Defence after foisting poll tax on the party, to its ultimate stupefaction, and after the 1987 election, in which the Scots formed an informal anti-Tory coalition to punish the party severely, watched his successor Malcolm Rifkind suffer an extraordinary series of overt and covert attacks. In the opinion of some senior Conservatives Younger was the perfect Secretary of State, poll tax apart.

The devolution years were not entirely without fruit. Much more time was given in the Eighties to Scottish parliamentary business. Various reports of the Scots Law Commission, tidying up and modernising the law, were taken from their shelves, dusted down, and put through Parliament, although the mechanism used, that of Bills containing 'miscellaneous provisions', was not ideal. In the early Eighties the Grand Committee began to meet in Edinburgh amid an almost complete lack of public interest. But increasingly the approach was simply to assume that devolution had 'gone away' and was no longer an issue. Along with his fellow veteran devolutionaries Michael Ancram, Douglas Hurd, Ian Lang and Malcolm Rifkind, Younger found office in the Thatcher administration to be what James Mitchell called an 'adequate corrective'.

It was left to a hard core of Scottish Tories to keep the issue alive. Among them were Brian Meek and Struan Stevenson (prominent in local government in Ayrshire). In the middle Eighties interest revived in the issue as the Conservatives began to be aware of their growing unpopularity. Around that time Meek had his first encounter with Michael Forsyth, at a Scottish Tory conference, and they became devoted enemies. Meek recalled:

> Forsyth was a junior figure in the Scottish Office at the time. We said hello. We had a pro-devolution fringe meeting and a lot of kids turned up with 'Devolution sucks' written on their tee-shirts. I asked this kid where he came from. He said, 'emel 'empstead and added, The only good union is the Union of the Crowns. That night there was an anti-devolution fringe meeting. Forsyth, a minister of the Crown, stood in front of a banner which said 'Devolution sucks'. That was when we realised we would for ever more be implacable foes. Even some of the old ladies in the party were put out. What does 'sucks' mean? they asked. Then devolution went away again and didn't really come until the 1992 election.

Younger kept the office of Secretary of State in good standing in Scotland by sheer personal charm. Labour leaders, smarting over the latest financial diktats from St Andrews House, would storm in mob-handed to see Younger and his officials. They found themselves accepting tea and sympathy. They would depart reflecting ruefully on the fact that they had got nothing out of him; but at least Younger had listened. Younger was very much in the tradition of Tory Secretaries of State. He was a gent but we were all, toffs and tinkers, in it together. He sought consensus and harmony. He fought to retard industrial change and delayed the closure of Ravenscraig, endorsing the stand taken by the then chairman of the party in Scotland, Michael Ancram, and making clear that for him its closure was a resigning matter.

But times were changing. Not only was the New Right beginning its bid for control of the Scottish machine. Not only had consensus, the great goal of the Scottish Office since the days of Tom Johnston, become a dirty word. The Scottish Office was operating in an environment at Westminster and in Whitehall that had become much less favourable to it. The age of planning, which had reached its highest point with George Brown's ambitious national plan of 1965, was receding. It is common to associate Mrs Thatcher with the attack both on public spending and the retreat from macro-planning. In fact the process had begun much earlier. In 1976 the International Monetary Fund lent Britain £2,300 billion to avoid economic policies which the Labour Chancellor Denis Healey said would lead to rioting in the streets. The price was expenditure constraint. By 1978, when Sir William Fraser took over as Permanent Under-Secretary of State at the Scottish Office, much of his work was occupied with cutting staff numbers. The process continued under Thatcher and into the Nineties with the Major administration, with privatisation, sub-contracting, market-testing and the allocation of public services to agencies all being used in the name of increasing efficiency on the supply side. Their chief result seemed to be that they were driving down wages and otherwise impoverishing the conditions of the lower-paid groups in the labour force.

For the Scottish Office the culture shock was traumatic, because it had helped to create the planning culture with which Government was imbued. During the war Tom Johnston had continued its development into a unique department of state, territorially based, staffed mostly by Scottish civil servants, but regarding itself also as an integral part of the Whitehall machine. The Scottish Secretary had sat in Cabinet from 1892 but the post was not elevated to that of full Secretary of State until 1926. In 1928 began its transformation into the creature we know today. The old boards (themselves pre-dating the Scottish Office) mutated into departments. In 1939 the Scottish Office as such migrated to Edinburgh from Dover House, which it retains as its London centre. The Scottish Ministers work in London from Tuesday to Thursday in an environment of elegance. When St Andrews House opened its doors in 1939, the Second World War had begun.

John S. Gibson wrote that the war found Scotland at the nadir of her fortunes. It had every appearance of being both a social and economic disaster. The great house-building programme, offering an end at last to slums, was halted abruptly. More and more Scottish labour was being drafted south. The switch from civil to military manufacture led to factory closures. Output soared on the Clyde but memories of the first war's boom and slump were strong enough to sustain cynicism.

Johnston, a hero to his staff, reacted creatively and energetically. A Council of State, consisting of all those still alive who had held the office of Secretary of State, united the party interests and maximised influence in Whitehall. On his appointment Johnston secured Churchill's agreement that its decisions would be supported. It was, wrote Gibson, a 'political jemmy'. The drain of labour to military industry in the south was reversed. By 1943 Scotland's share of war production had risen from three-and-a-half per cent to 13 per cent. Johnston saw off attempts by Whitehall to make housing and planning UK matters. He was the father of the hydro-electric board, seeing it as an instrument of economic growth in the Highlands. But his most influential legacy was the Clyde Valley Regional Plan. He commissioned it before the end of the war from a team led by Sir Patrick Abercrombie and Sir Robert Matthew. Published in 1946, it foresaw the decline of shipbuilding and the Lanarkshire coalfield, the need to disperse the overcrowded urban population and the role of New Towns in a strategy of renewal. Its philosophy suffused the Scottish Office for at least 20 years.

Immediately after the war, too, the Scottish Council Development and Industry was formed, bringing together in one forum industry, local government, the universities and the trade unions. It was the finest flower of the Scottish Office's genius for building consensus. With it the Scottish Office performed a double act in Whitehall, persuading the Board of Trade to locate industry in Scotland using its new powers of industrial direction. The crowning – and enduring – achievement of that period was the decision by IBM to locate a Scottish plant at Spango Valley, Greenock. Not all the prizes of inward investment were impermanent, and despite IBM's corporate retrenchment, it was still in Greenock in 1993 though casting an apprehensive eye on the rise of China as a manufacturer of the new generations of miniaturised electronic products.

The Scottish Council, in close conspiracy with the Scottish Office, sponsored the Toothill Report of 1961. It came up with the concepts of growth points supported by co-ordinated promotion; the Scottish Office's job was to improve the infrastructure. Two gifted civil servants, Douglas Haddow and James McGuinness, skilfully developed the policy. The office of Secretary of State increasingly had an industrial content as far as its public was concerned. Old Scottish hands say that since the war the Secretaries of State with the highest standing at the centre were James Stuart (1951–57) and Willie Ross (1964–70 and 1974–76). John Maclay (Viscount Muirshiel) and Michael Noble were Tory incumbents associated with promoting new heavy industry.

Ross enjoyed a close rapport with Harold Wilson. His achievements included the Highlands and Islands Board of 1965 and the Scottish Development Agency of 1975. In that year he also won a famous victory by gaining control of selective grants to industry from the Department of Trade. When I lunched with Willie Ross in London in the early 1970s, while he was in Opposition, this historic battle with the old Board of Trade and now the DTI, much more than any question of devolution, was uppermost in his mind. In the late 1970s another round was fought in the battle when the Scottish Office combined with the SDA in 'Locate in Scotland' to fight off a takeover bid by Whitehall, this time led by Norman Tebbit, for overseas industrial promotion.

Malcolm Rifkind, while Secretary of State between 1986 and 1990, told me he thought it was during the Ross-Wilson 'condominium' that Scotland had developed a really significant advantage in public spending per head. By this time Scotland's apparently favoured treatment was the subject of hostile comment throughout Whitehall and Westminster. Rifkind and his officials had to use every conceivable argument to justify it. All of the arguments had validity – for example, greater need, demonstrable from many statistics, especially those of public health, or the higher unit cost of delivering services. This last point is easily shown by the following calculation. A mile of motorway costs the same north and south of the border, more or less. But in Scotland its cost per head is vastly greater because of the low population density. Such arguments have a sting in them, of course, because lower population density may imply a lesser need, but the uneven distribution of population in Scotland also creates the need for more delivery points for services. Donald Dewar argues that if you took a slice of England with a similar population and class profile you would get figures of public spending per head much the same as for those in Scotland, a point with which Ian Lang agreed when we discussed the matter in 1993.

At any event, the Scottish Office, by the time Younger became Scottish Secretary in 1979, was beginning to feel embattled. Old hands date its difficulties from the creation of the Welsh Office in 1964. From then there was a growing 'metooism'. It is a reasonable hypothesis that the British state, around that time, began to seek ways of moderating the influence of the Scots. For that reason Haddow was none too pleased when the agitation for home rule woke dogs he would rather have left asleep. On the Tory side the southern MPs, including Scottish expatriates, grew increasingly unaccommodating; on the Labour benches the North of England MPs became extremely suspicious.

When a formula for apportioning tax revenues was developed by the then Chancellor, George Goschen, in 1888, it was based on rounded population figures from the most recent census. In 1881 Scotland's population was 15.3 per cent. The Scottish Office breached the Goschen principle in 1925 after Baldwin had been to

Glasgow to see for himself Glasgow's special housing needs. For 20 years, between 1958 and 1978, the formula largely fell into abeyance, though it survived in the calculation for rate support grants, and Scottish Office officials operated with great success in Whitehall in securing funds. In addition to a 'block' of recurring expenditure, they were able to get a share for Scotland of other programmes.

By the time Joel Barnett, then Chief Secretary to the Treasury, agreed the new formula in 1978 with the then Secretary of State, Bruce Millan, the relativities had greatly changed. The 1991 census showed Scotland's population dipping under five million. By this time the Scottish population (4,957,000) was 10.7 per cent of England's (46,161,000). A new formula was agreed in 1992 for calculating Scotland's share of changes in spending programmes for 1993–94 and beyond. It meant what officials called a 'trivial' shift to England and Wales in the share of new resources.

In 1979 the Scottish Office was not only grappling with a retreat from macro-economic planning. The more dogmatic conservatism of the New Right began to create serious tensions. Thatcherite conservatism had come out of Scotland, in the sense that its inspiration was Adam Smith, but never put down strong roots there. As Paul Scott has shown, it was in any case highly selective in its debt to the master. It was also heavily influenced by the work of economists like Hayek and Friedman who rejected the post-war Keynesian orthodoxy.

A generation of Young Turks sat at the feet of Professor James Wilkie Nisbet, who took up the chair of political economy at St Andrews University in 1947. Wilkie Nisbet himself was a pupil of William Robert Scott (1868–1940), Adam Smith Professor of Political Economy at Glasgow University. Scott sat on many committees on marketing and industries, edited Smith's *Wealth of Nations* and was a governor of the National Institute of Economic and Social Research. In 1947 Nisbet said in his professorial address:

> In the helter-skelter rush towards a middle-class paradise, paved with lavish promises of cheap and wonderful homes, family allowances, short working hours, holidays with pay, insurance from cradle to grave, health services free for all, education to the heart's desire – in all this sound and fury Chalmers and Mill and Scott, as true disciples of Adam Smith, urge us to pause and count the cost to the taxpayer, to the ratepayer and, above all else, to human character.

Douglas Mason was one of the founder members of the right-wing St Andrews University Conservative Club. (Later he became domestic policy adviser of the Adam Smith Institute.) He was a student at St Andrews from 1960, graduating in geology in 1964. Thereafter he sat through the political economy course for three years at his own expense. His view, quoted by Lorn Macintyre, was that Wilkie Nisbet was not a decisive influence on the emergence of a school of radical Tory politicians. The right-wing radical organisation was already established at the university when he went there. 'I would think the major influence was much more a reaction against the consensus politics of the Fifties and Sixties.'

Ralph (Lord) Harris (of High Cross) was a lecturer in political economy at the university from 1949 to 1956. Harris, quoted by Macintyre in an article in *The Herald* in 1989, recalled that Nisbet withstood the whole of the post-war fashion, not merely about Keynesianism or Beveridgeism; he thought that all those were well-intentioned but unsustainable impulses. There is a legend at St Andrews that

Nisbet was such an anti-Keynesian that he would not allow the new economics to be taught. But one of his staff gave secret tutorials on Keynes. In 1956 Harris became a leader writer on *The Glasgow Herald*. Then he went south and founded the Institute of Economic Affairs, in 1957, which became the leading generator of liberal free-market economics. It inspired much of the thinking of Keith Joseph, Mrs Thatcher's sponsor and mentor. Its work also encouraged Madsen Pirie and Eamonn Butler to set up the Adam Smith Institute in 1977 but this had other origins too.

A Reform Group had been established in the Sixties and Pirie, its president and a former Conservative Party election agent who was studying philosophy and history at Edinburgh University, was co-author with Douglas Mason of its first pamphlet. It advocated commercial radio. The second was an attack on the Potato Marketing Board called *Plough Them Under!* The fourth pamphlet, written by Richard Henderson and Eamonn Butler's brother Stuart M. Butler, called for the repeal of the Rent Act, means tests for council tenants, the sale of existing council houses and the abolition of local authority housing altogether.

Among the people moving in this milieu was Allan Stewart, in 1993 a Junior Minister at the Scottish Office but at that time a prospective Tory candidate and a member of the staff of the department of political economy at St Andrews. In 1959 John MacGregor, by 1993 Secretary of State for Transport, graduated from St Andrews with first-class honours in modern history and political economy. And economics was part of the course for the 1976 MA degree of Michael Forsyth, whose close rapport with Mrs Thatcher, and whose very considerable political skills, became in the Eighties a source of increasing discomfort for the Secretary of State for Scotland and the party establishment.

Born in 1954 and brought up in a council house in Arbroath, Forsyth had a true hatred for what he saw as the enfeebling impact on Scottish life of the socialist consensus and tried to transform the comfortable, gentrified old Tories into a group of hard-nosed professionals who ideologically would take no prisoners. He had broken through to national attention in 1976 when he became chairman of the National Federation of Conservative Students. In 1983 he was one of the founding members, with Harris and Peter Lilley, of the No Turning Back Group, the praetorian guard of the Thatcherite revolution.

It was against this background that George Younger led the party into the disaster of the poll tax. He produced it, like a rabbit out of a hat, to buy off a revolt in the Tory heartlands. Home-owners and small shopkeepers alike were incensed by the swingeing results of revaluation. Nigel Lawson, in his memoirs, gives a disdainful account of how Younger handled the poll tax, with what he called an uncharacteristic lack of political skill. Even Younger's best friends in the Cabinet felt this to be true. The real error, Younger suggested in an interview he gave me in 1993, was that the problem was not dealt with for what it was – an essentially and uniquely Scottish affair. Younger had a strong alliance in Cabinet with Whitelaw, who as custodian of the traditional values of the Conservative Party exercised a moderating influence on Mrs Thatcher, and Sir Geoffrey Howe. He was able largely to ignore the yappings of the New Right and what he identified as the hostility of Nigel Lawson.

When we talked in 1993 Lord Lawson denied that he was anti-Scottish. He thought that other spending Ministers, like Kenneth Baker, then at education, would have found him hostile for the same reason – his reluctance to agree to increased expenditures. But he liked Scotland and the Scots, visited it more often than most Cabinet ministers and always enjoyed his visits. But he did confess to a certain disappointment with Scotland and its 'chippiness'. Despite the fact that, in his view, the Scottish economy had benefited from Conservative policies and had nothing to fear from them, the new entrepreneurial culture had made less impact in Scotland than in any other part of the UK. He also found Scottish businessmen frustratingly reluctant to say in public what they said in private. They were not prepared to stand up and be counted, even though they might represent substantial companies. He acknowledged that this might be because they were more dependent on public-sector patronage than their counterparts in England. They felt they were being discriminated against but were nervous of speaking out. He also found the Scots excessively thin-skinned. They were always looking for insults or denigration. Speaking to a Scottish audience tended to be hazardous. Care had to be taken that no imagined insult could be found where none was intended.

There were only two respects in which Lord Lawson agreed that he was hostile to the Scottish Office. One was its enthusiasm for the poll tax which had arisen from 'the mess' over the Scottish rates revaluation which had been badly handled. No attempt was made to phase it in and even after its unpopularity was clear Malcolm Rifkind defended it warmly in Cabinet, as did Gerry Malone in a speech to conference. Lord Lawson very much regretted that he had not gone to the meeting at Chequers on 31 March 1985, convened by Mrs Thatcher, where the fateful decision to go ahead with the poll tax was made. He had preferred to devote Sunday to his family.

The other issue on which he crossed swords with Younger, though at the level of Chief Secretary to the Treasury, was over spending. In his memoirs he said, in the context of the poll tax, that he had thought for too long that the Scottish tail wagged the English dog. In our conversation he said there was a general tendency for Scottish Secretaries to 'ask for money'. They tended to deploy Scottish political arguments which, I gathered, Lawson often found unclear and unconvincing, incantation rather than argument. In any case, he pointed out, the application for money was decided by Cabinet and not by the Chancellor. On a number of occasions when he became involved with Younger, for example on a dispute with Scottish teachers, they found each other perfectly reasonable.

When we talked Lord Younger acknowledged that he had been successful in getting what he wanted whenever he wanted it badly enough. But he put that down to the support of Lord Whitelaw and Sir Geoffrey Howe. What is revealing, if one contrasts his remarks with those of Lord Lawson, was that he himself explicity rejected the new culture which Lawson wished the Scots to embrace with more enthusiasm. If Scotland was deficient in its response to Thatcherism, the problem started at the very top of the Scottish Office.

In his interview Lord Younger could not have made his rejection and dislike of the new confrontational attitudes of the Right more explicit:

I left the Scottish Office in January 1986. By that time I felt we had got through the agonies of 1980, 1981 with very good consensus and extremely good relations. If you think of the relations between us and the STUC – they were superb. They were as proud of it as we were. They couldn't really describe it, because the TUC had made such a mess of it down south. That went very well. Even with the local authorities, where we criticised each other in public, we got on extremely well in private. I also felt and still feel that that was when you first saw in reality the new Scottish economy: all these new big inward investments that we got have totally created a different animal now which is standing us in good stead at the moment.

Were you aware of the draught coming from the ideologues? Were you conscious of the English backlash?

I wasn't, no; nor did I have any trouble from the right wing, the so-called New Right in Scotland. I knew they were around but they weren't any problem to me.

You were in the tradition of the Conservative Secretaries of State. You were trying to put the Scottish interest in a broader way than just on party lines?

Yes. One of the interesting messages from Scotland since the war, and it's epitomised by the Scottish Council, which at times looks as if it doesn't matter. But in fact what has happened all through the years, through successive governments, is that we've had endless meetings, seminars and conferences which have thrashed out the next thing that needed to be done in Scotland. And everyone has then pushed really in all parties in the same direction. And we've gently and quietly got our way, if a bit slowly, on most things. The Scots are underestimated as lobbyists.

The poll tax was forced on Younger by the quinquennial revaluation, required by law in Scotland but not in England. To this day some former members of the Cabinet believe that Younger could have postponed the revaluation. He insisted that there was no choice but they suspect he was coerced by the assessors in cahoots with Scottish Office officials who believed that the integrity of the rating system had to be maintained. If so, then Younger's advisers allowed punctiliousness to overrule political judgment, and the Scottish Office was to pay dearly for it. To be fair to its senior officials, they did advise the Government consistently that the poll tax would not work. Younger continued:

In Scotland it [revaluation] was done by the assessors, who in Scotland are the last remaining trade union. They are very much a law unto themselves. They weren't under the Inland Revenue as in England which was a pity. The poll tax ... they failed to see the real nub of it. The whole thing, including the English bit of it which went so badly wrong, was to deal with an endemic Scottish problem. They don't like to admit it but it was.

The five-year revaluations became more and more unpopular right across the parties. David Lambie [MP for Central Ayrshire and its successor constituency Cunninghame South since 1970] and I had a long alliance against the rates. He used to represent Troon at one time. He had such a miserable time that he got together with me and we dealt with them together. Rates were a Scottish problem. And by the 1984/85 revaluation there came a point beyond which we couldn't take more pain.

There had been a progressive reduction in central support for local government expenditure, going back to Healey and the IMF?

Yes, that's right. We were certainly in a position from the spring of 1984 that it wasn't an option for the Conservatives in Scotland to say: No, the rates are better than almost anything else and stick to it, chaps, because they weren't buying that any more. We had to do something. Nigel's account – he's perfectly entitled to say he was against it all along. Perfectly true. And as he says himself in the book he possibly wasn't as assiduous himself about it as he might have been.

Once we had to do something, we forced them into taking it seriously. Mrs Thatcher was delighted of course. She hated the rates. She had during one of the Heath elections of 1974 given a press conference proposing their abolition. When we thrashed out with the English colleagues what the alternatives should be, we went through that awful process of looking at all of them and finding they all had difficulties. Since we couldn't go back to the rates, we eventually came to the conclusion that the poll tax had the least number of difficulties. That's how it came. Now this is maybe being a little wise after the event: but it was going to follow in England and one thing you couldn't do was successfully get through a poll tax in England without having had a revaluation. If you'd had a revaluation in England they would have been crying for the poll tax.

Would the poll tax have worked eventually in Scotland?

It was just about working when they got rid of it! I now get waylaid by people who say the new council tax is just as bad as the rates. You're back to where you started! I respond by saying, Well, where were you if you were so fond of the poll tax when we were in such trouble?

A misjudgment by Mrs Thatcher?

Well, I do think it was a misjudgment by us all really. And that's only half a statement really because no one will say what we should have done instead of it. We couldn't have stuck with the rates. It simply wasn't possible. Nobody wants the rates, including the Labour Party, they've never disagreed with that, but I don't agree with Nigel that it was anything like the main factor that removed her.

The story of the poll tax is full of ironies. Intellectually it came out of Scotland and the New Right, arising from the strong feelings that people like Michael Forsyth had about the iniquities of a local taxation system that meant the chief beneficiaries of local services paid least tax and had therefore no incentive to throw out prodigal councils. Another irony was that the Cabinet, to be fair to it, was not imposing the poll tax on Scotland. It was giving the Secretary of State something he advised them was politically desirable. In this advice he was supported by the party leadership in Scotland. The Cabinet rushed it through before the 1987 election because it wanted to do Younger a favour! In retrospect that seems barmy but it was the truth. In the event Scotland thought the Cabinet was 'trying it on the dog' before seeing whether the English could be made to accept it. Finally, there was the irony that Scotland had cried wolf once too often. In his memoirs Lawson confessed he thought if the poll tax were tried out in Scotland its unpopularity would become clear and it would not be imposed in England. But because Scotland habitually complained about anything and everything that emanated from the Government its protests were discounted. Had the Scots cried wolf too long? Younger said:

I think it's a bit right. Lawson was certainly rather inimical to the Scots. He was as inimical as Geoffrey Howe was favourable. Geoffrey was enormously helpful.

Because of Younger's good relationship with Whitelaw, in Cabinet he had enough weight 'to get through within reason anything we wanted'.

I never had anything that was important for Scotland that I was eventually turned down on. I was even offered, as you know, £5 million a year for five years to keep the smelter open at Invergordon. It was only that Alcan, the operators, didn't accept it – it wasn't anything else. That was 1982. I got that from Mrs Thatcher. Nigel Lawson was furious about it when he heard about it. He was in Energy at that time. In the end it was never taken up because Alcan wouldn't do it even at that. But I never asked for anything that really mattered for Scotland that I didn't get and that was because we always had Willie Whitelaw, who was very powerful if he was on your side, which he was, and Geoffrey Howe who was quite powerful for a long time. We could get through more or less what we wanted.

In December 1987 Lord Whitelaw had a stroke at a carol service and early the following year decided to withdraw from active politics. The loss of his moderating influence sent Mrs Thatcher into a bunker where she listened to acolytes rather than clear-eyed friends. Whitelaw was, like Younger, a consensualist who strove for wise government rather than revolutionary leaps. He was highly conscious of Scotland's complex web of social and political attitudes, and respected its distinctive nature. But now the ideologues were to have their chance. For the Scottish Office winter had begun.

CHAPTER TWENTY-ONE

Death of the SDA

In Scotland the results of the 1987 election were disastrous for the Conservatives. The Tory share of the Scottish vote fell by only four points to 24 per cent. But the first-past-the-post system is like a game of snakes and ladders and that was enough to drive the party down. The number of Tory seats collapsed from 21 to ten.

Mrs Thatcher's accumulated suspicion of the Scottish Tory establishment now found a new focus. Its sponsorship of the poll tax, and its belief that this would win votes, made its judgment deeply suspect. Its advice on devolution had been consistently wrong. The Scottish Office had resisted Thatcherism with the support of George Younger himself. He had got away with it only because of the protection of Lord Whitelaw and Sir Geoffrey Howe. She had bent over backwards to give Scotland what she thought it wanted. The result was an electoral disaster. Teddy Taylor told me in 1993:

> She was bitterly resentful of the people who were constantly complaining, asking for things, and taking up a lot of her time when they couldn't deliver anything at all. Her view was, You start winning some seats, mate, and then we'll listen to you.

It did not seem to occur to the ideologues that there might be perfectly simple explanations for the informal anti-Conservative coalition that had been constructed by Scottish voters. Apart from the poll tax, Mrs Thatcher's enthusiastic attacks on the public sector alarmed many professional groups in Scotland who depended on it for a living, either directly or via the patronage of local authorities and other public bodies. Instead the hunt was on for scapegoats. It could not be that Thatcherism was misguided in a Scottish context. That could not possibly be right; Mrs Thatcher could not possibly be wrong. Scotland was where Thatcherism had come from in the first place via Adam Smith, and the Scots were famous for their thrift and industry. The only convincing explanation was that they were being prevented from getting the message about the new culture by the Scottish Office, the Conservative Party's own hierarchy and administrators, and the Scottish press. There was a conspiracy obfuscating the true faith. A chill wind began to blow around New St Andrews House and the party headquarters at Chester Street, Edinburgh.

Michael Forsyth had entered Parliament in 1983 and was made a Junior Minister at the Scottish Office in 1987. His exceptional political gifts had become obvious. He had confounded dire opinion poll findings to retain his seat, by a

185

majority of 548 (he repeated his Houdini-style escape from defeat in 1992). Forsyth is an accomplished grass-roots politician and has mastered the modern arts of electoral campaigning, with its computer analyses and telephone canvassing. He is also an able parliamentarian, much respected for his work in committee as a junior Minister at the Scottish Office and his total dedication to his parliamentary duties. But the exceptional strength of his ideological feelings and his zealous loyalty to Mrs Thatcher and her rhetoric make it difficult for him to indulge those in a different camp even if they are set in authority over him; in this trait he invites comparison with Jim Sillars, though in his consistency he does not.

At first, I think, Malcolm Rifkind had no real idea of how difficult life was to become. He was an enthusiastic advocate of the poll tax, which he had inherited from George Younger. Lawson dealt with Rifkind's commitment to it in his memoirs in typically sardonic fashion:

> At the time these discussions were taking place [1989], the poll tax had been in force in Scotland for some six months, and stories of disaffection and non-payment were widespread. But since the Scots had made a practice over the years of complaining bitterly about every initiative the Government had ever taken, this occasioned little surprise, let alone alarm. In any event, we were regularly assured by the then Scottish Secretary, Malcolm Rifkind, who had inherited his enthusiasm for the tax from his predecessor George Younger, that in reality it was all working out pretty well. No doubt he was keenly conscious of the key role the Scottish Conservatives had played in bringing the poll tax about in the first place.

One Saturday morning George McKechnie, editor of the *Evening Times,* and I were summoned by Rifkind to a meeting at the Royal Scottish Automobile Club. There he attempted to convince us that the poll tax was a Good Thing. We demurred, we were not convinced, but Malcolm made a pretty good case for it. As we left, I remarked to George that if I were ever on a hanging charge I would ask Malcolm to defend me.

Signs of distress began to emerge as the New Right put on the pressure and Forsyth began to take advantage of his close personal friendship with Mrs Thatcher, whom he adored. He was in the magic circle; Rifkind was not. By 1988 it was becoming obvious that Mrs Thatcher had become genuinely attached to Forsyth. When they were together on her tours of Scotland there was, observers said, nobody else at the party. Rifkind and the rest were as wallflowers at a hop. Old hands tell you that Mrs Thatcher admired Rifkind but did not like him. She never really forgave his resignation in 1976. She suspected him of being a closet devolutionary and that he dripped with 'wetness'.

Rifkind moved to disarm the gathering hostility to the Scottish Office and all its works. He responded to the 1987 election with a series of speeches. His first aim was to kill the argument that the Conservative Government of the United Kingdom had no mandate to govern in Scotland. The second was to show Downing Street that the Scottish Office espoused the chief principles of Thatcherism – its dislike of the bureaucratic state and the local government machine, and its idea of devolving power to citizens at the level of the individual rather than that of the regional or district council (which in central Scotland at least would almost certainly be controlled by Labour). When we talked in 1993, Nigel Lawson acknowledged that

Rifkind had moved quite far from wet to dry; other senior Conservatives believed that in truth it was impossible for him to do so.

Rifkind delivered one of the series to the dinner held at the Scottish Council's annual forum. I was in the audience and observed its disappointment that Rifkind had abandoned his usual practice, much enjoyed, of speaking extempore and without notes but with remarkable grasp of content and shape. In 1993 I was delighted to observe, when I heard him address a lunch in London, that he was back to something like his old form. As Secretary of State for Defence he gave us a review of policy issues that showed all the old intelligence and dry wit.

Rifkind will never convince his friends that he is an ideologue. Essentially he is of the Whitelaw school, which believes in sagacious government. Brian Meek is one of Rifkind's oldest friends. He campaigned for him. Perhaps the best service he rendered him was to give him honest if unpalatable advice. He told me in 1993:

> During the Thatcher years he had tried to become a kind of Thatcherite. It was appalling. It was a mistake. I told him it was a mistake.

Scottish Office insiders first began to suspect that Forsyth was going up the 'back stairs' to Mrs Thatcher when Sir William Kerr Fraser retired as the chief civil servant at the Scottish Office. He was Permanent Under-Secretary of State for ten years to 1988, when he became principal of Glasgow University. Mrs Thatcher didn't like him either. She suspected him and the Scottish Office of working against the grain of her policies. It lacked 'bottle' in its approach to local government. William Reid, the man thought by his peers to be the candidate of choice to succeed Sir William, was unacceptable. He had worked with Mrs Thatcher in the Department of Education before the days of her leadership and she had not forgotten. Reid eventually became ombudsman for the health service and Russell Hillhouse was chosen as a compromise candidate after unsuccessful attempts had at the instigation of Downing Street been made to find a suitable applicant from the South. This search reflected the desire of the ideological purists to dilute the consensualist traditions of the Scottish Office.

The Thatcherites were also highly suspicious of the Scottish Development Agency, a creation of Willie Ross and a Labour administration but essentially the invention of the Scottish Office which stood between it and the Treasury, allowing it a certain freedom of action. The SDA made little attempt to ingratiate itself with the Government in general or the Conservative ministerial regime at the Scottish Office in particular. It valued its capacity to operate at arm's length. At a time when Mrs Thatcher was denouncing the levels of state expenditure, it was quietly getting on with the restoration of Glasgow's fabric in partnership with the private sector and the Labour local authorities. Its boss, George Mathewson (now chief executive of the Royal Bank), maintained a high profile for the agency. For Rifkind the SDA became a serious embarrassment because, despite the millions of public money being pumped into Glasgow, the Government got no credit and no votes.

A power vacuum of an unprecedented kind had thus developed. The Scottish Office, the main instrument of government in Scotland, was discredited by the Government itself. The Secretary of State for Scotland found himself treated by the Prime Minister with increasing distance, if always with respect. Into the void stepped a man with more or less no political experience. Somewhat to his own surprise, one suspects, Bill Hughes had more political influence in a few months than most people can expect to exercise in a lifetime. There came that tide in the affairs of man which, if taken at the flood, leads on to great things.

Bill Hughes was born in Lancashire of Scottish parents. Both grandfathers had been miners in the Lanarkshire coalfield. His father was a metallurgist and his mother a nurse. When he was 17, and a pupil at Sheffield Grammar School, his father came to Scotland to work and Bill went with the family. He took an honours degree in pharmacy at Glasgow University and a doctorate at Strathclyde. For two years he lectured at Heriot-Watt University before going into business as a retail pharmacist. He built up a substantial chain of chemist's shops within the Guinness Group. In 1976, at 36, he joined Grampian Holdings as its chief executive; in 1985 he became chairman also. He joined the CBI in the early Eighties, became involved in questions of education and training, worked with the Scottish Office to develop new policies, served on the Scottish committee of the Manpower Services Commission, and in 1987 became chairman of the CBI in Scotland. It was in this capacity that he came up with the idea of merging training and industrial development and replacing the SDA with Scottish Enterprise. He had become highly frustrated by the various Government training schemes. 'They were not hitting the mark at all, they were so bureaucratic, they were dominated by the Treasury. The money was going down a hole and wasn't being properly directed,' he said.

As for the SDA, he thought it was 'only half an organisation'. But he was aware, within the Conservative Party, that Mrs Thatcher was 'totally disenchanted' with it. Hughes himself was not a great supporter of Government intervention but believed that in a traumatic period of rapid economic change there was a need for it. 'You need a blood transfusion, not a life support machine.' The SDA, he felt, had been badly sold to Mrs Thatcher. She didn't understand it. He continued:

> And it had come from the wrong roots. Everything of that nature she had got rid of – the National Enterprise Board for example. If one of us in the party in Scotland hadn't done something about the SDA, I think Mrs Thatcher would have abolished it. It would have been doomed. I believed that the public and private sectors were not pulling well together and that any development body should be headed by the private sector.

To prosecute his ideas Hughes more or less by-passed Malcolm Rifkind and the Scottish Office. He said:

> Malcolm is one of the most interesting politicians to have come out of Scotland in the last decade. You could sit down with Malcolm. He's one of the nicest guys to have 20 minutes with. He would be most receptive and you would go away absolutely confident that you'd got your point over and something would happen. With Malcolm nothing ever happens.

Rifkind's standing, and that of the Scottish Office, were low at the time, of course, and initiatives from that quarter would probably have been dismissed by Mrs Thatcher; and the SDA, said Hughes, was the creature of the Scottish Office. The civil servants there 'believed that they should control it'.

Hughes spoke not only with Rifkind but also with Jim (later Lord) Goold, chairman of the party from 1983 to 1989. He was 'all powerful and had very much Mrs Thatcher's ear'. On the advice of Gerry O'Brien, at that time CBI Scotland's press officer, he decided to float his idea with Alf Young, *The Herald*'s influential economics editor. 'If it's presented by Alf, people will listen to it,' he said. In 1988 Alf ran the story and elaborated it in his Monday column. *The Herald* followed with an editorial on the Tuesday. In the Commons that week Rifkind disavowed it, said Hughes, 'though he had been well briefed by me.'

At the end of that week Hughes received a phone call from the No. 10 policy unit and asked if he could come down to see the Prime Minister. Within a fortnight he had a meeting with her. He continued:

> We didn't muck about. I had never met her before. We talked for about half an hour. I had been well briefed by Jim Goold not to faff, to make sure everything was one-two-three-four and was crystal clear.

The idea was that Scottish Enterprise should combine the development functions of the SDA and acquire the training functions of the Department of Employment. These would be administered by a network of local enterprise companies directed by local businessmen. At the centre of the network Scottish Enterprise would retain the strategic and supervisory role. Hughes put forward both economic and political arguments for the change. He said:

> The political argument above all was the stimulation of the enterprise culture in Scotland, with more involvement of the private sector and less involvement by the bureaucracy. That was the tone I followed.
>
> There and then she took out her diary and pencilled in the last Saturday in August, six or seven weeks ahead, for a full day on Scotland at Chequers. She said to me, Who should be there? Obviously, Malcolm was top of the list. Norman Fowler because he was at Employment at the time. Sir David Nickson who was designate for the CBI chairmanship at the time. And Sir Hector Laing [of United Biscuits] who all this time was one of the biggest influences on Mrs Thatcher about Scotland. He spoke to her on the phone at least about once a week, privately. I kept close to him at this period. I knew him well, having worked with him on Scottish Business in the Community [a CBI programme].

When the day came Rifkind and Hughes arrived at Chequers off the first shuttle. Mrs Thatcher's first remark was about the price of wheat in Scotland. She had heard, from that morning's farming programme, that it had fallen. What did they think of that? 'Malcolm looked at me and I looked at Malcolm. We decided that we didn't know very much about the price of wheat in Scotland.' Hughes was impressed by her references to this and various press items. On the plane going home he asked Rifkind where she found the time. He replied: 'It's quite easy, Bill. She does it at four or five in the morning when she's waiting for the farming programme to come on!' Of the day itself, Hughes said:

> The whole day was one of impatience with Scotland. She said, Why will you not come to me with solutions to your problems? To me Scotland is a problem. It's nothing but problems and you won't give me solutions to them. I'm not inhibiting you in any way. Why don't you come to me with ideas?
>
> The only reason my idea was so readily accepted was it was an idea offering something different for Scotland. She was frustrated with Scotland. She couldn't understand why it had not accepted Thatcherism. It had its Adam Smith pedigree. It was born for Thatcherism. Why would my Scottish Ministers,

why would my Scottish people not give me solutions? Take everything I believe in and apply it to Scotland and I'm happy. What she wasn't going to do was compromise her Thatcherism. If there was an interpretation of Thatcherism which would accommodate the Scottish dimension she would accept it straight away.

Hughes had talked earlier of his ideas to Campbell Christie, general secretary of the STUC, who had told him: 'Bill, there's no way that will ever be accepted. The Treasury will kill that from day one. They will never let that training budget escape from their grasp. Just forget about it.'

At lunch that day Hughes sat beside Mrs Thatcher. It was served by cadets and Hughes was impressed by her rapport with them and the human side she revealed. He continued:

> She said to me, My frustration is this: I'm still finding it difficult to find people – all I need is three or four people, five at the most – who believe exactly as I do. I have yet to get those five people. She was talking not in a Scottish context but in a general context. I took this to mean that she felt she had very few truly loyal people and that there was a number she felt had betrayed her. She was very frank about people. She confided, a little dangerously in my opinion.

The identity of the SDA, into which so much creative work had been poured, on which so many millions had been spent, was lost and it was replaced by Scottish Enterprise. Tensions quickly developed between the centre and the network of local enterprise companies. Their performance was uneven. Some of the local business-men serving on the boards seemed to have one eye on their 'gongs' and there was a tendency for their boards to be averse to risk. In 1993 Professor Donald MacKay, the distinguished economist and consultant, was appointed chairman of Scottish Enterprise and expressed his hope that a strong central intelligence could co-exist with the local enterprise companies. Ian Lang, when we talked in 1993, was strongly committed to Scottish Enterprise and its chairman who, for his part, was anxious that painful memories should be forgotten and a new beginning made.

CHAPTER TWENTY-TWO

The Forsyth interregnum

D r Alexander Stone is a Glasgow lawyer, merchant banker and philanthropist who, with Ross Harper, has raised more money for the Conservative Party in Scotland than any other person in recent times. Dr Stone is a kindly man of erudition and charm. He received me one day in 1993 in his office in Glasgow and told me how he became involved in fund-raising for the party. An old friend, with whom he had been in business in Gibraltar, told him proudly that he had held a party in Ayrshire attended by George Younger, to gather donations for the Tories. How much had he raised? The answer, a couple of hundred pounds, did not seem much to Dr Stone. After some preliminary efforts he set up the Friends of the Scottish Conservative Party. He and Ross Harper were its treasurers. Dr Stone was able to influence people whom he had encountered in his charitable work with the Alexander Stone Foundation. He held a fund-raising party in his home in 1985. It was attended by Denis Thatcher; he had been persuaded to come by Norman Macfarlane who from time to time played golf with him and had asked him up to open a factory. The party was modestly successful, though only after Dr Stone had gone round the guests individually and exacted a little more from them. He remitted a series of cheques to the Scottish party treasurer, the financier and industrialist Sir Matthew Goodwin, and set himself a target of £200,000. By November 1989 he and the Friends had achieved it. He threw a party in his house in Pollokshields. The handsome invitation carried a happy picture of Mrs Thatcher on its front cover. The guest of honour was Malcolm Rifkind. On this sparkling occasion the cheque for £35,750, bringing the total up to the magic £200,000, was to be handed over.

About 100 people attended the party. The other guests included Michael Forsyth, who on 6 July 1989 had been appointed the Scottish chairman by Mrs Thatcher; and John J. MacKay (now Lord MacKay of Ardbrecknish), then chief executive of the party in Scotland and uneasily under Forsyth's command. With understandable pride Dr Stone stood on the steps inside his house and, after a short speech, presented the cheque to Forsyth who accepted it gracefully. He deposited it not in the main party account in the bank near its headquarters in Edinburgh but in a Number 2 account that had for some years been maintained as a 'kitty' out of the grasp of Central Office in London and used to help local constituencies fight elections and by-elections. John MacKay had inherited this account and had continued to find it convenient. The costs and revenues of one-day conferences – not the main conference – would be passed through it, and a small surplus could usually be expected. From this constituency associations would be given short-term loans in times of need but they would have to repay them from funds they raised. It had been little more than a petty cash account and stood at no more than about £1500 when Dr Stone's cheque was deposited. Forsyth had complained about the account when it was discovered, and the fact that it was unaudited. Bill Hughes, appointed deputy chairman to Forsyth, told me in 1993:

> This account had been established for many years. It was an account that had been personally administered and signed by John MacKay. It was after this incident that I shut this Number 2 account and we had only one master account.

The fact that the money bypassed the main bank account had caused resentment and quite unsubstantiated rumours that it had somehow disappeared. Dr Stone wished he had given it to Sir Matthew Goodwin, who subsequently resigned as treasurer. According to some accounts he left because he had been bypassed and because he found Forsyth uncongenial; according to Hughes, Forsyth wanted him to go as part of his reform of the machine. In our talk Dr Stone blamed his own naivety for having caused a rift between Sir Matthew and Forsyth. He liked Forsyth and admired his rhetorical talents but thought he had a habit of rubbing people up the wrong way.

The most convincing explanation I was given, by a senior Conservative, was that Sir Matthew was offended by what he regarded as a serious breach of etiquette involving not only this but other cheques. One of the inviolable rules of the party, and this applied also to branch treasurers, was that the treasurer was responsible for banking. It was quite common for Ministers – even the Prime Minister – to be given cheques by well-wishers. Sometimes they were made out in favour of them personally, sometimes in the name of the party or a branch. It was normal practice for them to be handed in at once to the treasurer, who then acknowledged them. The reasons for doing this are obvious: any misunderstanding could lead to a scandal even many years later.

Those who observed events at the party reported that after Forsyth had accepted the cheque, Sir Matthew asked him to hand it over. Forsyth said he wanted to write a letter of personal thanks to Dr Stone and would send it on. Sir Matthew did not receive it, although he made a number of requests for it. Early in December of that year (1989) he tendered his resignation to the Prime Minister because of his unsatisfactory relationship with the chairman. His friends on the Scottish Conservative and Unionist Association, representing the voluntary wing, were informed not of his resignation (he was treasurer of it also) but of his intention not to stand for re-election: they were grateful to him for his desire to avoid publicity.

The Stone donation, now lodged in the Number 2 account, was used to support Forsyth's aggressive attempt to bypass the party structures and address the grass roots. He employed right-wing friends at a public relations consultancy, Leith Communications, to produce a glossy party newspaper and provide other services. Hughes said:

> Michael had this idea early on that the key to the strength of the party was in the grass roots. He had a feeling all the time that the system as we knew it, working through agents, what you might call the traditional bureaucracy of the party, was an inhibitor. He saw the structure of the party as antiquated. He thought the agents were invariably second-raters. They were people who had failed to do anything else in life and therefore had become party agents. They

were not accountable to anybody. They were in a very localised system whereby they worked to the local party organisation. He felt that whole structure could be brought into the twentieth century.

One of the ways of bypassing that was to a create a new form of communication, which would be the magazine, *Scottish Conservative*. His idea was to do it about four times a year. If he could get it off the ground and circulate about 40,000 or 50,000 copies it could actually be an interesting advertising medium. He did a certain amount of research on other magazines and decided that there was an opportunity here and it would become self-financing.

Forsyth's appointment as chairman was a serious setback for Rifkind. For the Secretary of State to have a junior minister with direct access to the Prime Minister was unsettling to say the least. It was as tolerable for him as the presence of Sir Alan Walters was for Nigel Lawson. Rifkind had made clear his preference for Ross Harper, the Glasgow lawyer who that year had been elected as president of the Scottish Conservative and Unionist Association, the organisation representing the voluntary wing. Harper, as a former activist in the Heathite Tory Reform Group, was ideologically unacceptable to the new puritans, but Rifkind felt confident that he would get his way: he advised Harper that he would have to give up the SCUA presidency on taking up the chairmanship. Rifkind went to Downing Street to propose him for the job, but apparently Mrs Thatcher had already decided to appoint Forsyth, probably on the recommendation of Lord Goold. Gerry Malone had also been on the short-leet. Brian Meek believed, when we talked in 1993, that Rifkind could have preserved the Scottish Development Agency and prevented the appointment of Forsyth had he stood up to Mrs Thatcher.

Soon after Forsyth's appointment as chairman there came an incident which caused profound embarrassment. It arose from the desire of *The Sun* to discomfit Rifkind and its readiness to float a story with as many holes in it as a sieve; Arthur Bell, Scottish chairman of the Tory Reform Group, told me in 1993 that it was a 'classic political set-up' although I could find no evidence to support this contention.

On the morning of Mrs Thatcher's visit to Scotland in July of 1989, *The Sun* published a story about Ross Harper. There was a risible aspect to the allegations and Professor Harper's position as president immediately became untenable. He resigned two days afterwards.

Jack Irvine was Scottish editor of *The Sun* at the time. He and his pal Steve Sampson were much involved in playing jolly japes on the great and the good, and building up *The Sun*'s circulation in rivalry to Irvine's old paper *The Record*. He told me in 1993 that the instructions from Sun editor Kelvin Mackenzie had for a time been to treat Rifkind favourably. Shortly before the Harper episode the instructions changed. It was now acceptable, said Mackenzie by phone, to 'put the boot in' to Rifkind. The closeness of the Murdoch press to the Thatcher camp has often been noted. Lawson's memoirs describe how Bernard Ingham, Mrs Thatcher's press secretary, would brief *The Sun*. Teddy Taylor told me:

> There's no doubt at all that Michael Forsyth enjoyed the support of *The Sun*, and had it very strongly. How *The Sun* interpreted this is a matter for them. But there was a battle going on. There's no point in hiding it.

Irvine denies that a manipulative intelligence set up the story. The source, Irvine told me, was a left-wing social worker. Friends of Ross Harper said in 1993 that he also accepted that this was the origin of the story. He himself, as a part of his libel settlement with *The Sun*, could make no comment. Irvine claimed that the coincidence of the story's publication on the morning of Mrs Thatcher's visit was explained by a clumsy but well-meaning intervention by John MacKay. Irvine told me in 1993 that the paper had been given the story by a regular informant. The paper had been investigating it for three months but had insufficient material to publish anything. MacKay came to see him in his office. It is believed MacKay was tipped off that *The Sun* had the story by 'a little bird' and that it nested in a Tory tree – it was a party member. After a fencing conversation, during which MacKay tried to dissuade Irvine from running the story, MacKay left the office and, Irvine claimed, was followed by *Sun* reporters. His subsequent actions and the responses those triggered convinced Irvine that there was substance to the allegations and he decided to run them. In fact it was a lamentable and porous piece of journalism. *The Sun* muddled up two of the central characters, ascribing the alleged action of one to the other and then, when it realised its mistake, muddying the issue in subsequent stories. Rather naively, Jack Irvine when we talked in 1993 blamed the subjects' manipulative conduct for the error. Since his entire story was based on their evidence, he perhaps should have thought of that earlier. A tape recording was inaudible and subsequently lost. I doubt if Irvine would have run the story if open season on Rifkind had not been declared. I made a useless protest against it by refusing to publish anything in *The Herald* the next day. My colleagues told me that it was a lapse of professional judgment in that the story had, like it or not, become a political event. They were proved right the next day when Harper resigned as SCUA president. The professor accepted a sum from *The Sun* in settlement of his libel case. The newspaper also printed an apology and a retraction, and paid Harper's indemnity costs – what in England would be called full judicial and extrajudicial costs – which must have been very substantial. Harper could have gone for higher damages and almost certainly got them, but the alleged details would have been paraded through the courts.

What was incontrovertible was the damage the publication of the story did to Rifkind. Quite apart from ruining Mrs Thatcher's visit, it made his judgment in supporting Harper for the chairmanship seem deeply suspect. Forsyth, according to Hughes, was equally distressed. It wrecked Mrs Thatcher's first visit to Scotland during his term as chairman.

Forsyth got on with his mission to Thatcherise the party. When he was appointed, Meek commented: 'We shall have to judge Mr Forsyth by his actions. I'm as surprised at the appointment as many other people are.' *Herald* chief reporter Derek Douglas wrote on 7 September 1990, after Forsyth had vacated the chairmanship and Lord Sanderson had taken over:

> Meek and others did not have long to wait for Forsyth to act. Out from the Chester Street headquarters in Edinburgh went senior departmental directors like Bob Balfour and Peter Smith and in came young right-wingers like chief of staff Russell Walters, and Simon Turner, the man who took over the role of chief agent. The attitudes and gung-ho approach of the discredited Federation of Conservative Students which had been Forsyth's political training ground came to be the accepted norm. John MacKay, the former Scottish Office Minister who had been chief executive, found himself sidelined.

Party moderates viewed the changes with growing alarm. Forsyth was involved in an unseemly row at the party conference in Blackpool, during which the freemasonry of constituency agents expressed their great displeasure at what was happening in Scotland and the memorable phrase 'Mr Forsyth's sinister brotherhood' was coined.

At the start of Forsyth's tenure there appeared an American adviser, Grover Norquist. He had apparently been a member of the Republican team which had destabilised the Dukakis presidential campaign of 1988. He was supposed to be the master of the blacker arts of disinformation. According to anecdote he travelled round Scotland talking to people and compiling a 'hit list' of the politically incorrect in the party. John MacKay was said to have spent an uncomfortable day in his company visiting the Borders. Hughes confirmed that his services had been paid for by a Right-wing American organisation though he could not recall its name. (It was, in fact, the Heritage Foundation.) Hughes had an hour or so with him. He told him: 'You might be good for the States but I doubt if you're applicable to Scotland.' He did not think much came of his recommendations. But it is a fair deduction, admittedly from circumstantial evidence, that a decision was taken to purge the list of parliamentary candidates of 'unsuitable' names.

For John MacKay the next few months were a nightmare that had to be endured in silence and even in 1993 he refused to talk about it. But it was well known in moderate circles that he had been treated with abominable discourtesy. After Forsyth had taken over as chairman, he came into the office to find it staffed by the new brooms. The tired old brooms were reconciled to leaving. The pictures of Heath had been taken from the wall and replaced by more ideologically acceptable material. The new brigade could not conceal its contempt for those of the wrong persuasion. They referred throughout the interregnum to 'Rifkind' and 'Lang', using the courtesy title 'Mr' only for more politically acceptable brethren. MacKay kept his counsel and went off on holiday. When he returned he found that all the filing cabinets, including those in his office, had been searched by means of keys cut by a locksmith. Of chief interest to the searchers had been the files of parliamentary candidates. Material unfavourable to those of New Right was removed.

The style of the new team was peremptory. When the St Andrews University association fell behind with payments its account was summarily closed. At the subsequent meeting, the local office-bearers – engaged on restoring this association historically associated with the Right to a more moderate position – were treated to a display of autocratic table-thumping by the Young Turks. The situation for MacKay was unsustainable. Bill Hughes recognised that it could not go on and brought him through to Glasgow. Hughes told me:

> There was no way John and Michael could have got on. John hates Michael. Michael and he had nothing in common. I felt it was my responsibility to somehow or other separate them. There was an uneasy calm before I could do it. John's got a certain number of skills. He wasn't a top administrator but was a super stand-in for anything. With ten MPs there were so many gaps in putting over the Conservative case it wasn't believable. John was a most willing horse. That was what he was doing most of the time. We had a number of talks and it was decided he would head up the Glasgow office.

For MacKay the final insult came when John Corrie and he were invited to apply for the parliamentary candidacy at Ayr, where George Younger was standing down. The two former MPs were submitted to a calculated humiliation. Phil Gallie, from the demotic wing and now the sitting MP, was preferred. MacKay got to hear of the decision not from the party but from the press. He came from a day's fishing to find the phone ringing. It was Bill Clark of *The Herald*, asking for his reaction. MacKay eventually departed with a settlement negotiated by Hughes and described by Hughes as 'very fair'.

Like Teddy Taylor Forsyth believed that the working class was not irretrievably lost to the Tories. Indeed, he had proved it in his own constituency. But Teddy thought the establishment was out of touch with this truth. Although he conceded that Michael had appointed some 'silly young blokes', he felt they never had a chance because of the hostility of the Scottish Tory establishment. Teddy recalled in 1993 that Forsyth had turned to him for help in bypassing it:

> Michael Forsyth asked me to come back to Scotland. We had long discussions. I came up in an unofficial capacity. I told them that would be better because there were people up there who didn't like me. I remember people in Scotland saying to me, Don't go to Easterhouse or Castlemilk [two Glasgow housing schemes] because things have changed and they'll throw stones at you.
>
> The day I came up to start on the initiative for Michael we went to Castlemilk and had a glorious reception from people in the shopping centre and held fabulous meetings. I said, This shows the Tories are still there if you'll go for them. We had a meeting in Campbeltown, the first time we'd held a meeting there for years. It was a huge success.
>
> The initiative unfortunately caused all sorts of resentment. I was given the instruction, Look, we still want you to come but please don't publicise it. Apparently the fact that we got a lot of publicity caused great disharmony. Poor Michael had to say, Teddy, I still want you to come, but please don't publicise it.

For Forsyth things began to go badly wrong. His new staff showed themselves to be inexperienced, naive, offensive and barely competent. Derek Douglas reported:

> With the departure of MacKay, a new Chester Street boss was headhunted. Douglas Young, a Jardine-Mathieson accountant, was appointed as the campaigns and operations director who was going to get the organisation fighting fit again. Young made a disastrous appearance as a party spokesman on a TV political talk show and he and Forsyth soon discovered that, despite their common membership of FCS, a lot of water had passed under the political bridge since then. He was not really a libertarian right-winger in the Forsyth-Walters-Turner mould.
>
> Then, at Christmas [1989], Russell Walters announced his resignation. Young had won the battle of wills. But the campaigns and operations director himself did not last much longer. By the summer of this year [1990], he, too, was out and administrative leadership at Chester Street fell into the hands of the youngster Turner.

Forsyth felt able to ignore the increasing resistance to his regime because he knew he had Mrs Thatcher's complete support. Hughes took some of the blame. He said:

> We had met twice, no more. I was approached directly by Mrs Thatcher, as he

was, and asked to become deputy chairman. In retrospect it was a strange combination. My problem was I had not come up the party system. I knew very little about the voluntary side. It was strong, important, with its own structure. Michael was very popular with the voluntary side but there was a certain element in it, the non-Thatcherites, which was frightened of him. I was identified as Thatcherite, from the business side, and I knew nothing of the way the party was run. So for the first six or nine months I was a very bad counsellor to Michael if he was going over the top in any direction. I felt very naked for the first nine months because I didn't have a feel for the party. So I don't think the combination was going to be helpful because there was no moderating influence on Michael. His feeling was that because he had her 100 per cent backing he really wasn't concerned about obstacles in the way.

Hughes accepted that the *Scottish Conservative* had been a mistake and that Leith Communications was questionable in its performance. In *The Herald* in October 1991 Bill Clark reported:

The Scottish Conservative extreme right wing suffered a severe double blow when one parliamentary candidate resigned and another's Tory PR business was involved in insolvency proceedings. District Councillor Stephen Morrison, 30, has told Leith constituency in Edinburgh that he is to devote himself to full-time law studies at Dundee University.

His friend and one-time business colleague, Mr Brian Monteith, nick-named the Blue Trot and prospective candidate for Monklands East, the seat of Shadow Chancellor Mr John Smith, has had insolvency specialists called in at his public relations firm, Leith Communications.

The Conservative Central Office in London is named among his 59 creditors, which could be an embarrassment to the party in Scotland since Mr Monteith's firm was responsible for the glossy *Conservative News* magazine.

It was edited by MP Sir Nicholas Fairbairn, and reckoned to have cost the party around £200,000 before it ceased publication after just four issues. It was replaced by a cheaper newspaper format.

Leith Communications was set up by Mr Monteith, 34, and his wife Shirley in 1986, and also handled contracts for the Scottish Central Office. At one stage it had a turnover of £78,000, but now has creditors all over Britain including the Inland Revenue, Department of Social Security, and the BBC.

Mr Monteith, a former chairman of the now banned Federation of Conservative Students and of the Young Conservatives, was unavailable for comment yesterday. Calls to his business were intercepted by an answering machine. At one stage in his career, Mr Monteith was severely criticised by Scottish Conservative chairman Lord Sanderson of Bowden. Mr Monteith failed last year to land the nomination at Angus East before being chosen for the industrial Monklands seat.

It was during Mr Monteith's chairmanship of the Young Conservatives that Foreign Secretary Douglas Hurd, then an anti-hanging Home Secretary, was greeted with boos and cries of 'Hang the bastard' when he attended their Peebles conference. Nooses were waved during his speech.

In Hughes's judgment Forsyth was guilty of immaturity, impatience and poor judgment. Hughes claimed that, Leith Communications apart, the office ran to budget under Forsyth, but others believed that there was a serious deterioration in its financial position because of numerous sackings and their consequences. This led to strained relationships with Central Office in London. And some were now beginning to formulate a more serious charge: that he was disloyal to his ministerial boss, Malcolm Rifkind.

CHAPTER TWENTY-THREE

Rifkind's ordeal

Arthur Bell owes his dislike of the New Right to his days in student politics at Edinburgh in the Sixties. He owed his decision to oppose the Forsyth Interregnum at Chester Street, at least in part, to what the Church of Scotland did to his father. More than once, when gathering material for this book, I was struck by the influence of personal experience on political attitudes. William Wolfe walked into his father's study one day and found *Scouting for Boys*. Much later, troubled by his country's rapid industrial decline, he was repelled by the Englishness of scouting literature. Bell is a Unionist partly because his forebears were among the Scots who went to Ulster in the Plantation; and he was the son of a Scottish manse (he was born in Brechin in 1946) because his grandfather was among those who later returned.

Bell met his wife Susan at Edinburgh University. She was a member of the Thistle Group. She has been a staunch companion in his political campaigns. He was UK vice-chairman of the Federation of Conservative Students at a time when it was still resisting the attempts of the St Andrews Young Tories to take control of it for the New Right. Bell remembers their campaigns. The St Andrews shock troops were the leaders of the student Right. That was when, he said, they began to 'learn their tricks'. He added: 'Forsyth was the breakthrough for the Right in the youth movement of the party and it's never come back.'

Now the odd thing about all this is that Arthur and Susan Bell are, you would have thought, the perfect realisation of the Thatcherite dream for the Scots. They are entrepreneurs. They have built up a thriving business in marketing and mail order. One night in April 1993 they royally entertained me in their delightful Georgian house near Biggar. We were in Arcadia. The fire crackled in the hearth as we chatted; and then we repaired for a delicious meal to the dining room with its view of the house's graceful park. Beyond the lawns, the trees parted in an avenue which ended, in the distance, in a ha-ha. It was hard to believe that we were in Lanarkshire. But it was because we were, and because Bell in 1979 had once contested a seat against Judith Hart (MP for Lanark, later Clydesdale, from 1959 to 1987), that he believed that Thatcherism was inappropriate in Scotland. He particularly resented the idea that it should be imposed from above.

The Bells are simultaneously Scottish, British and European. They are fiercely Unionist. They rejected Thatcherism because they feared it would destroy the Conservative Party in Scotland and therefore the Union itself. But for an explanation of why they decided to fight the Forsyth regime in 1989 and 1990 we have to go back to 1970 and 1971. On Christmas Eve, 1970, as he lay in the Western

General Hospital, Edinburgh, having suffered a heart attack, Bell's father, Leonard Bell, was sacked by the Church of Scotland. To be more precise, he received a letter from the publicity and publications committee terminating his appointment as editor of the Kirk's magazine, *Life & Work*. No reason was given but Arthur and Susan Bell told me it was because his father had published as a front cover a reproduction of Botticelli's *Madonna and Child*, recently acquired by the National Gallery. This was seen by the Kirk's Old Guard as papish. The flames of the Reformation, and its rejection of Mariolatry and the worship of graven images, still burned in their hearts. The row caused Leonard Bell's heart attack and ultimately his death because of the acute worry. Losing his job meant losing his house. Bell said his mother never got over it. He and his brother decided to fight. In May 1971 they took it all the way to the Supreme Court of the Church of Scotland. The television cameras were switched off and a packed General Assembly heard the pleas of counsel Harry Keith, QC (later the judge Lord Keith). By an overwhelming vote the General Assembly reinstated Leonard Bell and the convener of the committee resigned. Leonard Bell, who as minister at Brechin had been very much on the liberal wing, for example eschewing all connection with the masonic movement, was dead within the year.

This experience did two things to Arthur Bell. It left him with a strong dislike of those who abused authority and it taught him how to run a campaign. He learned how to communicate with the press and engage the interest and sympathy of journalists. After he left university Susan and he stood as Conservative candidates at various places but after 1979 found selection committees unsympathetic to Conservatism of their kind. Susan had worked for a time as an investment analyst but left to found and build up, with Arthur, their various businesses and bring up their children.

Their experience had taught them that you had to have a peg to hang your hat on if you wanted to have a locus in any political argument. Throughout their career in politics outside the mainstream, they have shown considerable skill in either using existing formations or in creating them *ad hoc*. Susan founded the Conservative Candidates' Association and both served at various points as its chairman. Even before the Forsyth new broom began to sweep away their old friends from Chester Street, the Bells were alarmed by the party's lurch to the Right after the 1987 general election. Before Forsyth's appointment as chairman, they decided to give a little shake to the Scottish Conservative and Unionist Association, a 'little coup d'état'. This was a hitherto sleepy body, composed of about 130 constituency chairmen and other office-bearers, that ran on the principle of 'Buggins Turn'. The Bells ran a slate of candidates. Susan would stand against them to deter others and, when the coast was clear, withdraw. The strategem worked. Ross Harper became president after the 1989 party conference and Brian Meek vice-president.

When Forsyth took over and began to get rid of the old faithfuls from Chester Street, the Bells were enraged. These were old friends. They had done nothing wrong. They had not been well paid. Their sin was that their Toryism was of the wrong kind, with a strong social content. They were the Tories of the 'Celtic conscience', as Susan put it. Arthur Bell said:

> He started doing to friends of mine what a small clique in the Church of Scotland had done to my father. I thought, What are these people going to do? They were suddenly kicked out of a job in front of the television cameras which just happened to have been called along.

They were further incensed when Forsyth brought in Grover Norquist. But it was what Bell believed to have been the 'set-up' of Ross Harper which made him decide to fight. He said:

It made me so angry. I said, Right, chaps. This is a declaration of war.

The chosen vehicle for resistance was the Tory Reform Group, Peter Walker's refuge for Heathites, or, as Bell put it, the 'Government in exile'. He contrived to become its Scottish chairman. His first, highly provocative, move was to convene a conference entitled 'Does the Scottish Conservative Party have a future?' After two hours on the phone he persuaded the former Scottish party chairman Russell Fairgrieve to attend. No journalist could resist such an event, and it received wide publicity although it was attended by only about 30 people. A few days before the fateful party conference in May 1990 he showed his media skills again. On behalf of the STG he issued a statement asking if the Scottish party were like 'the *Herald of Free Enterprise*, heading out to sea with its mouth open?' He chose the tasteless simile with care and was rewarded with widespread publicity. It ran on every Radio Scotland bulletin throughout that day and ensured that when he arrived at the conference he was treated as a pariah. 'I was totally *persona non grata*,' he recalled.

On the eve of the conference Arthur and Susan became aware of the strange activities of Bill ('Biggles') Walker, the MP for Tayside North, vice-chairman of the party in Scotland and well-known as a Forsyth loyalist. That morning Stuart Trotter reported exclusively in *The Herald* on a move inspired by Walker to install Forsyth as Secretary of State for Scotland. That night at a reception given by Grampian Television, Walker was telling anyone who cared to listen of his ideas. The next day he went on Radio Scotland to tell the whole nation of them. They were reported by Stuart Trotter and Bill Clark in *The Herald* of 11 May:

[Mr Walker] said that he wanted to see 'two Scots in the Cabinet' instead of the present one. He believes Mr Rifkind's successor should be Scottish Health Minister and party chairman, Mr Michael Forsyth, who had earlier dismissed the *Glasgow Herald* report about moves to put him in charge at the Scottish Office as 'a silly season story'. Mr Walker . . . made clear that there is support near the top of the party for a change.

It was not so silly. Trotter and Clark added that 'senior Conservative MPs' at Westminster were saying privately that a move for Rifkind in the next Cabinet reshuffle could not be ruled out. In fact he was appointed Transport Minister later that year. The report added:

At Westminster the Prime Minister described Mr Rifkind as 'one of the best' Secretaries of State Scotland had ever had when Clydesdale Labour MP, Mr Jimmy Hood, asked if she would be giving full support to him when she speaks at the Scottish Tory conference in Aberdeen tomorrow although Scots Tory back benchers wanted him sacked.

Next morning the nightmare grew worse. Because of the security arrangements, delegates were brought into the conference centre by bus. Arthur Bell recalled that he was sitting in front of Rifkind and Meek. Both looked miserable. Above the bus a Grampian police helicopter fussed officiously. Meek said: 'You'd better duck, Arthur. That's Biggles after you.' Meek takes up the story:

> We had gone to Aberdeen instead of Perth because we were supposed to be going to win seats in the north-east and the *Press & Journal* had always been sympathetic. I came down to breakfast and picked up the *P&J* and read: Plan to oust Rifkind. And I thought, How really wonderful. And then I heard Walker had been on the radio and said he was acting in Rifkind's best interests.
>
> Malcolm is beside himself with rage. Walker is denying it at the same time he is giving interviews. Forsyth is going around saying, What's everybody getting so excited about? Mrs Rifkind arrived and we all went to this trailer at the back of the stage. I managed to persuade Malcolm to make a joke of it. I said, When you go on look at your watch and say, It's 12 o'clock and I'm still here. He did that and it brought the house down.
>
> It was the right way to handle it but behind the scenes internecine warfare was going on. I remember walking down this long corridor and for some reason there seemed to be only me going this way and coming towards me were Forsyth and one of the Right-wingers. We walked past each other without a word. This was in the party where we were all trying to work for the same ends. That experience taught Rifkind that your friends are the people you know and taught him something politically. I think he now realised that he would never be able to join this gang.

That morning the conference was silent, as if in shock. Bell said: 'The audience was dead. Not a single word had been raised in defence of Malcolm. The party was absolutely in crisis.' He had demanded to speak in the poll tax debate, the third item on the morning's agenda, on a motion moved by the then candidate for Central Edinburgh, Paul Martin. Bell continued:

> I said, It is a remarkable coincidence that the motion has been moved by the candidate for Central Edinburgh. I remember 20 years ago a candidate for Central Edinburgh coming back from his honeymoon to campaign in the 1970 general election. And he's with us today. And I'd just like this conference to say, Happy anniversary, Malcolm and Edith Rifkind. And there was a great burst of applause. We want to give you this message, Malcolm: This party needs you and wants you in Scotland. The place just exploded. It was very emotional because they all liked Malcolm.

Trotter and Clark reported:

> Delegates closed ranks around the beleaguered Mr Rifkind, making clear with constant affectionate, warm applause that there would be fierce resistance to any attempts to oust him and replace him with Mr Forsyth . . . A strained-looking Mr Rifkind said: 'It is a free country and he [Walker] is entitled to his views. He was in my company last night and did not have the courtesy to tell me of his views. I do not feel threatened. People have three days at this conference to express their views, let them have the guts to come forward.'

Time and again, the report continued, tributes were paid to Rifkind.

Mr Forsyth joined in the applause. In an aside in his chairman's speech, he tried to stem the flood of speculation in the hall about his intentions, saying: 'Let there be no doubt, I have quite enough on my plate at present.' In a furious attack on his critics in the party, he said: 'Those calling for lifeboats are a sad crew. Loyalty is the currency of success – not mutiny.' Defending hard-line Thatcherism, he insisted: 'Radical policies do pay dividends. Being weak-kneed will neither achieve our objectives nor win us support. Where we show we shall not waver we reap the dividends.' He . . . ended by claiming that 'the faint hearts have been found out'.

Whereas Mr Rifkind had earlier received a total standing ovation from the hall almost a third remained seated at the end of Mr Forsyth's speech. Several delegates, including two West of Scotland parliamentary candidates, left making it clear where their loyalties lay. Glasgow councillor John Young, prospective parliamentary candidate for Cathcart, said: 'Mr Forsyth is a man of consider-able ability and energy but as he said he has enough on his plate. Mr Rifkind is the greatest asset this party has in Scotland. If he were moved to a UK Ministry a lot of people would be quite horrified. He still has a lot of work to do in Scotland.'

Throughout the day Walker sought to explain his action in writing to the Prime Minister complaining about Rifkind's 'mishandling' of the poll tax rebate issue in the Budget – rebates for England had been announced but none for Scotland and Rifkind was blamed for not having demurred in Cabinet – and his support for Mr Forsyth. Trotter and Clark continued:

> It led to the spectacle of his being followed around the conference centre by gaggles of newsmen, with radio and television journalists claiming he was giving conflicting versions. Mr Walker snapped at one point: 'There is a grain of truth which is being blown out of all proportion.'
>
> He tried to explain his position to conference in the poll tax debate but his claim of misinformation was given a cool response. He invited delegates to consider his record as an MP for North Tayside for 11 years. A senior Tory said: 'If Bill is behind the coup then Rifkind's quite safe.' Another added: 'I didn't know Scotland was a West African republic, because that's where flight-lieuten-ants normally lead coup attempts.'
>
> The general feeling was that if indeed it was a coup attempt then all it had succeeded in doing was to improve Mr Rifkind's stock in the party and make them ultra-protective towards him.

That night, over drinks and dinner, there met a group that might be called the *salon des refusées*. It was composed of former office-bearers and activists who had received no invitation to the official dinner. Apart from the Bells, it included Russell Fairgrieve. As the discussion progressed, the Bells discovered that others shared their unhappiness. It was at this point, the Bells believed, that the coalition that eventually forced Forsyth out of the chairmanship was formed. They were prom-ised support, and Mrs Thatcher thereafter began to be bombarded with letters telling her of the crisis.

There followed a war of press leaks. Bell began building up a dossier. Although he did not know it, others were doing likewise. John MacKay kept some of his old contacts in London in touch. The ideologues made their main target Ian

Lang, Rifkind's Minister of State. He was the stalking horse. Hostile press leaks appeared, in particular under the by-line of Derek Bateman in *Scotland on Sunday*. The bitterness again broke out into the open. On 4 July, *Herald* parliamentary correspondent Stephen McGregor reported that Arthur Bell had been called a 'pig-ignorant pipsqueak' by Allan Stewart, who added that he felt this description was unfair to pigs. The remark was made in the Commons committee considering the Scottish law reform Bill. It had been discussing remarks made by Bell over the weekend. McGregor continued:

> He [Bell] criticised the behaviour on the committee of Scottish Tory vice-chairman Mr Bill Walker, who voted against the Government on two occasions last Thursday, and called for him to be sacked. Mr Bell also was reported as saying that if Mr Walker was not 'reined in', then his mentor, Scottish Health Minister and Scottish Tory Party chairman Mr Michael Forsyth, should go too.

At one point Forsyth denounced Bell on Radio Scotland. It was well known, he said, that Bell was the 'stupidest man in the Scottish Conservative Party'. It was a sign, Bell believed, that Forsyth had lost his nerve. 'This was no Mr Cool.'

Scottish political journalists were now bombarded daily with leak and counter-leak as the warring factions fought it out. The stories being circulated by the moderates became more and more scurrilous to the point that even today their publication would attract libel writs.

At Westminster Rifkind, who had been slow to accept that there was anyone working against him, realised that all was not as it should be. A senior moderate Conservative told me in 1993:

> Malcolm took I don't remember how many weeks and months to accept what was happening. I remember going along to the Commons and having dinner with Rifkind. Ian [Lang] was there. I said, Look, Malcolm, you'd better believe it. A major destabilising effort is going on. Every time we turn around we pick it up.

What convinced Rifkind he must act was a series of events at Westminster. Forsyth gave tacit endorsement to a revolt led by Walker against the provisions of the Miscellaneous Provisions Bill. One of the series of portmanteau measures used to tidy up and modernise Scots law, the Bill would, among other things, have ended Scots lawyers' monopoly in conveyancing.

The revolt saw an alliance between the Forsythites – Walker and Allan Stewart – and the Old Guard of Sir Hector Monro and the idiosyncratic Sir Nicholas Fairbairn. Walker and Sir Nicholas were united by a personal dislike of Rifkind. Bill Hughes told me that they never had a good word to say for him. Monro and Sir Nicholas were genuinely concerned about the impact of the legislation on the viability of legal practices in the old market towns. Walker and Stewart had a different agenda. If, as has been suggested, Walker was an 'unguided missile', Forsyth did nothing to seal him in a silo. Hughes told me that Forsyth was 'fed up' with Rifkind's 'own goals'. Apart from the mishandled poll tax rebate, these included his support, out of fealty to George Younger in whose constituency it was, for the continued monopoly as Scotland's international airport of Prestwick. (Rifkind had to concede to intense pressure from the business lobby in March 1990, opening the way for Glasgow's overdue development as an international airport.)

In a famous column in *The Herald* Brian Meek attacked Forsyth's ambivalence towards Rifkind who, having made a strong public stand on the Bill, was forced into a humiliating reversal. Hughes said:

> Michael did nothing to contain or control Bill Walker. He was quite happy to let him cause Malcolm the maximum discomfort. Michael no way was pulling the string. Bill Walker was not controllable. He was his own guy and did his own thing. But Michael almost took pleasure in Malcolm's discomfort because they were not pulling together. And Michael knew there wasn't a great deal of love between Malcolm and Mrs Thatcher, either.

The Bill was short of parliamentary time and the rebels threatened to vote against the guillotine motion. Rifkind was forced to eat his words and accept substantial changes. This caused further damage to his standing in Cabinet. 'Rifkind can't deliver' began to be heard in the corridors. It was, of course, a supreme irony that the Right, in its eagerness to discredit Rifkind, should have opposed a measure which had flowed from the purest founts of Thatcherism. It was the behaviour of Forsyth on this issue, rather than anything that happened in Scotland, that drove Rifkind at last to demand his removal as chairman. He did so in an interview with Mrs Thatcher. He pointed out that Forsyth was in breach of a chairman's duty of loyalty to the Government. Senior colleagues believe he added that if Forsyth did not go he would resign. She listened to him and suggested that he take a little time to reflect. He went on holiday.

Had Rifkind's been the only voice, Forsyth might have survived as chairman. To some extent the influence of the Bells was regarded by both camps as like that of the gadfly – an irritant – and Mrs Thatcher might have defied the advice even of Lord Whitelaw. The dossier compiled by the Tory Reform Group was sent to chief whip Timothy Renton. It was designed to show that there had been a concerted campaign by influential people within the party to undermine and discredit Rifkind. Whitelaw was visited at the House of Lords by Bell, who showed him the dossier and explained his views. One suspects that, like Rifkind, Whitelaw was a little embarrassed by Bell's energetic pursuit of the cause. Bell, after all, had not been elected to any significant office and his party career had been on the voluntary wing. But from his and other evidence Whitelaw too decided that the situation was 'unsustainable' – a favourite word for such moments. At that point he was generally taking a back seat but thought this matter was sufficiently serious for him to draw it to the attention of the Prime Minister. He saw Mrs Thatcher and told her that Forsyth could not continue as chairman. Younger added his voice.

The decisive voice, and one that Mrs Thatcher could not ignore, was that of the Scottish Conservative Business Group, chaired by James Gulliver. The public turbulence in the party was having a negative impact on donations. Gulliver confirmed in conversation that the group, which he chaired, indicated its belief that the situation had become unsustainable and affirmed its support for Rifkind. A secret meeting of this group was held two days before Forsyth's resignation as chairman. Correspondence to Downing Street resulted: Lord Goold was present at the meeting and probably reinforced the letters with a personal report to Mrs Thatcher.

On the Saturday before Forsyth resigned from the chairmanship, there was a special meeting of the SCUA executive. In 1993 Meek recalled;

We unanimously said we've got to go and tell the chairman he can't go on behaving like this. The office-bearers were deputised to do so. We went to the Carlton Hotel. I remember Micky [Hirst, the president] saying, I think we should have a drink. I said, No, I don't think we should because if we have a drink we'll just have a fight. We went down the road and were ushered into Forsyth's office in New St Andrews House. He was expecting Micky but didn't know the other office-bearers were coming and wasn't best pleased. Then all the recriminations started. He tried to draw the conversation to an end. Adrian [Shinwell] said, No, I'm sorry, I've another 18 points to put.

At one point Forsyth burst out and said, If this is how you feel I'm going to resign. And there was a deathly hush. Nobody said anything. He said, Well, I'm not going on with this meeting. Then we went off and had large drinks at the Hilton. We reckoned he had talked himself into a situation where he would have to go. We knew that people like George Younger and others were telling Mrs Thatcher that the situation could not go on. If Forsyth didn't resign a large number of prominent Scottish Tories would do so.

Some friends of Rifkind, however, believed that it was not until Bill Hughes withdrew his support from Forsyth's chairmanship that she finally decided she had to yield. On the night before Forsyth gave up the chairmanship, Hughes returned from a trip to the US to receive a call from a senior aide at Downing Street. Hughes said:

He asked me if I had any viewpoint on what was happening. I said that it did appear from what he told me that we had passed the point of no return, that it wasn't a sustainable position. He said, What about your position in these circumstances. I said, My position is my position. I wouldn't see the departure of Michael as any grounds for my resignation. I was appointed by the Prime Minister, not Michael Forsyth. I will retain my loyalty to her and do the job. He said, That's all I wanted to know.

Mrs Thatcher bowed to the pressure. But she could not accept defeat entirely. She simultaneously promoted him to be Minister of State. In Bell's view that enraged many of the moderates, and the situation retained some of its inherent instability. Rifkind moved quickly to re-establish his authority, making it clear that Forsyth as his junior Minister reported to him on questions of policy. At least Forsyth's formal access to Mrs Thatcher was ended even though informally the link remained as firm as ever. When Ian Lang became Secretary of State in 1990 he soldiered on rather uncomfortably with Forsyth as Minister of State until Major moved Forsyth to the Department of Employment in 1992. Here his boss, Gillian Sheppard, learned to appreciate his qualities as a subordinate. When she moved to Agriculture in May 1993, John Major showed that he was not bereft of a sense of humour by moving the leading Wet, David Hunt, from the Welsh Office to take over as Forsyth's boss at Employment.

Forsyth's successor as chairman was Russell (Lord) Sanderson. He was in France on holiday when the call came. He insisted on completing his holiday. He 'let the dust settle' for about a fortnight. During that period Hughes took temporary charge. A story was leaked to *The Sunday Times* that all the locks had been changed at Chester Street. Hughes recalled:

The Sunday Times had it on the Sunday. Then I got a phone call from Gerry O'Brien saying *The Sun* was going to run it on Monday. I spoke to Steve Sampson and told him it was a pack of lies. I was the only person with the keys and they had never been changed. If they wanted to come and photograph them they were free to do so. To which he said, Bill, it's a super story; I'm running it.

Sanderson was by then an influential figure in the party's voluntary wing. From 1981–86 he had been chairman of the National Union Executive Committee. His appointment reflected the feeling of the first Thatcher administration, before the asperities of the post-1987 period set in, that Scotland should be brought into the family. He could speak with genuine authority about Scotland, because as a businessman in textiles he travelled all over the country and had a good feel for its pulse. As a result of his service on the NUEC he became respected also by English Conservatives. He believed the Forsyth way was not the way for Scotland. He had never before come across a party headquarters that had become a hotbed of factional politics.

He had observed that while Mrs Thatcher had regard for Rifkind's abilities the chemistry between them was not good. Forsyth was one of the coterie in whom she confided, that magic circle, one of us. She would tell him things before she told them to Rifkind if she told him at all. Sanderson believed that the situation was unstable from the start. To have a chairman 'going up the back stairs' to No. 10 would have been undermining even if he and the Secretary of State had been the best of friends.

Sanderson cleansed headquarters of its ideologues more or less on the morning he took over. He installed instead experienced political organisers, indeed he had made a condition of his appointment that he should be able to do so. The Forsyth interregnum was over. Its only survivor was Simon Turner, who became Forsyth's agent in Stirling.

Ian Lang's relative success in the 1992 election – successful because he avoided the widely predicted extinction of Scottish Conservative seats and turned the party's share of the vote upwards again – was a turning point for the Conservatives in Scotland, the more so because of his close relationship with Major, with whom he spent five years in the whips' office and whose campaign for the leadership he openly supported. It was a setback for the Forsythite Right, which now could be excluded from the party's inner councils in Scotland though not expunged from the grass roots. It was a defeat, too, for devolutionaries in the party like Bell and Meek. They had warned that without devolution in their manifesto the Tories could face disaster.

In constructing this account of events, I have been at a disadvantage in that Forsyth declined to talk to me about them. He let it be known that he did not want to re-open old wounds. Teddy Taylor, a sympathetic colleague, believed that Forsyth was the victim rather than the author of any conspiracy. He said:

I came to the conclusion that most of the rumours going round were rubbish. It was just rumour upon rumour. There was this divide between the establishment and Michael, who was trying to move the party in a certain way. They just didn't like it. Most of the alleged plotting which Lord Whitelaw eventually recognised – it didn't take place at all.

It would have been too much to assert, writing in 1993, that Ian Lang had restored the tradition of consensus but I was beginning to sense he was moving in that direction. He did seem receptive to Bell's view that the Tory Party in Scotland was not just a broad church but an 'amorphous mass'. True, the proposed privatisation of water was highly controversial, though he was pursuing the compromise of franchising; and the reversion to single-tier local government was being resisted by the Labour barons who dominated the Convention of Scottish Local Authorities.

The ordeal taught Rifkind something. As a young politician he had been precocious. His gifts propelled him up the ladder and away from the in-fighting of the political life below. He was slow to realise what was happening, though his unwillingness to believe the worst gave him dignity too. He continues to attract the virulent hatred of the New Right. In 1993 the *Evening Standard* in London carried a vicious attack on him because he had had the temerity to resist Lady Thatcher's remedies for the civil war in Bosnia. There were sneers about his Scottishness and his old Jewish father (now dead and remembered by Brian Meek as a delightfu man). But just as Ian Lang had been a stalking horse for Rifkind, so had Rifkind now become a stalking horse for John Major. The praetorian guard, with its privileged access to the Murdoch press and other newspapers, was still armed to the teeth.

Most people with whom I discussed this episode had good things to say about Forsyth. They admired his abilities. What went wrong during his chairmanship was that his zeal to serve Mrs Thatcher overcame his judgment and the Young Turks got out of hand. The last word in this chapter I leave to Lord Lawson. The Forsyth interregnum represented an attempt by Forsyth to fulfil Mrs Thatcher's wishes. 'He was doing what she wanted – or he thought he was,' he said.

CHAPTER TWENTY-FOUR

Portrait of a lady

Why did Mrs Thatcher and the Scots not get on? Of course, she had zealous admirers north of the Border. Yet the generalisation holds true. My mother entertained a dislike of her which was almost pathological. Whenever Mrs Thatcher appeared on television, she would say in tones of inexpressible contempt: 'That woman!' It was not that my mother was a socialist. Coming from the United Free Church, she would have had a Liberal political upbringing, though I never heard her talk of it. What offended her, I think, was Mrs Thatcher's homilies on thrift and the principles of good housekeeping. My mother had grown up in Rosehearty in some poverty. The older children, after they progressed through university, would help support the younger ones in turn. Mrs Thatcher's occasional forays into questions of interior decoration, also, inspired scorn. Dennis Canavan, in a memorable phrase during an election campaign, advised his electors in 1979: 'Don't let that witch hang up her curtains in Downing Street!' This sentence combines chauvinism – with its underlying idea that a woman might not be fit for high office – with an appeal to female dislike of a woman who had got above herself.

From the particular resentments of Scots like my mother grew a more general dislike, shared by many Scots, of Mrs Thatcher's insistence that she knew best. She attempted to impose her policies rather than convince Scotland of their merit, although the most hated policy of all, the poll tax, was imposed on the advice of Scottish Ministers and office-bearers. Scotland had, through the only democratic means available to it, indicated its dislike of her Government. Yet she decided that Scotland was wrong because she had to be right, and Scotland found itself, as a result, with much reduced political leverage. After 1987 much of the Conservative rhetoric about Scotland became abusive and insulting, with some particularly offensive examples in *The Sunday Times* (edited by a Scot) and *The Evening Standard*.

I met Mrs Thatcher on several occasions, and found myself in a paradoxical position. I disliked many of her policies. I thought she knew little of Scotland and, I suspected, cared less. I was a child of the Attlee years and of the Scottish Office's consensualist tradition, and I instinctively resented the attempt to impose a narrow doctrinal mindset on a complex set of economic, social and political issues. Yet I recognised that the reforms of the labour laws over which she had presided had released my own industry from a raft of restrictions and obsolete technologies if at some cost to its decency and the wages and conditions it offered to its servants, its foot-soldiers especially. I also found her a personality of compelling power and charm with considerable sex appeal.

When she visited *The Herald* on the occasion of its bicentenary in 1983 she gave a display of personal magnetism that made us realise, if we had been sufficiently obtuse not already to have done so, that here was a politician of the highest class. The machine room's union representatives had made it clear that she would not be welcome in the press hall. The management was perfectly willing to disregard this statement but Downing Street indicated it would prefer not to be the cause of any embarrassment. The machine room was omitted from the itinerary. Mrs Thatcher came late from the Chamber of Commerce's bicentenary dinner (we both celebrated this anniversary that year). We lined up to greet her. Harry Reid, my deputy and a Thatcher fan, kissed her hand. He did so to win a wager with his wife but Mrs Thatcher seemed highly delighted. Then she toured the building. In editorial she kicked off her shoes and chatted with the news desk, the reporters and the subs. In the composing room she knocked them cold. These old trade unionists leapt about in great excitement. She posed for their photographs. Before she left she crushed Michael Kelly, accompanying her in his capacity as Lord Provost. One of our leader writers, Bob McLaughlan (another fan), presented her with the scholarly Glasgow University edition of Adam Smith. She said: 'Adam Smith got it right.' Kelly said Smith might have got it right then but he hadn't got it right now. She rounded on him: 'Well, laddie,' she said, 'Your lot haven't got it right yet.' (Incidentally Teddy Taylor told me that while she wanted to crush the Nats she had no such ambitions for Labour: a bipolar system needs its north and south, its left and right.) Her visit was regal, more so than that of the Queen some weeks later. She talked to all the waitresses in the boardroom before departing. The next day the machine room put in an official complaint: why had she not visited them?

There were several occasions when I met her with other editors. During my term as chairman of the West of Scotland branch of the Newspaper Press Fund she generously came to one of our lunches, ensuring that it was a magnificent fund-raising success. I had the privilege of sitting beside her and found her a most agreeable companion. At a dinner given for the Prime Minister by the editors' council of the Scottish Daily Newspaper Society I had a hilarious evening in the company of Denis Thatcher, who enjoyed playing up to the caricature in the 'Dear Bill' letters of *Private Eye*. The Thatchers had just been to the Salzburg Festival and he told me this story about the famous musical autocrat, the late Herbert von Karajan:

> We were allowed into a dress rehearsal of the Berlin Phil. The orchestra was playing splendidly without a conductor. Eventually they brought this chap out on a wheelchair and propped him up on the podium. It was von Karajan. He swayed about a bit and the orchestra played on. I didn't notice much difference in their performance.
>
> That night at a reception I met von Karajan. I said to him: Von Karajan, old boy, if you don't mind me saying so, you don't seem to do very much, do you? Ach so, he replied: it's a splendid orchestra and I just let them get on with it!

When Geoffrey Parkhouse and I interviewed Mrs Thatcher for *The Herald* in 1989, we were given another insight into her professional skills. For about an hour she stuck to a dreary brief provided, I suspect, by the Scottish Office (that would have set her against it from the start). We were given a list of Government achievements in Scotland. Bernard Ingham, her press secretary, prowled about in the background, interjecting from time to time some muttered imprecation about Yorkshire (he resented what he conceived to be Scotland's special treatment). At the end of the hour we had not very much, except an extempore dictum that every citizen aspired to a conservatory. She was aware that it was dull stuff. Suddenly she shifted gear. She began to talk of her sadness about how it occasionally became necessary for the older statesmen to move over and let the young talent through. She also issued a remarkable encomium of Lord Mackay of Clashfern, the Scottish lawyer she had appointed Lord Chancellor. She trusted that when Lord Mackay died, the Good Lord would prepare a resounding fanfare with which to welcome him to heaven. It was an engaging characteristic that she did not hesitate to give advice even to the Man Upstairs. Her remark about older statesmen was interpreted as referring to Sir Geoffrey Howe, and her final rupture with him paved the way for her removal from the leadership in 1990.

Many commentators have discussed the reasons why Mrs Thatcher lost her sensitivity to public and political opinion towards the end of her premiership. From a Scottish point of view, the retreat of Lord Whitelaw to a less active role was a decisive factor as was Mrs Thatcher's quarrel with Sir Geoffrey and Nigel Lawson. This latter estrangement was made inevitable by her decision to retain Sir Alan Walters as her personal financial adviser. For any Chancellor that was a barely tolerable situation but completely intolerable when the argument was conducted in public. At the heart of the disagreement was the policy on European economic union. It had for years been a festering sore at the heart of the Government. Sir Geoffrey and Lawson were committed to joining the exchange rate mechanism of the European monetary system, and had begun trying to make sterling track the Mark. Mrs Thatcher, advised by Walters, thought it disastrous. After Major took over the premiership, Britain crashed out of the ERM but it is too soon to say that history has proved her right.

Nigel Lawson in his memoirs has recounted how she treated Sir Geoffrey habitually as some sort of punchbag, despite his loyal service as Chancellor and then as Foreign Secretary. A senior Conservative said: 'We all agree she was a great leader but even great leaders need somebody to tidy up. Geoffrey was very good at tidying up behind her.' Bill Hughes has a recollection of a lunch at Downing Street in July 1990 towards the end of her tenure:

> I was invited to a Downing Street lunch on Tuesday. I was sitting on her right. There were about 12 of us. Michael Portillo was there. There was no doubt that he was viewed by her as very bright, as very high in the succession stakes though not immediate. She had obviously a lot of time for him. He was a very confident presenter and totally at ease with her. Sitting opposite her that day was Geoffrey Howe. Michael Forsyth was sitting at the far end of the table – this was just before he left as chairman in Scotland. We went through lunch and I spoke to her a lot. I came away from lunch with Michael, who said, What do you think of that lunch? Staggering, isn't it, Michael, I replied. Yes, he said, it's very disappointing. Geoffrey had sat opposite her and they never looked at one another and never spoke through the whole lunch. Michael had been a PPS to Geoffrey Howe and had a lot of time for him. He went away distinctly worried, as I was, that that type of chemistry between a Prime Minister and her deputy was completely unsustainable.

There is a savage portrait of Ingham in the Lawson memoirs. He was much resented by senior Cabinet ministers; Lord Whitelaw at one point, according to Lawson, advised her to change her press secretary. I have known Bernard on and off for many years. I worked with him on *The Guardian* in the early Sixties in the days when he was old-school Labour. I always liked him. His fault was not that he became rabidly Thatcherite. It was more that he became an excessively loyal hound who brought the Government news machine to a level of effectiveness that perhaps was against the public interest. He used a mixture of manipulative skill, favouritism and plain bullying to get results and drilled his team like an old-fashioned news editor. His anti-Scottishness lay in his refusal to recognise that Scotland was any different from Yorkshire; he is, like Sir Marcus Fox, a Yorkshire nationalist. Such advice must have influenced her judgment of Scottish questions and led her to underestimate the significance of Scottish national sentiment. After 1987 she was 'walking on water' and she lost the caution that had characterised her early period. Her withdrawal from the party's commitment to devolution was a long ritual dance of graceful disengagement. Ian Lang in conversation has pointed out that in the early days her rhetoric was much more radical than her actions. Later, the doctrines of the New Right swept Eastern Europe. There was an illusion that if totalitarian states subscribed to democracy and the free market they could look forward to prosperity more or less overnight. In 1993 John Gray, a theologian of the New Right, published a book called *Beyond the New Right*, where he recognised that its triumphalism had been overweening. History had not, to adapt the famous phrase, come to an end, and Conservatism must struggle to find a post-Thatcher doctrine which gave more weight to community values. Ian Lang expressed similar ideas in a speech in Glasgow in April 1993. But for the moment Thatcherism seemed imbued with the infallibility of papal teaching or Marxist orthodoxy.

The fairest way of summing up her relationship with Scotland is that Scotland did not understand her and she did not understand it. She sincerely tried to do so but nobody could give her the advice she sought which would reconcile her principles with a coherent view of the way ahead in Scotland. For most of Scotland she remained, as for my mother, 'that woman'.

My own tentative conclusion is that the rapid pace of industrial decline and a relatively high degree of reliance on the public sector produced a reaction in Scotland that made it fearful of her rhetoric and its results. Thatcherism also seemed at odds with concepts of social coherence and mutual obligation that had until then been constant values in Scottish political transactions. Much of what was achieved during her administration in Scotland will stand the test of time – the increased proportion of home ownership (now more than 50 per cent), the emergence of a more variegated economic base, the survival of a development agency even if in mutated form – though it cannot yet be said that Scotland is a dynamic country. Yet it is hardly surprising that rapid industrial decline, culminating in the closure of Ravenscraig, should have produced feelings of confusion, anxiety and resentment which found their outlet in a generalised dislike of Mrs Thatcher. She united us, in 1987, to a remarkable degree, if in a somewhat negative way.

At the time of writing she was continuing her political activities in the Lords, organising the campaign against Maastricht, revealing that she herself is a nationalist of a vibrant kind. The campaign had become not only hostile to the treaty but also to Major, her stop-gap successor who proved to be his own man. In her campaigns she was in cahoots with her old friend Teddy Taylor. Teddy is not a team man, a senior Conservative told me, but a brilliant campaigner. With characteristic frankness Teddy told me what the Right's aims were. They thought they had about 12 Cabinet Ministers on their side on the question of ERM and there would be mass resignations if Britain rejoined. They recognised that Major must stay because there was no immediate replacement but demanded a reshuffle which would give a higher profile to two eventual leadership candidates – Michael Portillo and Peter Lilley – who, Teddy said, were on the right side on the European question. By no stretch of the imagination could the party be said to be at peace. The war of succession rumbled on. The reshuffle of May 1993 did not placate the Right.

CHAPTER TWENTY-FIVE

Symbols of a modern Scotland

Twice a year when we were young my father would take us to Murrayfield to watch Scotland play in the rugby internationals. They were in those days douce affairs. Opponents were applauded and they were allowed to take their penalty kicks in silence; and the crowd would occasionally raise the genteel cry of 'Feet, Scotland, Feet' (having despaired, no doubt, of anything coming by hand). These internationals were mostly bourgeois festivals, although the cheerful and sporting Welsh supporters who held revels in Edinburgh for days before the match were clearly working-class. It was a pleasant ritual. We caught the bus from St Andrew's Square and walked the short distance to the ground past the one-man band who, it was said, had made so much money from his art that he owned a luxurious bungalow in Murrayfield. He wore a tammy and played mouth-organ and squeeze box; to the beat of his bass drum he added the clash of the cymbals attached to his elbows.

It was at Hampden or, on alternate years, Wembley that our national passions were more fiercely on display. Football was the great game. As we played our own childish games in the park, the roar of the crowd would be carried on the air from Easter Road where the 'Famous Five' were delighting the Hibernian faithful. Their names still roll off my tongue: Smith, Johnstone, Reilly, Turnbull and Ormond. My father eventually took me to see them and I became a Hibs fan. He rather disapproved, preferring the Hearts with their 'Terrible Trio' of Bauld, Conn and Wardhaugh, and I did not realise until later that this was a residue of his presbyterian spirit. Hibs were, at one time, the Irish team. For similar reasons he opposed our membership of the Wolf Cub troop at the episcopal church up the road at Goldenacre, to which we went with neighbouring children, but he eventually gave in to our demands. In those days football attracted enormous crowds. The late Jimmy Wardhaugh, the great Hearts inside forward, told me once that 20,000 had attended a reserve match between Hearts and Rangers at Tynecastle. We listened to the annual Scotland-England game with fraught attention. We despaired when Willie Bauld hit the bar and the frenzied commentator, Peter Thomson, shouted, 'It's a goal – no it's no.' We exulted when Lawrie Reilly scored a last-minute equaliser at Wembley to the evident stupefaction of the patronising Raymond Glendinning: 'I say, this looks dangerous! Scotland has scored!'

A great change has come over Scotland since those days. The football team is a dull affair and Scotland's national passion is now paraded at Murrayfield where the crowd sings *Flower of Scotland* and reviles the English. Today Hampden and Murrayfield stand as symbols of modern Scotland. The first has been shabby, forlorn and, in the rain, squalid. The second is plumply modern with its new stands which, to my regret, obscure the traditional view of the railway line. The innocence of the old internationals is gone, the players have professional attitudes, and on match day the marquees are full of corporate officers and their guests with their snouts lodged deeply in the trough of business entertaining. It is fat, complacent and not particularly attractive. But it is mercantile Scotland at play. Here is wealth, here is comfort, here is entrenched Unionism. Why, then, do they sing *Flower of Scotland* with such passion and is there anything more peculiar than the sight of some perjink Edinburgh insurance broker, Unionist to his fingertips, unleashing a volley of abuse at the English team and all its works?

Into the switch from football to rugby we may read many things but the simplest explanation may be that the Scottish football teams have been dreary since the heady dreams of Ally McLeod imploded in Argentina in 1978. Indeed they have become something of an international joke. These words are being written in Venice and I have just read in the *International Herald Tribune* a dismissive report of Scotland's 3–0 victory over Estonia, who have a perfect no-win record: New Scotland, the headline runs, Play Like Old.

Football, of course, was the game of industrial Scotland and rugby, outside the Borders, of the middle classes. The laws of football are simple, those of rugby obscure even to the players, a preparation for the professional life. And industrial Scotland is on the way out. Population is draining away from the old industrial heartlands. Bourgeois, dormitory Scotland is on the increase, driving to work unprecedented distances on its new roads. Murrayfield is bourgeois Scotland's temple.

In the politics of football we find a story of decline, schism and jealousy. This downward progress was punctuated by two extraordinary events. The first was the Wembley international against England of 1977. For many Scots football supporters Wembley was a great biennial festival. The famous victory of the Wembley Wizards against a fancied English team in 1928 was part of folklore. On the occasions I attended the game, the English had the ungracious habit of winning, sometimes by an embarrassingly large margin. On one occasion my brother Robbie and I watched Don Revie's English team knock five goals past another hapless Scottish goalkeeper more or less before we had settled into our seats. By the early Seventies the fixture was increasingly spoiled by the drunkenness of the Scots fans. At the time, as London editor of *The Scotsman,* I was living in Harrow and was well aware of the resentment, and even fear, aroused among the locals by the arrival of bus-loads of Scottish drunks.

In 1977 I was back in Scotland. A party of us drove down and stayed with a friend who lived near Wembley. Next day drink was taken and we made our way to the stadium where I had a ticket for the press box (sitting beside Jim Reynolds, later to be my colleague on *The Herald*). The English sports writers tended to dismiss their Scottish colleagues as fans with typewriters but it always seemed to me that if anything they were worse. Scotland won a scrappy game that day by two goals to one, but the quality of the play did not matter. At the end the Scottish fans invaded the pitch, broke the goalposts and departed with sections of the sacred turf as souvenirs. A Scottish MP was with us that day. He hopped over the wall and got his piece of greensward. Luckily the Metropolitan Police stood back and let them do it; otherwise it might have been a Donnybrook. In truth it was bacchanalian rather than violent. But from television screens throughout the land boomed the outraged comments of Kenneth Wolstenholme (whom Scots always found irritatingly patronising). In following years drunken jollification deteriorated into nasty hooliganism. The English authorities had enough. Since 1981 the fixture has been played furtively and without passion.

From this incident and others of the period came the incidents which led to the Act of Parliament which prohibited the consumption of alcohol at sports grounds or on buses and trains going to them. It was a strikingly successful piece of legislation and the fans' behaviour has since improved greatly. There followed a period when English fans became notorious. National perversity has given the Scots supporters another reason for behaving well – it shows the English up.

Then along came Ally McLeod's finest moment, quickly followed by his and our humiliation. Amid euphoria we qualified for the 1978 finals in Argentina. Only in Scotland, I think, could the squad have gone to Hampden and taken a lap of honour in front of an ecstatic crowd before kicking a ball in the finals. Scotland was in a high state of excitement. We had an 'easy draw'. Peru would be a walkover, a sentiment immortalised in Alan Bold's verse:

> Poor poor Peru
> If only you knew
> What the boys in blue
> Are going to do to you.
> Too true!

All over Scotland people gathered to watch the massacre. A million cans of lager were opened in anticipation of the toasts to follow. But Peru had not read Alan Bold's script. They could play a bit and had the temerity to beat Scotland. Anguish. Despair. Although Scotland later recovered their spirit sufficiently to beat Holland, life was never going to be the same again. Subsequent managers or coaches, such as Jock Stein and Andy Roxburgh, went around like worried actuaries. Stein would warn us not to expect too much and by the time Roxburgh took over we had learned to keep our expectations low. Modesty and Scottish football never went well together and a lot of the fun and excitement drained away with the end of Ally's dream.

This was the public face of Scottish football. But more serious tensions behind the scenes stultified its development. The Heath Government of 1970–74 was prepared to make a substantial contribution to the improvement of Hampden. The late Sir Alex Fletcher, then Tory MP for Edinburgh North, told me that the Government offer was withdrawn after protracted negotiations. Rangers, then embarking on the improvement of their own ground at Ibrox, did not want a competitor in the shape of another ground of excellence. With the help of clients and allies in the Scottish League and the Scottish Football Association, he told me, Rangers killed the improvement to Hampden and proceeded to develop Ibrox. There was no point, said Alex, in forcing the money on them. In 1993 more stringent standards demanded by the football authorities and Hampden's failure to meet them obliged the SFA to use Ibrox for internationals. Given the sectarian undertones to football in the West of Scotland, and the resentment that the dominance of Rangers has aroused in Scotland furth of Glasgow, it was not an option that appealed to the SFA but it had become Hobson's Choice. The SFA was plodding on with improvements to Hampden, still owned by the amateur club, Queen's Park. Its relationship with Rangers was by no means cordial. Celtic, relatively impoverished at Parkhead, riven by boardroom jealousies and pursuing schemes for a new stadium for which the requisite funding was not available, were impotently watching Rangers, with their ambitious programme of signing English stars, emerge as the dominant force in Scottish football. Rangers' run in the European Cup in 1993 won them more friends in the rest of Scotland than anything in their previous history; but neither Ibrox nor Rangers can unite Scottish sentiment. Hampden has symbolised the tendency of Scots to quarrel among themselves.

And this brings us back to the nationalism of the Murrayfield crowd. What are we to make of its anti-Englishness and its espousal of the song, *Flower of Scotland,* adopted by the highly conservative and Unionist SRU as a defensive and pre-emptive gesture in the face of the supporters' rampantly nationalist feelings? Its limping lines make even some nationalists wince. At the World Cup sevens in 1993 the Scots crowd supported anyone rather than the English (who duly gave the perfect answer – they won the trophy). English friends are offended by this crass anti-Englishness and I am embarrassed when I hear it. Douglas Henderson found in it, when we talked, an encouraging sign of incipient nationalist recovery. John Smith found it unattractive, as I do. But he did not attach too much importance to it; he would be more worried if it were heard at Ibrox or Hampden.

Murrayfield nationalism is a kind of vapour rising from the Union, a venting of resentments and jealousies. Perhaps Scottish political nationalism has a similar explanation. It may be a weapon kept in reserve by the Scottish people as a kind of warning that their commitment to the Union is not beyond peradventure. A Union between partners of such uneven size is bound to cause problems. The English faults are paraded every day in the media and in politics. Some English commentators and pundits are arrogant, patronising and, worst of all, they do not recognise the existence of Scotland as a nation. Winston Churchill cynically exploited Scottish national sentiment and then imposed on Scotland an English view of history. In government John Smith managed to change the name of a draft accord from the Anglo-Norwegian to the British-Norwegian oil agreement. But even he has given up trying to insist that it is not the Anglo-Irish Agreement (for a while I insisted that *The Herald* called it the British-Irish Agreement but I too have given up). In 1993, in a speech to the US press club, Chris Patten, the governor-general of Hong Kong, referred throughout to England in his references to the United Kingdom. It was fairly typical.

The faults of the Scots are also the function of size. We are, in Nigel Lawson's word, chippy. We take offence too easily and imagine slights where none is intended. When John Major came to Scotland as part of his promise to 'take stock' of the Union he remarked that Scotland defined its nationalism with reference to England. With an eye on his Maastricht rebels, he added that England defined its nationalism with reference to France and Germany. And it is true that in the activities of the Maastricht rebels may be discerned, above all, English nationalism – or in the case of Teddy Taylor, British nationalism. It is interesting that many of the same people who most virulently opposed devolution also have fought fiercely against Maastricht – for example Lord Tebbit and Sir George Gardiner. An exception is Tam Dalyell, who in 1993 was fiercely pro-European; this much-loved politician defies prediction.

Despite its uneasy moments the Unionist coalition in Scotland remains strong, comprising all the political parties except the SNP. Its strength may be seen from the voting behaviour of the Scottish people – even in 1987 when they constructed an informal anti-Tory coalition they did not endorse independence – and from the failure of political extremism in Scotland. Since the days of John MacCormick's

Covenant there has been an intermittent series of terrorist trials in Scotland and the authorities have always taken the threat of Scottish political terrorism seriously, particularly in the West of Scotland where the fear of sectarian infection from Northern Ireland is a constant anxiety (so far, it seems, diminished by the use of both sides of Glasgow and the West as a 'safe house'). In the Seventies senior politicians like Michael Foot warned that the failure of devolution would lead to rioting in Scotland, and there were those in the Home Office who believed him. Scotland, in truth, has shown no sign of being sufficiently alienated from the Union to contemplate terrorism or to give it succour. The apparent incompetence of the Scottish terrorist reflects at least three factors. First, the authorities have successfully infiltrated and negated incipient terrorism by the use of *agents provocateurs* and police spies and informers. Secondly, potentially effective terrorists have been compromised by their association with common criminals. This was true, for example, of Matt Lygate, of the Maoist Workers Party of Scotland, who was freed in 1983 after serving eleven-and-a-half years of a 24-year prison sentence for his part in a series of bank robberies. His sentence makes the third point: the Scottish judiciary has been prepared to hand out exemplary sentences in political cases.

An account of the intermittent terrorist activity since the days of the Covenant is to be found in the book *Britain's Secret War*. It contains many unsubtantiated statements and tends towards the conspiracist view of the British state, working through its intelligence arm, as all-powerful, omniscient and pervasive. There does seem no doubt, however, that a rapid build-up in Special Branch activities did take place in Scotland in the Seventies when there was a growth of 'copy-cat' terrorist groups inspired by the IRA. The Special Branch remains active and intermittent campaigns of letter-bombs take place. Two members of the Scottish National Liberation Army continue to take an interest in Scotland. Both are in exile. One is in Dublin where he has formed a connection with the Provisional IRA. He successfully evaded extradition. The second, who did not, is somewhere in Europe. The authorities in Edinburgh remain anxious to interview both.

Since the 1992 general election, the Major administration has adopted a new tone towards Scotland. The document which appeared as a result of 'taking stock' contains a specific recognition of Scotland's nationhood within the Union. The Edinburgh EC summit was the first attempt to give that dimension more reality. This new sensitivity is welcome. The Government, like so many of its predecessors of all political complexions, has turned to the Grand Committee as a palliative vehicle. It is to be peripatetic, with the power to 'take evidence' from Scottish Ministers. Such devices are unlikely to make much impact because they remain well-meaning but cosmetic. As John Smith remarked when we talked in 1993, the real issue is the transfer to Scotland of political power over its own affairs.

That, I believe, is ultimately inevitable. There are at least three ways in which the institutions of the Union may develop. There may, as Teddy Taylor predicted, be a surge of support for the SNP as a reaction against European Union. Labour may ultimately withdraw its support for the Union. That could happen if the present gifted generation of Scottish Labour front-benchers were to be consistently rejected by the English electorate. They may begin to feel, as their predecessors felt in 1918, that Scotland is the more promising political arena. Thirdly, the Westminster Parliament may prove capable of reforming itself and finding a more satisfactory way, perhaps through the development of its committee system, of dealing with the Scottish dimension, of simultaneously giving it more attention and reducing the extent to which it impinges on the whole House. That is the way, one suspects, that would be most congenial to the Scots and to the British state itself. The 'big bang' of independence seems a less attractive vision than that of an evolving relationship. The British state hates binding rules. It needs the freedom to change imperceptibly. Westminster is capable of producing a kind of *de facto* federalism by convention and use; but it would be highly reluctant to formalise it too precisely. Sir Alec's proposals of 1970 still seem to me to have much interest. They avoid the duplication of the executive function; they retain the ultimate rights of the Union or federal Parliament at Westminster; but they do transfer powers to an elected legislative body in Scotland which could, by convention, be open to Westminster over-ride only if they impinged on the rest of the UK or involved the allocation of extra resources. This is not, however, the place to produce yet more devolutionary schemes. There is a large pile of them on the shelves. With goodwill Labour's plan, to which John Smith and Donald Dewar are so committed, can also be made to work, although the criticism that it would create an inherently unstable relationship between Edinburgh and London has got to be taken seriously.

For myself I remain a Scottish nationalist of the John Buchan or the Lord Cooper variety. I believe that Scotland is a nation with its inalienable rights vested in the Treaty of Union. It is neither a region nor a province. But I value also the Union and our new connection with Europe. When I look at resurgent nationalism in Eastern Europe, the Balkans and elsewhere I am reminded of the value to be placed on order and good government, and on the ability of different races and peoples to live together in a complex modern state.

The nation state itself is a concept that should be obsolete but is obstinately persistent. Partly this is the response of nations to the suppression of their identity, for example in the former Soviet Union, or to the insensitivity of the majority or central power within a state, as in the United Kingdom and parts of Europe. We need a new kind of state. Markets and zones of influence pay less and less attention to national boundaries. Modern political science is devoting much attention to the problem of building states which can accommodate varied groups within them, and the concept of 'mutual veto' has acquired some currency. By this is meant the right of minorities to block actions by the majority if they are perceived as oppressive or not disinterested. Ideas of this kind are to be found in the new South African constitution being so painfully negotiated at the time of writing. They are also present in the constitutions of Switzerland and Belgium, and might be useful in any new all-Ireland settlement. English politicians have historically treated Scotland in the spirit of mutual veto by largely letting it get on with its own domestic affairs. This principle, however, was notably breached during the Thatcher years, as we have seen. Scotland has reverted to the status of a 'managed' territory and its quite modest aspirations for democratic control over its domestic affairs have not only been ignored; they have sometimes been reviled. In their future relationship Scotland and England must struggle to define those matters which are domestic and those which are quasi-federal. Water privatisation, deeply unpopular in Scotland, has put this issue to the test again.

Like most Scots I am confused about the political consequences of our national identity. For almost 300 years we have lived in a Union with a bigger partner which has often had the irritating fancy that it has absorbed us. We resist this fate. Indeed our very resistance and his very presence sustain our sense of nationhood. But where does our resistance lead us? We are not alone in our confusion. England must now come to terms with political union with a larger partner. It does not find it easy, either. But more than most nations, the English have the gift of compromise and of creating flexible institutions. I remain out of sympathy with the Thatcher school of government – the idea that the state is some kind of corporation, the Prime Minister its chief executive and that certitude is in itself some kind of virtue. The art of politics is more complex than that and of course Mrs Thatcher's simplifying rhetoric was often belied by her own actions. The Whitelaw school, by contrast, values wise and sagacious government which moderates conflict in society through conciliation, negotiation and honest administration.

Nationalism is no longer an adequate foundation on which to build the edifice of the state or to base a political programme. It is a matter of sentiment and identity; but its potency and its destabilising force are undeniable. A successful political Union must recognise that truth and find ways of accommodating it.

Scottish electoral behaviour since 1945

Column I: percentage share of the vote by party
Column II: number of seats

	Lab		Con		SNP		Lib*	
	I	II	I	II	I	II	I	II
1945	49.4	40	41.1	27	1.2		5.0	
1950	46.2	37	44.8	32	0.4		6.6	2
1951	47.9	35	48.6	35	0.3		2.7	1
1955	46.7	34	50.1	36	0.5		1.9	1
1959	46.7	38	47.2	31	0.5		4.1	1
1964	48.7	43	40.6	24	2.4		7.6	4
1966	49.9	46	37.7	20	5.0		6.8	5
1970	44.5	44	38.0	23	11.4	1	5.5	3
1974								
Feb	36.6	40	32.9	21	21.9	7	8.0	3
Oct	36.3	41	24.7	16	30.4	11	8.3	3
1979	41.5	44	31.4	22	17.3	2	9.0	3
1983	35.1	41	28.4	21	11.7	2	24.5	8
1987	42.4	50	24.0	10	14.0	3	19.4	9
1992	39.0	49	25.7	11	21.5	3	13.1	9

Note 1:
Percentages do not round to 100 because 'others' have been omitted. In 1945 'others' won 3.3% and 4 seats. The Labour total for 1945 includes 1.8% and 4 seats won by the Independent Labour Party, whose MPs joined Labour in 1947.

Note 2:
For the purposes of the table the heading Liberal is used. The Liberals fought the 1983 and 1987 elections in the Alliance with the Social Democrats. Since then they have stood under the title of Liberal Democrats.

Sources:
Scottish Political Facts by Richard Parry (T & T Clark 1988); John Bochel and David Denver on 'The 1992 General Election in Scotland' in Scottish Affairs No 1, Autumn 1992 (University of Edinburgh).

Devolution: a chronology

1967   Mrs Winifred Ewing wins Hamilton by-election from Labour.

1968   Declaration of Perth.
Heath commits himself to a constitutional review.

1969   Wilson appoints Crowther (later Kilbrandon) Commission on the UK Constitution.

Wheatley Royal Commission proposes a two-tier system of local government for Scotland, including a large West region (later called Strathclyde).

1970   Sir Alec Douglas-Home's Conservative Party committee recommends devolutionary scheme based on a directly elected Scottish convention subordinate to Westminster. The Conservative manifesto of that year states that this report will form the basis of proposals which a Conservative Government will place before Parliament.

In June election, Conservatives under Heath win surprise victory. SNP secures one seat. Queen's Speech gives legislative priority to local government reform.

1973   *25 October*
Local Government (Scotland) Bill is enacted.

31 October
The Kilbrandon Commission reports.

8 November
Margo MacDonald wins the Glasgow Govan by-election.

1974   *28 February*
Labour, with no manifesto commitment to devolution, narrowly wins indecisive general election, having more seats but fewer votes than Conservatives. SNP wins seven seats.

7 September
A White Paper proposes directly elected assemblies for Scotland and Wales.

10 October
Labour, now with a manifesto commitment to devolution, wins with overall majority of three over all other parties. SNP returned in 11 seats.

1975   *10 February*
Mrs Thatcher elected Conservative leader.

5 July
In referendum Britain votes to stay within EC.

22 November
A White Paper, *Our Changing Democracy*, calls for a legislative assembly with a cabinet and chief executive in Scotland, but only an executive assembly for Wales, run on the committee system.

1976   *18 January*
The Scottish Labour Party is established, with two Labour MPs, Jim Sillars and John Roberston.

16 March
Wilson surprises the country by announcing his resignation 'because he has reached 60'.

5 April
Callaghan becomes Labour Prime Minister. Michael Foot, Lord President of the Council and Leader of the House, takes charge of devolution. John Smith, as Minister of State, become responsible for legislative progress in the Commons and John (Lord) McCluskey, Solicitor-General, in the Lords.

7 July
David Steel elected Liberal leader after resignation of Jeremy Thorpe.

24 November
Foot introduces first devolution Bill, providing for separate assemblies in Scotland and Wales. Indicates Government is willing to consider a referendum.

1 December
Shadow Cabinet agrees to oppose Bill. Alick Buchanan-Smith, shadow Scottish Secretary, and his deputy, Malcolm Rifkind, argue for abstention at this stage. When shadow Cabinet enforces doctrine of collective responsibility Buchanan-Smith resigns from it and Rifkind resigns also from his junior portfolio.

6 December
Heath defies Conservative leadership by supporting full and effective devolution in Scotland.

16 December
Devolution Bill is given a second reading by 292 to 247 votes.

1977   *22 February*
Government defeated on bid to apply timetable to devolution Bill, by 312 to 283 votes, with 22 Labour MPs voting against and 15 abstaining. This means that Bill cannot become law because of a shortage of time.

17 March
The Aircraft and Shipbuilding Industries Bill, providing for public ownership, is enacted.

23 March
The Government survives no confidence vote by 322 to 298 after Callaghan and Steel announce Lib-Lab Pact.

21 May
Scottish Conservatives withdraw their call for a directly elected assembly.

14 November
The Scotland Bill, providing for a Scottish assembly, is given a second reading by 307 to 263 votes. A separate Bill for Wales passes this stage by 295 to 264 votes.

16 November
A timetable is imposed on the Scotland and Wales Bills.

1978   *25 January*
An amendment to the Scotland Bill, providing for the repeal of the measure if 40 per cent of the registered electorate do not agree to devolution in a referendum, is passed against government wishes by 166 to 151 votes.

22 February
Attempts to remove the 40 per cent rule fail at report stage and the Scotland Bill is given a third reading by 297 to 257 votes.

13 April
Donald Dewar romps back to Parliament by winning the Garscadden by-election, with 45.4 per cent of the vote. The SNP has 32.9 per cent.

25 May
Steel announces the end of the Lib-Lab Pact.

31 May
SNP obtains only 33.4 per cent of the vote in the Hamilton by-election. George Robertson wins it for Labour with 59.6 per cent.

30 July
John P. Mackintosh, the Labour MP who is perhaps the most fluent advocate of devolution of all, dies.

31 July
The Scotland Bill and the Wales Bill are enacted.

7 September
Callaghan announces there will be no autumn election.

1 November
The Queen's Speech promises five more seats for Northern Ireland, reflecting Callaghan's desire to win more support from Ulster Unionist MPs.

Callaghan announces on the same day that referenda will take place in Scotland and Wales on 1 March 1979.

1979   *1 March: the referendum.*
        I: Percentage of votes cast. II: Percentage of total electorate.

	Yes	No	Turnout	Did not vote
Borders				
I:	40.3	59.7	66.4	
II:	26.7	39.7		33.6
Central				
I:	54.7	45.3	65.9	
II:	36.1	29.9		34.1
Dumfries & Galloway				
I:	40.3	59.7	64.1	
II:	25.8	38.3		35.9
Fife				
I:	53.7	46.3	65.3	
II:	35.1	30.3		34.7
Grampian				
I:	48.3	51.6	57.2	
II:	27.6	29.5		48.4
Highland				
I:	51.0	49.0	64.7	
II:	33.0	31.7		35.3
Lothian				
I:	50.1	49.9	65.9	
II:	33.0	32.9		34.1
Strathclyde				
I:	54.0	46.0	62.5	
II:	33.7	28.7		37.5

Tayside
I: 49.5   50.5   63.0
II: 31.2   31.8   37.0

Orkney
I: 27.9   72.1   54.1
II: 15.1   39.0   45.9

Shetland
I: 27.0   73.0   50.3
II: 13.6   36.7   49.7

Western Isles
I: 55.8   44.2   49.9
II: 27.8   22.1   50.1

Scotland
I: 51.6   48.4   62.9
II: 32.5   30.4   37.1

Wales votes heavily against devolution by 46.9 per cent to 11.9 per cent.

22 March
Callaghan announces that the repeal of the Scotland Bill will be laid before Parliament without delay.

28 March
The Government is defeated on a motion of no confidence by 311 to 310 votes.

For the Opposition: 279 Conservatives, 13 Liberals, 11 Scottish Nationalists, 8 Ulster Unionists.

For the Government: 303 Labour, 3 Welsh Nationalists, 2 Scottish Labour Party, 2 Ulster Unionists. Gerry Fitt (Belfast West) and Frank Maguire (Fermanagh and South Tyrone) both abstain.

The Government is forced into an election.

3 May
The Conservatives win the election with an overall majority of 44. The SNP retain two seats.

Works cited and consulted

Barnett, Correlli. *The Audit of War: The Illusion and Reality of Britain as a Great Nation*. Macmillan 1986.

Benn, Tony. *Conflicts of Interest: Diaries 1977–80*. Hutchinson 1990.

Bold, Alan. *MacDiarmid*. John Murray 1988.

Bower, Tom. *Tiny Rowland: A Rebel Tycoon*. Heinemann 1993.

Brown, Rev Thomas. *Annals of the Disruption*. Edinburgh 1890.

Buchan, John. *Witch Wood*. Canongate Classics 1988.

Campbell, John. *Edward Heath*. Jonathan Cape 1993.

Checkland, Olive and Sydney. *Industry and Ethos: Scotland 1832–1914*. Edinburgh University Press 1989.

Cockburn, Henry (Lord). *Memorials of His Times*. The Mercat Press 1988.

Cooney, John. *Scotland and the Papacy*. Paul Harris 1982.

Cooper, Lord, of Culross. *Selected Papers*. Oliver and Boyd 1957.

Crichton Smith, Iain. *Collected Poems*. Carcanet 1992.

Cunningham, George. 'Burns Night Massacre'. The Spectator, 28 January 1989

Devine, T. M. (Ed.). *Conflict and Stability in Scottish Society 1700–1850*. John Donald 1990.

Dewar Gibb, Andrew. *Scottish Empire*. London 1937.

Dicey, A. V. *England's Case Against Home Rule*. Richmond 1973 (1886).

Dickson, A. D. R. and Treble, J. H. (Ed.). Brown, Callum, and Knox, W. (contributors). *People and Society in Scotland: Volume III*. John Donald 1992.

Dickson, Tony (Ed.). *Scottish Capitalism*. Lawrence and Wishart 1980.

Donaldson, Gordon (ed.). *Four Centuries: Edinburgh University Life 1583–1983*. Edinburgh University Press 1983.

Donoughue, Bernard. *Prime Minister: The Conduct of Policy under Harold Wilson & James Callaghan*. Jonathan Cape 1987.

Drucker, H. M. *Breakaway: The Scottish Labour Party*. Edinburgh 1977.

Ferguson, Adam. *An Essay on the History of Civil Society*. 1767.

Foote, Geoffrey. *The Chronology of Post-war British Politics*. Croom Helm 1988.

Fry, Michael. *Patronage and Principle: A Political History of Modern Scotland*. Aberdeen University Press 1987.

Fry, Michael. *The Dundas Despotism*. Edinburgh University Press 1992.

Garioch, Robert. 'The Wire'. In the *Faber Book of Twentieth-Century Scottish Poetry*, edited by Douglas Dunn. Faber and Faber 1992.

Gibson, John S. *The Thistle and the Crown: A History of the Scottish Office*. HMSO 1985.

Hamilton, Ian. *A Touch of Treason*. Lochar 1990.

Hanham, H. J. *Scottish Nationalism*. Faber and Faber 1969.

Johnston, Thomas. *Memories*. Collins 1952.

Keating, Michael, and Bleiman, David. *Labour and Scottish Nationalism*. Macmillan 1979.

Kellas, James G. *Modern Scotland: The Nation since 1870*. Pall Mall Press 1968.

Kellas, James G. *The Politics of Nationalism and Ethnicity*. Macmillan 1991.

Kellas, James G. *The Scottish Political System*. Third Edition. Cambridge University Press 1984.

Kemp, Robert. *The Malacca Cane*. Duckworth 1954.

King, Elspeth. *The Hidden History of Glasgow Women: The Thenew Factor*. Mainstream 1993.

Lawson, Nigel. *The View from No 11*. Bantam 1992.

Lynch, Michael. *Scotland: A New History*. Century 1991.

MacKay, Donald (Ed.). *Scotland 1980: The Economics of Self-Government*. Q Press, Edinburgh, 1977.

Mackie, Allister. *The Trade Unionist and the Tycoon*. *The Herald* and Mainstream 1992.

Magnusson, Magnus, and others. *The Glorious Privilege*. Nelson 1967.

Magnusson, Magnus. *The Clacken and the Slate*. Collins 1974.

Marr, Andrew. *The Battle for Scotland*. Penguin 1992.

Maynes, Charles William. 'Containing Ethnic Conflict'. Published in *Foreign Policy* No. 90. Washington DC 1990.

McCrone, David. *Understanding Scotland: The Sociology of a Stateless Nation*. Routledge 1992.

McCrone, David; Kendrick, Stephen; and Straw, Pat (Ed.). *The Making of Scotland: Nation, Culture and Social Change*. Edinburgh University Press 1989.

Midwinter, Arthur; Keating, Michael; and Mitchell, James. *Politics and Public Policy in Scotland*. Macmillan 1991.

Miller, Karl (Ed.). *Memoirs of a Modern Scotland*. Faber 1970.

Mitchell, James. *Conservatives and the Union*. Edinburgh University Press 1990.

Mitchison, Rosalind (Ed.) *The Roots of Nationalism: Studies in Northern Europe*. John Donald 1980.

Mitchison, Rosalind. *A History of Scotland*. Second Edition. Methuen 1982.

Moffat, Robbie (Ed.). *Scotland's Constitution*. Moffat & Co, The Quadrangle, Ruchill Street, Glasgow G20 9PX. 1993.

Muir, Edwin. *Scott and Scotland*. Polygon 1982.

Nairn, Tom. *The Breakup of Britain*. Verso 1981.

Parry, Richard. *Scottish Political Facts*. T & T Clark 1988.

Regan, Donald T. *For the Record: From Wall Street to Washington*. Harcourt Brace Jovanovich 1988.

Rodger, Richard (Ed.). *Scottish Housing in the Twentieth Century*. Leicester University Press 1989.

Scott, Andrew Murray, and Macleay, Iain. *Britain's Secret War: Tartan Terrorism and the Anglo-American State*. Mainstream 1990.

Scott, Paul Henderson. *Walter Scott and Scotland*. William Blackwood 1981.

Scott, Sir Walter. *The Journal*. Edinburgh 1891.

Sillars, Jim. *Scotland: The Case for Optimism*. Polygon 1986.

Spark, Muriel. *The Prime of Miss Jean Brodie*. 1961.

Warr, Charles L. *The Glimmering Landscape*. Hodder and Stoughton 1960.

Watkins, Alan. *A Conservative Coup*. Duckworth 1991.
Williams, Philip M. (Ed.). *The Diaries of Hugh Gaiskell 1945–1956*. Jonathan Cape 1983.
Young, Douglas. 'A sketch history of Scottish nationalism' in *The Scottish Debate*, edited by Neil MacCormick. Oxford 1970.
Young, James D. *John Maclean: Clydeside Socialist*. Clydeside Press 1992.
Youngson, A. J. *The Making of Classical Edinburgh*. Edinburgh University Press 1966.

Index

Saltire Society, 82, 100
Sampson, Steve, 193, 207
Sanderson, Russell (Lord), 194, 197, 206 *et seq*
Saunders, Ernest, 61 *et seq*
Scholey, (Sir) Robert, 59
Scotch Education Department, 78
Scotland on Sunday, 204
Scotland, Kenny, 20
Scots Independent, 80, 82, 86, 97, 98
Scots Law Commission, 175
Scots National League, 80
Scotsman, 22, 28, 31, 35–38, 73, 96, 114, 140, 151, 159, 215
Scott, C.P., 15
Scott, Jane, 98
Scott, Norman, 147
Scott, Paul, 179
Scott, Professor William Robert, 179
Scott, Sir Walter, 17, 23, 87, 90
Scottish & Universal Newspapers, 42
Scottish and Universal Investments (SUITs), 39–50, 66
Scottish Convention, 86, 91, 92
Scottish Council Development and Industry, 40, 84, 177, 178
Scottish Covenant, 82, 86, 92–93, 97, 218
Scottish Daily Express, 54, 56, 83, 100, 129
Scottish Daily News, 56–57
Scottish Development Agency (SDA), 59, 139, 185–190, 193
Scottish Enterprise, 58, 59, 188 *et seq*
Scottish Football Association, 216
Scottish Grand Committee, 79, 85, 91, 113, 122, 176, 218
Scottish Home Department, 93
Scottish International, 105
Scottish Labour Party, 112, 127, 128, 140, 154–161
Scottish League, 216
Scottish National Congress, 82, 97
Scottish National Liberation Army, 218
Scottish National Movement, 80
Scottish National Party (SNP), 17, 41, 75, 85, 86, 87, 96–106, 110, 117, 124–132, 134, 145 *et seq*, 155 *et seq*, 166–172, 217, 218

Scottish Office, 57, 98, 102, 119, 121, 134, 139, 176–184, 185–190, 209, 210
Scottish Rugby Union, 217
Scottish Select Committee, 113
Scottish Socialist Society, 170
Scottish Standing Committees, 91, 113
Scottish Television, 38
Scottish Unionist Party: *see* Conservative Party
Secretary of State for Scotland (office of), 79
Sheppard, Gillian, 206
Shinwell, Adrian, 206
Shipbuilding, 53, 54
Short, Edward (Lord), 139
Sillars, Jim, 112, 118, 127, 128, 131, 140, 141, 154–165, 167 *et seq*, 186
Sim, Alastair, 29
Simpson, David, 124
Singers, 58
Siol nan Gaidheal (Seed of the Gael), 103, 166, 167, 168–169
Small, Willie, 116
Smith, Adam, 179, 185, 189, 210
Smith, Gordon, 214
Smith, John, 87, 90, 93, 108, 116, 126, 129, 131, 140 *et seq*, 155, 159, 164, 197, 217, 218, 219
Smith, Maggie, 24
Smith, Peter, 194
Smith, Sheriff Irvine, 42
Social Democratic Labour Party (SDLP), 147, 148
Social Democratic Party, 171
Spark, Muriel, 20
Spectator, 143, 148
Spence, Lewis, 80
Spencer, Nick, 114
Sproat, Iain, 106, 123, 133, 134, 137
St Andrews University, 179–180, 195, 199
St George's School, 21
St Rollox, 52
Steel, (Sir) David, 128, 142
Stein, Jock, 216
Stephen: Alex Stephen of Linthouse, 55
Stevenson, Struan, 176
Stewart, Allan, 137, 180, 204